FREYA STARK
Letters

FREYA STARK
Letters

EDITED BY LUCY MOOREHEAD

VOLUME SIX

THE BROKEN ROAD

1947–52

MICHAEL RUSSELL

© Freya Stark 1981

First published in Great Britain 1981 by
Michael Russell (Publishing) Ltd
The Chantry, Wilton, Salisbury, Wiltshire
and printed in Great Britain by
Western Printing Services Ltd
Chittening Estate, Avonmouth, Bristol

Set in Linotype Granjon

ISBN 0 85955 081 8

Publisher's Note

It is a matter of the greatest sadness to record that Lucy Moorehead was killed in a road accident in Italy during the preparation of this volume. The editing of the text had been completed; we have had only to supply the footnotes. If there is any cause for consolation, it is that the publication of the letters will continue to be served by Moorehead family skills. Caroline Moorehead, Mrs. Moorehead's daughter and herself an author and journalist, has undertaken the editing of the final volumes.

Foreword

There is no rule about length in collected letters, nor any fixed law other than that the reader should know his author better after he has read them than before, and that pleasure is desirable. This volume and its fellows try to combine these two qualities and the only obstacles I have asked my indulgent editor to avoid are, in ascending scale, repetition too frequent, criticism too temporary, and the giving of pain to a few living people. The 'Broken Road' of this volume's title alludes as much to an abandoned marriage as to a pause from serious travel. There were, inevitably, passages in the letters which even now might give pain when there is no wish to do so, and the privacy of their nature has been respected.

Asolo 1980

FREYA STARK

GERALD DE GAURY[1]   Windsor Castle
                                                   14 January 1947
My dear Gerald,

   I am doing a wonderful deal with Jock Murray:[2] my copyrights when I die
for a mink coat now! A mink costs £4,000. Jock is very perturbed as there
is no means of knowing who gains by this transaction. I know, however, that
I prefer a mink on my back to a copyright in the tomb.

   I have been staying with Pam[3] in this exalted place, and since then I have
had 'flu and have only just crept out of bed two days ago in time to go to
Scotland to lecture with no voice. It fills me with fear and horror: I would
like to arrange my life never to have to lecture again.

   I hope you *will* write soon or I shall think you are still cross and depressed.

                                                   Yours affectionately,
                                                   FREYA

GERALD DE GAURY   Paris
                                                   9 February 1947
My dear Gerald,

   It was very nice to hear from you, just in the last two days when life in
London was far too much of a rush to do anything in the way of answering.
Now I am here, with Juliette Huxley[4] who is Queen of Unesco.

   Do you know the latest romance? Biddy Carlisle[5] and Walter Monckton.[6]

---

   [1] F.S. had first met him in Baghdad in 1931–32. Resident in Kuwait before the war,
he returned to Baghdad for wartime service as Attaché to the British Legation.
   [2] F.S.'s publisher and friend of long standing.
   [3] Widow of the first Earl of Gowrie's eldest son (who had died of wounds in North
Africa in 1942). Raised to the rank of Viscountess Ruthven of Canberra, so long as she
remained a widow, in June 1945. Extra Woman of the Bedchamber to Queen Elizabeth
the Queen Mother 1948–51. Married Major Derek Cooper in 1952.
   [4] Wife of Julian Huxley, the distinguished biologist and scientist.
   [5] Eldest daughter of the tenth Lord Ruthven; married to the Earl of Carlisle.
   [6] Sir Walter (later Viscount) Monckton, lawyer and politician.

They are looking rejuvenated and radiant and are hoping to be divorced and married this year. For some extraordinary reason, they thought I might disapprove of it (as if I ever worried about people's private affairs!) until Pam saw them and I was asked to dine. They are living very quietly indeed just now and it is not being talked of yet, but no doubt will be soon.

London is altogether a hopeless place for seeing one's friends and I think another time I will go straight to Oxford, which still preserves a pleasant atmosphere of civilisation, where you can find your friends at home and pleased to see you if you happen to pass by. Isaiah Berlin[7] was in bed with a chill in New College, lying, as he described it, 'like a prostitute – people come knocking at my door all day.' I lunched with the David Cecils,[8] and found Lionel Smith,[9] who showed me the cross that still shows the place on the pavement where Cranmer was burned. It was snowing and, in London, most people's pipes had burst. What other country would let them do this every year and not put them *inside* the houses? There was general gloom over Palestine, India, coal, and everything else.

Here it is a little less cold, but on the other hand, there is even less fuel. Only the Embassy is lavishly warmed. I went to the Salon Vert last night and found Diana[10] surrounded by Generals, and Mr. Masaryk[11] looking like a pleasant and intelligent frog. General Morgan, just on his way to take Jumbo's[12] place in Washington, told me he had left blocks of ice in the Venice Lagoon.

I had one very pleasant evening before leaving, with Harold Nicolson[13] at John Murray's. We got him to talk about all sorts of people – among others Edmund Gosse, who was once visited by an old lady who had inherited the mss. diary of Byron's doctor and wanted to know what to do with it. Gosse himself told Harold that he 'advised her to burn it', which she probably did.

He also told a nice story about Churchill, who, when complimented on his obituary speech on Chamberlain, said he hoped the Divine Providence would

<hr>

[7] Now back in Oxford as philosopher and academic. F.S. had met him in the United States in 1943; he had been posted there with the Ministry of Information and later served at the Embassy in Washington.

[8] Lord and Lady David Cecil, old friends of F.S. Lord David became Goldsmith Professor of English Literature at Oxford the following year.

[9] Lionel Smith, sometime Rector of Edinburgh Academy, and another old friend. He had been Adviser to the Ministry of Education in Baghdad when F.S. was there in 1929.

[10] Lady Diana Cooper, wife of Duff Cooper, the British Ambassador.

[11] Jan Masaryk, Czech Foreign Minister.

[12] sc. Field-Marshal Lord Wilson, Head of British Joint Staff Mission in Washington 1945–47.

[13] Author and (1935–45) Member of Parliament. Married to Vita Sackville-West.

spare his ever having to make one for Baldwin. In spite of this, when Baldwin was out of everything, he invited him to lunch and, instead of taking his usual afternoon nap, took him all over the secret rooms where the invasion of France was being mapped and planned, knowing too much how he must feel, being kept away from all the news.

Yours affectionately,

FREYA

STEWART PEROWNE[14]   Paris

9 February 1947

My dear Stewart,

A letter of yours has been waiting for weeks for an answer, but you know what the last days are in London. One feels as if emerging from a football scrum. Now I am here for a few days, picking up a Molyneux *and* a Schiaparelli, *and* a very intriguing little hat, and thinking of Asolo in a week's time with much nostalgia. My visit to Greece is again postponed. This time it is the British Council's budget: it seems they have overspent three years' income in one, and have to make it good. So I shall be in Asolo or round about, and very happy to be so, and expect you as early as possible in May. Diana and Duff hope to come to Venice for that month.

I saw the British Council people and must say I am losing faith in that and any other of these huge monsters of our age. I think they (without knowing they were doing so) pointed out to me the fundamental flaw which will always make these unwieldy machines expensively useless: I said the whole secret lay in having people who know and like the Italians in Italy (and the same for any other place). They say this is impossible in a big concern, where people have to be transferred from one country to another. Jeffery Amherst[15] rightly remarked that it is like giving the leading parts in a play to the general utility men. It means all one's recruits on a lower level and that we try to do with our third-rate people what other countries, who base their propaganda on individuals, do with their *first-rate*. And we can't succeed.

Another depressing subject – Palestine. I urged on the Arab bureau to think seriously now of a boycott of oil, and air landings. They are all in favour of sabotage, which will be pushed into a dark corner of the newspapers and never get through to Americans in Congress, where the Zionists are

---

[14] The orientalist and historian, whom F.S. was to marry. At this time in the Colonial Service.

[15] Earl Amherst, a friend from the wartime Middle East.

presenting the whole thing as a Jewish–British quarrel with no mention of the Arabs at all. But if one gets a good headline – 'Arab League Stops Oil Supplies' – I believe there would be a change in the U.S.A. in a month.

I didn't see much of the Arabs; in fact, only got glimpses of people all round. London was *bitterly* cold, snow, sleet, and slush, and Mr. Shinwell[16] cutting all the warmth (though there is still far more than in Italy). I went one evening to the ballet and that was charming – *Giselle* all in white tulle and spangles, and little dancers floating on wires. Off the stage Covent Garden is all very drab, everyone in utility day-clothes. I will write from Asolo. Love meanwhile.

Your

FREYA

JOHN GREY MURRAY   Paris
                                            11 February 1947
Dearest Jock,

This is being left to greet you and Diana on arrival; and I hope you will find a nice springlike Paris, and not be frozen as I was for the first two days. Then the sun came out and Juliette and I walked in the Bois.

I met a man in a pushtin on the boat, who greeted me warmly. After two days I discovered, without betraying myself, his name, and he's asked me to dine in a little bistro in S. Sulpice with French journalists, and Janet Flanner of the *New Yorker*, who told me when we parted that I was 'just marvellous' – wonderful American rapidity! The stranger, who turns out to be a gardener and wise about roses, was quite overcome because I said I was buying a 'gown'. He told me his grandmother was the last person he had heard using such a word. How trying it is not to be able even to *talk* like other people.

A young A.D.C. at Diana's had met me at the 13th Corps Ball at Duino. I said the ladies seemed rather 'varied', and he confessed that, as they had been short, they had relied on a young subaltern who said he could produce twenty. So they sent him with a lorry, and he did. And that is what they looked like.

Love to you,

FREYA

---

[16] Emanuel Shinwell, then Minister of Fuel and Power in the Attlee Government.

22 February 1947

My dearest Jock,

I hope your week in Paris was not all slush, snow, and icy cold like Northern Italy. A glorious vision as one came down into Domodossola out of the Alps. Dazzling sun and snow and lake like turquoise, but then the clouds came down, and the whole of the plain was buried in ice. The irony is that it has snowed very little high up where the water-power is produced, so that one has a cold winter combined with next to no electricity. The same wails as in England; though, as we are happily not organised, we do not suffer so much. I am now back, after another visit to Pavia, Cremona and Mantova (the whole Gonzaga palace and Mantegna, which one can't see enough). There is a fascinating gilt maze forming one of the ceilings in the palace, called 'Forse che sì, forse che nò'. It seems that the Gonzaga, who was captured by the Turks, was put into a maze and promised his freedom if he found the way out; and he went along saying those words and *did* find the way, and built the ceiling in memory of it.

There are food problems, and Emma and Checchi[17] have burnt up all my wood-store; the baths are still as they were for want of electricity for the marble saws, and the boiler burst. Apart from this and the cold, it is lovely to be home. The silver teapot and the milk jug are a great joy and have almost cheered up Emma, who is gloomy over the thought of having her baby and says her 'life is ended'.

Love,
FREYA

22 February 1947

My dear Stewart,

You will be delighted to hear that I saw two bottles of Carpano in a *patisserie* in Mantova and bought them against your arrival. I came back two days ago – loaded with Schiaparellis – and picked up Cici[18] on the way.

I have a fascinating book for you to read: a description of field sports in the light of quotations from Shakespeare. Hawking, coursing, stag-hunting – he explains them in the way they were done and ever so many sayings emerge into clarity and sense. It shows what a real countryman Shakespeare was.

[17] The maid and the gardener.
[18] Costanza Boido, F.S.'s niece.

I hope to settle down now to write till Lulie[19] comes in April, when I have promised to do another of my little tours and take her as far as Florence.

Much love,

FREYA

SIR SYDNEY COCKERELL[20]   Asolo

22 February 1947

My dearest Sydney,

I have just got home again — it was lovely to find your letter and to hear that you are really better. I think, perhaps, the illness was a blessing: it kept you in bed when that was the only good place to be in. I had an excellent, luxurious journey out, with a train and sleeper just as easy as before the war. Woke up to look at the Alps shining in the early light across the Lake of Geneva, and burst through the tunnel into Italy with all that old Northern feeling of rapture. Turin was lovely to look at with its Alpine crown, but the roads in any strip of shadow, and down all the long cobbled streets of the old towns, were slabs of thick transparent green ice with lorries marooned sideways here and there. I visited my reading centres[21] in their various places: a beautiful old city palace in Alessandria, with empire gilt columns and ceilings and old Chinese panels unexepected in the drab streets; an art student's room in Asti where he sits imitating Gauguin amid his very disapproving family; the Valdensian pastor at Torre Pellice, a most touching little community, poor, decent, and keeping somehow or other a care for the eternal values. An A.D.C. of Wellington's, a General Backwith, who lost a leg at Waterloo, read a history of the Valdensians and spent his life there, giving them a church, hospital, etc. His portrait hangs above a case with his decorations, clothes, and wooden leg: a decided old Victorian, with his wooden stump decently draped in cloth and a collie dog and romantic landscape behind him.

I am glad to be home, though it was good to see so many friends in London. But it is not a nice *way* of seeing them in such a hurry and I am looking forward to this quiet month or two as a luxury.

Your ever devoted

FREYA

[19] Lulie Abu'l Huda, who had worked on F.S.'s staff in the war.
[20] Man of letters, F.S.'s friend and literary adviser.
[21] After her return to Italy in 1945 F.S. had started numerous reading centres where the English press might be available.

Asolo

3 March 1947

Dearest Jock,

I am wrestling with Chapter One.[22] *What* a difficult book this is going to be. I am depressed because I know you do not think hopefully of it; but I feel I want to write it all down, and Montaigne says it is worth writing to please even a few people and if not a few, then only one – oneself! It is *still* threatening to snow. The winter seems never-ending.

I hope Diana got a fine hat. Love to her and the children and you.

FREYA

GERALD DE GAURY Asolo

3 March 1947

My dear Gerald,

Murray's had a board meeting and decided mink is immoral. Then when I said they could forget it and just buy my copyright and I would mink it myself, they offered me £1,500 which I repudiated, feeling like Julius Caesar when the pirates asked too small a ransom. So now I am looking for anyone who will gamble and offer me £4,000 for the copyright and I will then waste it in my own way. I feel very rebellious towards this taboo of everything that is better or more expensive or more frivolous than its exact counterpart machine-made for everyone else: a sort of abolishing of excellence. After all, if one has *one* luxury, and does without things like radio sets, motor cars, tobacco, or the *New Statesman*, why should one be disapproved of? Sydney Cockerell says no house is civilised that has not got a thirteenth-century manuscript! Anyway, I have decided never to save any money *ever*, and to collect things that are beautiful and precious whenever I can as a protest against this dreary evenness.

Much love, dear Gerald.

Your
FREYA

FIELD-MARSHAL LORD WAVELL[23] Asolo

9 March 1947

My dearest Chief,

This is so well out of the world that papers only reach us about a month after things have happened, so I only saw yesterday what the Government

---

[22] Of *Perseus in the Wind*.
[23] Viceroy and Governor-General of India 1943–47.

has been saying about India and that you are coming away. I very much long to hear more and especially to know whether you are glad or sorry. I sometimes think that to serve a government one must feel rather like one's pen might feel if it had ideas of its own about writing. And the strain of doing it different must be almost unbearable.

You must be terribly tired, and yet you have made so many people trust and like you, and will mind leaving them. And to what sort of a chaos? I am looking forward to Felicity's[24] coming, not only to see her but also to get news of you. Privately, in all this change, there is a hope of seeing you more often and with some leisure. There is no golf course here nearer than Venice, but I shall hope to lure you to Asolo just the same.

I am trying to write a book and find it very hard work. I thought I would put down my own Everywoman philosophy in as clear and simple way as I know. But *what* a labour it is to be clear and simple. If I can make it interesting as well, I shall be pleased and surprised. It is also very difficult to sit at a writing desk in the spring. If I can find a car I shall break away and take the honeymoon couple to Lake Garda for a day.

Alan Moorehead[25] has just been here to dine from Venice. He tells me he will never again write the life of anyone still alive, that he could have made a fascinating study of Montgomery and had to write what he knew to be a bad book instead.

I met General Morgan as I came through Paris. He was staying at the Duff Coopers', and the A.D.C.s were discussing with Diana whether some French show was fit to take him to or not. How you have to be guarded in the Army!

Your devoted

FREYA

SIR SYDNEY COCKERELL   Asolo
23 March 1947

My dearest Sydney,

I only get to my letters on Sunday now, as I am writing all mornings and the rest of the day is too short for all the rest which has to be crammed in. The garden and the bathrooms take an incredible amount of one's time. One has to see a plumber at work to realise the complications of modern civilisation. And mine is a nice man called Amadeo, but very dramatic, so when he comes

---

[24] Lord Wavell's second daughter, who had just married Major Peter Longmore.

[25] The author – and husband of the editor of these volumes. His *Montgomery* had been published the previous year.

and tells me that the hot water has got into the cold water pipe, he nearly gives me a fit (thinking I may be paying for the heating of the whole of the Asolo irrigation system), until he explains it as 'merely temporary pressure'. It makes one realise that mystery surrounds us.

I have done four chapters of my philosophy, and I am sending them to you. Not that they are in their final state, but I would like you to see the idea of the book. Perhaps you will think it dull. I am really writing it to please myself and clear my own thoughts. Anyway, I think it may be a book which my own friends will like to have.

Lulie and I leave for Tuscany on the 8th. Four days in Settignano with B.B.[26] and then down to Umbria. I hope to be back here on May 4th.

Dearest love,

FREYA

FIELD-MARSHAL LORD WAVELL   Asolo
31 March 1947

FIELD-MARSHAL LORD WAVELL

My dearest Chief,

The honeymoon couple arrived yesterday, alas not to stay, but they are coming I hope in May. In a day or two they will know where they are posted and I am hoping it may be Padua, right on my doorstep, so to say. It was very good to see them both looking so happy and so very comfortable with each other.

But, at last, I heard all the Indian story and have been almost suffocating ever since with shock and anger. It is not even so much for you. You are ever so far beyond the reach of those people, but it opens an abyss to realise that this is the sort of thing by which we are being governed. What hands to hold a rudder! What bankruptcy of everything that makes up a statesman! They bring these people up on formulas, and they are incapable of even imagining how one deals with human beings. Oh how I hope we may live to see a reaction against theories at second (or millionth) hand.

It must have been a grief to you to leave, but it would have been even harder in a year, and I do believe your work will make its way more and more. Perhaps even more so when you are no longer there.

Fizzy thinks you should live near Oxford. I spent a weekend and felt it the only town in England I should like to live in. I toyed with the idea of cutting out London altogether and going to England for a term a year in Oxford to

---

[26] Bernard Berenson, the art historian and critic.

9

read up things like the Crusades. How good it would be if you settled there, and I could come now and then to stay without curtseying!

Much love to you,

FREYA

CHARLES RANKIN[27]

Asolo
5 April 1947

My dear Charles,

It was very pleasant to have a good long letter and Lulie brought it quite safely and lost nothing on the way except her sleeper, of which she mislaid the day!

I don't think I have ever felt more disgusted with politicians than after hearing the Delhi story from Felicity. The poorest peasant couldn't behave like that and expect to be tolerated. I don't think there is a chance for civilisation until public and private manners and morals are brought under the same law. The whole thing fills me with disgust and nausea. I imagine that H.E., just by being himself, produces an inferiority complex in these miserable half-men and offends their vanity; and, of course, that is never forgiven.

Yours affectionately,
FREYA

SIR SYDNEY COCKERELL

Asolo
Easter Day 1947

Dearest Sydney,

This is a very hurried note, as everything here is happening all at once: Osbert Lancaster, Lulie, and the Wavell honeymoon pair are in the house; there are all the social calls and Easter greetings; this morning eleven children from the *tessoria*[28] (including the two youngest work girls) came to hunt for Easter eggs in the garden; and the bathroom is *still* being worked upon. We leave on our tour on Tuesday, so you see it is rather hectic and no writing will get done till I return, anyway. I enclose one more chapter and an improved ending to Chapter Four. I am most anxious to hear whether you think it is going to be a book worth writing.

[27] Charles Rankin had been an A.D.C. to Lord Wavell when F.S. stayed in New Delhi in 1945.

[28] The small silk-weaving factory in Asolo.

We have now had two fine days since mid-February and it seemed like a resurrection to sit out and have tea in the garden. There is very little there but grass. The few poor shoots and buds were crushed by hail so that the elements are really spitefully directed this year. I hope Tuscany and Umbria will be warm, but I am starting out in my tweeds all the same.

Osbert has brought a most enthralling book: the account of Hitler's last days gathered from all the evidence by a young don called Roper.[29] It is extremely well done and, of course, Hitler has succeeded in his *Gotterdammerung*. The story is so dramatic that it will never fade out of history. The awful *stupidity* of the Nazis is what shocks one most. I took the book up reluctantly, but am now unable to put it down.

Always your affectionate

FREYA

BERNARD BERENSON   Perugia
                                              22 April 1947

My very dear B.B.,

The days have been slipping by and we are still hopping from bough to bough. Today Bevagna and Montefalco: so much beauty that it seems impossible for one small land to contain it all, and one wonders how Italy can be discontented with her lot – surely no reasonable person would hesitate between austerity here and wealth in Manchester or Chicago? Anyway I feel as if I were now completely lined inside with gentle backgrounds painted on gold!

The four days with you gave more than the sight of lovely things – that feeling of not being alone in one's world which is the most blessed of all companionships. It is so precious and I value it for what it is. So that I will try to reach Vallombrosa and take you at your word.

Very much love,

FREYA

SIR SYDNEY COCKERELL   Rome
                                              26 April 1947

My dearest Sydney,

I was so very glad to find your long letter here when I arrived (*very* fatigued after visiting fifty-two churches interspersed among the reading centres). The

[29] Hugh Trevor-Roper, *The Last Days of Hitler* (1947).

most exciting of all were two very old ones, eighth to eleventh centuries and then abandoned, out among asphodels and judas trees in the *campagna* at Tuscania. It has all been a happy trip, only too rapid and too much to do every day. The sort of trip one enjoys more and more as one digests it afterwards.

I am sad about my book and that you are not going to like it. I am most grateful for all the suggestions you make for the various pages and glad of all you can say. The fact that there are so many is perhaps due to fatigue (I keep on saying I need a year's rest and no one pays any attention), but it may also be that I have never shown you any of my work in so unfinished a state, except the autobiography which is easy, being pure narration. This will need a good deal of polishing and I never contemplated it as being final in *detail* as yet. But I feel that you will not really like it apart from this, as it is vague and mystical and not agnostic at all. But that is a real difference of outlook which I can't and would not change. All I am trying to do is to give an easy picture of what values I believe in, and not to justify those values, and far less to present them as original. It would be rather sad to have original values in a world where people have been thinking for so long? All I want to do is to present them in a lively way.

I have four days here before returning to Asolo by Urbino and Ravenna. What lovely sights and horizons in one's mind! All that country from Florence to Siena and south is, I imagine, unsurpassed anywhere. Every little farm or cypress tree is placed as if it were in the background of one of the early pictures of its own region. By the way, I am more anxious than ever to possess one small Sienese primitive, and, if you find me a good one, will give anything up to £1,000. I would gladly sell out some capital and have that daily joy! B.B. says that London is the only place where one can chance upon such things at a possible price.

Ever so much love and thanks, dear Sydney.

Your

FREYA

JOHN GREY MURRAY

Rome
26 April 1947

My dearest Jock,

We reached Rome two days ago, happy and in perfect harmony, but Osbert has seen eighty-five churches since his arrival and I fifty-two, with all my reading centres added. Osbert is very tough, but I have been in bed with a temperature. I am up today and told Osbert that I could have a car from 4.30 to 7. 'Oh yes,' says he, 'there are two churches I am most anxious to see.' Insatiable!

I am delighted today to get your letter with Harold Nicolson's criticism and so pleased with it. I had hoped to give the effect of a tapestry, rather rich and not too sharply defined and it is a great joy when one's attempt is taken as it is made. And I must say that your first words, and especially S.C.'s, were *very* discouraging. Sydney has a kink against anything mystical or religious: it rouses a quite unintellectual animosity in him. So we will have to agree to differ, while considering his remarks on technical points. As a matter of fact, I would have been even more depressed, but I had showed it to B.B., who embraced me and said that we 'live in the same universe' and that it is the best I have done. Lulie and Cici, who are both sensitive and not particularly literary, said the same. So it is evidently one of those things that people either like or don't like.

I hope to get some more done when I get home. I thought of calling it 'Perseus in the Wind'. It is a title I thought of years ago when I saw the constellation at the head of all the Persian passes; and, as it refers to the stars that lit my path, it seems suitable, and I could get in a paragraph in the text to explain it.

Oh Jock, I *wish* you had come. *What* haven't we seen? Zig-zagging between Trecento and Renaissance like mad. Lulie lost something in every resting place; Osbert makes a habit of walking away with his hotel key, but is very expert in returning it; I only forgot my passport. We spent the last night on the shores of Lake Bolsena where the Corpus Domini was invented; otherwise it is only known for its eels.

Thanks for all,

FREYA

SIR SYDNEY COCKERELL

Asolo

7 May 1947

Dearest Sydney,

It is very pleasant to be home again, and I have missed the wistaria and the iris, but am in time for all the roses.

I was glad of H. Nicolson's verdict but do not agree as to the *cause* of your differing. Jock agreed with you and his age did not enter into it. I think that this book will succeed (if it does) by the qualities that make poetry rather than prose. Not everyone likes those sort of qualities, so I think it will arouse likes and dislikes. I don't know when the next chapters will be written as I have a stream of people coming. Stewart Perowne arrives any day next week, the Keelings on the 26th, Gerald de Gaury, Juliette Huxley, and Steven Runciman in June. For July and August, I go to L'Arma[30] and hope to have mornings for writing there.

Ever so much love and thanks, dearest Sydney.

FREYA

SIR SYDNEY COCKERELL   Asolo
                                                    17 May 1947
My dearest Sydney,

Pam and the two children are filling my garden with life, and Stewart came yesterday. Pam and I motored down to Venice in the evening to fetch him, took the wrong turning off the *vaporetto* landing, and walked into a strange cocktail party where a casual acquaintance invited us to pause and drink brandy cocktails. After this pleasantly unexpected episode, we found Stewart at the Luna and went to a *trattoria* to eat scampi and strawberries in marsala, and drove him back in the dark.

All this takes up my writing time. I have done one more chapter, but shall not sit down to real work till I get to L'Arma in July and hope to come back with more than half the book written. The roses all out and lily buds showing. It is not a good year. The fears for food and harvest, as well as general uncertainty of the world, are always there in the background of everyone's thought. But I never read a paper if I can help it, and have no radio. It is not escapism, but I feel a great need of a year or two of not thinking of daily events after all these years of a topical atmosphere.

Stewart is in very good form and full of Baghdad gossip. He has just told me of Mr. Churchill's definition of Mr. Attlee as 'a sheep in sheep's clothing', which you, no doubt, have heard but it delighted me.

Your loving
FREYA

JOHN GREY MURRAY   Venice
                                                    28 May 1947
My dearest Jock,

The only thing that spoils Venice is a feeling of poverty as soon as any little incident pierces the smooth surface of things. The crowd getting off at

[30] A small house near Ventimiglia which F.S. had made over to her niece Cici and Cici's husband, Franco.

Burano, for instance: all working people, with clothes patched and turned to the last possibility. So different to the smart neatness of the *piazza*.

It was lovely at Torcello, as if centuries of peace had soaked its vines and stones. Pam thinks of taking the children there for a few days to bathe and all staying in the little pub from Monday to Saturday so as to leave it clear for Sunday tourists. Mr. Cook's first trainload has arrived, and two more tours are due.

I am reading Motley's *Dutch Republic*, which fortifies one's Protestantism no end. What strikes one is how easily those circumstances and that sort of a spirit might return. Nor could one hope for much less savagery now. The beginning of British support for Holland is also characteristic: Queen Elizabeth refused to hand back the Spanish ships full of coin! 'Joindre l'utile à l'agréable' no doubt.

Your loving

FREYA

JOHN GREY MURRAY   Asolo

4 June 1947

My dearest Jock,

I get no time for letters, nor does my book get on at all. One more chapter I hope to send and hope L'Arma may be more inspiring. I must earn some money somehow – the house is *eating* it. The boiler bust, and a new one has to be got, and it costs half a million lire! One is going towards the astronomic currencies and loses all one's bearings. How glad I am that the two bathrooms at any rate are *done*, even if the water supply was washed away the very next day by a flood in the hills and all we can do is to get miserable little buckets full from the *piazza*. It is a mad year. We lit a fire a fortnight ago, the evening was so cold, and now it is as hot almost as Cairo, and a sirocco wind curling up all the leaves. The harvest poor, and a general uneasiness of hunger lurking just round the corner.

Love,

FREYA

SIR SYDNEY COCKERELL   Asolo

19 June 1947

My darling Sydney,

You (and everyone else) are being so neglected, but it is the fault of this book. I struggle to get a little time, and even so, it is very rare to have a clear morning. I am only in Chapter Eight, but hope to be at L'Arma in a fortnight and to work there every morning. Meanwhile, visitors come and go. A quiet little female party of Pam, Juliette Huxley and myself is being broken into by Steven Runciman tomorrow. It will be so nice to see him again, after last lunching with him in Jerusalem in 1942! Today a young buccaneering Irishman called Leigh Fermor[31] is coming to lunch with Joan Rayner who was Osbert Lancaster's secretary in Athens. But Pam and her two adorable boys are leaving. It has been a great joy to have seven weeks of nearness of such a real and dear friend.

The *tessoria* gives a good deal of work, but it has at last paid off its debt and we can buy our new lot of raw material out of our own resources. As for the garden, a *pink* lily has blossomed! I go and look at it with adoration at intervals through the day. If you see any very exciting and beautiful combinations of flowers at Kew, I shall be so glad to hear. It takes very long to try out colour schemes in gardens, as one has a year's interval with each effort. I now have a lovely mass of great Regal lilies under the ilex trees, and orange day lilies just beyond. The sun shines through them against the far background of the plain and they fill one's mind with peace.

I am buying a tiny motor bicycle left over by the commandos. It can pack into a suitcase, and will be very useful for getting about.

Dear love, dear Sydney,

FREYA

HON. A. J. WAVELL[32]   Asolo
                                                                    20 June 1947
My dear Archie John,

I was so delighted with yours, and glad to have real news of your father. I don't think anything for a very long time has made me feel so angry as the way he has been treated, and it is part of this miserable wave into which the world is plunging, of a belief that institutions are living things and not merely the consequences of whatever the people are wherever they are. Your father stands 'self-schooled, self-scanned, self-honoured, self-secure'. He is not in danger and I think his name will grow and grow as more is known. But who are *they*, these miserable Lilliputs, to chuck away our great men as if they were their miserable private property?

I am sure you are right to stay in India, where all sorts of things are bound to come out of the melting pot quite soon. Surely we shall be back in the

---

[31] The writer Patrick Leigh Fermor (subsequently married to Joan Rayner).
[32] Only son of Lord Wavell.

16

eighteenth century then, with a fine jungle for those who are tired of planned insecurity?

I shall read *Lear* carefully one of these days and write and tell you what I think, but, just offhand, it seems to me that what Shakespeare is interested in is not so much the consequences and punishment entailed by wickedness, as the terrible power of evil against good. I think Timon of Athens and Cressida put the problem of terrible and *undeserved* punishment; and the tragedies work out the answer that, so long as man endures and when he accepts, the power of evil ceases to matter. In *Lear* again you notice that the conclusion is stated, (in the scene with Gloucester) that 'ripeness is all'. I think the Gloucester episodes are a very important part of the play and perhaps the key to its philosophy. For there we have a good old father who had given no cause at all, of temper, or injustice, to make him hated; and it is pure evil in Edmund which costs his eyes.

'Wisdom and goodness to the vile seem vile.'

The whole play is full of this theme, and the only answer is endurance:

'Henceforth I'll bear
Affliction till it do cry out itself
"Enough, enough" and die.'

This is Gloucester again. The more I think of Shakespeare's tragedies, the more it seems to me that he isn't concerned so much with the consequences of individual faults, but with a huge body of evil in the world ready to take advantage of any moment of human vice, weakness, or even too gentle goodness, and his search for the answer and triumph over the incubus. He finds it in acceptance or endurance, which leaves the victor not a victor. Do read *Lear* in this light and tell me what you think.

Affectionately,
FREYA

SIR SYDNEY COCKERELL   L'Arma
                                                  7 July 1947

Dearest Sydney,

Your letter has followed and reached me just as I was going to write to you. I am here for two months now and hope, in a day or two, to settle down to write. At present, the sea and the sun, the mosquitoes and the heat all make life very *physical*. And there is still a lot of creaking in the life of this poor little shell-shocked house. All its gay paint and shining furniture has been defaced by war, bits chipped off, and the surface rained on or blistered by the sun. The drawing-room ceiling is propped up on beams, and the bathroom door won't shut because it alone supports a sagging wall. I shall have to spend more sums in getting the most urgent things done (at astronomic prices now), but hope to have got Cici a long lease for eight months of the year, and that will help.

The land looks cheerful again. All green with beans and tomatoes and carnations and another two years should make one able to forget the war. Let us hope there may not be another. It seems incredible even to imagine such a thing.

If only I can finish this caprice of a book this autumn. I shall devote all next year to the autobiography, just to please you!

Much love, dear Sydney,

FREYA

STEWART PEROWNE   L'Arma
                                                        7 July 1947
My dearest Stewart,

Do let me hear as soon as you know your future. It is so disheartening to work for H.M.G. One would think there would be a real welcome for you after all your years of such successful work. I am sure they want you very soon and then will be all smiles and favours; but, meanwhile, it gives a chill to the spirit and takes all the *joie de vivre* out of one's work. I think there is a basis of envy. I never believed it for years, but slowly one is forced to see it, and it is one of the most horrid things there are.

It is unusually hot here and lots of mosquitoes. It is like a countryside coming to life again, a lot of joints still creaking, but wonderful compared to the ruins of last year. The villas around are mostly re-inhabited and the terraces again filling with little rows of carnations for the black marketeers who, next winter, will be able to buy them.

Your loving
FREYA

SIR SYDNEY COCKERELL   L'Arma
                                                       21 July 1947
My darling Sydney,

It is an enchanting book.[33] I knew it would be, when you praised it so highly, and it is delighting me greatly. There is a wonderful directness of

[33] *Out of Africa* by Karen Blixen.

approach, a clear vision, so that one sees what the writer saw. I know that I have read the *Gothic Tales* long ago. I thought them very remarkable and meant to find more of hers, and I have forgotten all about them except this strong impression.

I went for a walk yesterday with my lunch in a little red bag with white spots and sat all alone under an olive tree to eat it. How pleasant often it is to be alone. You can't think how beautiful these hills are, going high quite suddenly and breaking into numerous steep valleys full of hot spicy smells: thyme, and lavender and broom, myrtle, cistus, olive and heath and pine. The dry gulleys have oleanders and brakes of cane; and every little easement of the slope is used for a patch of vines or roses, and has a stonework cistern or at least a *tub* for the water to irrigate near by. The country is lonely. All these patches are well cared for, but there was not a soul in sight while I walked over an hour, as it were in Psyche's garden. A lovely light breeze came from the sea, drawn toward the hills, and the olives looked black and silver on the slopes. One daren't lose one's way off the paths, as the country is still full of mines and will, I suppose, remain so indefinitely.

I have just lost a very dear old friend, Mrs. Buck, who died at the age of ninety-seven or ninety-eight (no one quite knows). So you see, eighty is quite juvenile. Many happy returns, dearest Sydney, for the joy of all your friends and dear love.

FREYA

GERALD DE GAURY   L'Arma
                                                              26 July 1947

My dear Gerald,
    How difficult life must be for you, if you are really broken in to travelling always with six motor cars, five A.D.C.s and the whole Iraqi court! But it was a very pleasant surprise to see you here on your way to Switzerland.

    We have had a great smuggler catch: a boatload of skins (snake, lizard, and all sorts desirable for bags and shoes) was landed at midnight. I saw a rapid boat rushing into our bay, but turned my face to the wall. The next thing was that three new and zealous 'guardie di finanze' came upon the lot in Herbert Olivier's[34] garage, and on a lorry just taking them away. The men all escaped. Luckily for them all, the sergeant of *carabinieri* is so deep in the traffic that he put his best foot forward to help. The skins are being quickly

[34] Herbert Olivier, a painter, was an old friend of F.S.'s parents. He had been so enchanted with L'Arma that he bought the house next door.

divided among the smugglers and the police (I thought of putting in for a handbag myself, but didn't!).

Love,

FREYA

JOHN GREY MURRAY
L'Arma
1 August 1947

My dearest Jock,

You shall sit in peace in Asolo. The house will be chaos, and perhaps I will rent La Mura next door for us all to sleep in; but we will keep the garden inviolate, and one little room if it rains. Let me know the dates and addresses exactly and I will pick you up on a lake if they send me a car. It is a happy thought to think of you and Diana so soon.

Have you forgotten all about my chapters, in your desk where '. . . they in trembling hope repose'? I hope you will send me a little list of suggestions, as you see I adopt practically all! I have now finished Chapter Eleven, on Words.

I am sure there ought not to be more than twenty chapters at the most, and it should be a *little* book the size of a Max Beerbohm (but alas, not the content!) or of Birrell's *Obiter Dicta*. Otherwise, it will be too stodgy. I would like to have a nice little arabesque at the beginning and end of each chapter? And a page of five or six quotations in front of each? (Very grateful if you think of any.) It doesn't call for illustrations, but perhaps a frontispiece of some sort. I *hope* you begin to like the poor little waif. He is costing me such trouble. Anyway, it is quite surprising and interesting to find out what I think about a lot of things myself.

Love, dear Jock,

FREYA

NIGEL CLIVE[35]
L'Arma
5 August 1947

My darling Nigel,

It would be lovely if, after your stay in Asolo, you would escort me over to Athens? I just *refuse* to go to Athens when you are not there. And it is good to think of you in Asolo to begin the year. We will have a big fire to sit over;

[35] Nigel Clive had been 'my young p.g.' in Baghdad in 1942 and held a special place in F.S.'s affections.

and, if you want anything active, we will dash up to the little pub in the Dolomites to ski (you can; I can only sit down very suddenly). My book should be written by then and in proof, so you can cast your eyes over it.

Did you ever come across a strange enthusiast called Carl Raswan? Lots of people thought him bogus or a spy, but I think he is just a single-hearted Arabo-maniac and rather touching. Anyway, he and his wife say they are going to buy Arab horses in Nejd in the spring for a Texas millionaire who pays all expenses, and have asked me to go. I don't think I can resist the thought of the black tents in the early spring. So that, *if* it comes off, I might go on from Athens for three months. I have never been into Nejd or Hejaz.

The whole Iraqi court, i.e. the Regent, two ministers (Nuri and Tahsin Haidari), five A.D.C.s, one dog, six cars, and Gerald de Gaury, all had lunch at the Mortola pub on their way to Switzerland. I was called by a little note which was handed to me in the sea. Gerald, on these occasions, looks like a benevolent Nanny who takes no responsibility for what the young Masters like to say or do!

Your loving
FREYA

SIR SYDNEY COCKERELL
L'Arma
20 August 1947

Darling Sydney,

I am so much interested in all you tell me about Karen Blixen and hope so much to meet her some day. It is sad that unhappiness seems necessary to bring people to their best. I have been thinking of this with my poor Cici, who has now opened her eyes and sees what a dreary young man she has married. She still hopes to make it a possible life and the distressing thing is that he is such a disinterestedly enamoured husband. He asked for no 'dot', which is remarkable in Italy, and is ready to adore her if she will only cease to be active on her own. She seems to have a strangely passive, indolent character, and perhaps may do so. What can one wish? I would, myself, rather be *actively* unhappy than passive altogether. One can't judge for others, but she has never been in love with anyone as yet, and a passive discontent is a poor thing to live on. Life itself will no doubt provide some way.

Meanwhile, there is a sort of weariness and gloom instead of the joy in a house of her own and all the things that open out before her. I suppose if it had not been for this indolence she would never have married a young man she didn't love. It is more and more borne in upon one what a monstrous thing it is to do this.

The sea is so quiet now and blue. The sky, too, and much darker; and one never gets tired of the olive branches and their little green berries so delicate against it. I wish you could see it here with me, dear Sydney.

Your ever loving

FREYA

LADY RUTHVEN   Asolo

2 September 1947

My darling Pam,

It never rains but it pours! I came here yesterday hoping to find tenants gone and workmen in, and found Georges Chavchavadze so enamoured of Asolo that he hoped to stay on, with or without me, and the wife of the French High Commissioner in Austria arriving with an A.D.C. They are all charming people, but the masons had to get in and were only just restrained from knocking down the walls of the A.D.C.'s room while he lay asleep inside. I said he was like Jericho, but he evidently doesn't know his Bible! Anyway, I have told Georges he can stay as long as he can bear it, and *I* have cleared out into the Mura for a month; and have let it from October 15th to Gerald, and already sublet it for him from October 15th to an unknown Scottish-Irish major who sounds rather eccentric, but has good bank references. Into this chaos the Mooreheads are arriving on the 6th, the Jock Murrays on the 8th, and now your letter about the Morpeths on the 8th. I think it will be all right. Everyone else I ever knew is asking to come for a day or two days or so, in September. Thank God this is to be the last of masons *inside* the house for a long time. It looks as if the whole place were coming down and not a room is free except the two bedrooms where guests will be parked among the splinters.

Love,

FREYA

NIGEL CLIVE   Asolo

14 September 1947

My dearest Nigel,

Such a peculiar thing has happened: I have promised to marry Stewart. I have not written to anyone to tell them yet; but I must say so at once to you, for you are very dear to me, nor do I feel that this or anything else will affect it. I hope you will feel this too, and make me happy by saying so. If you had been old, or I young, we might have lived our lives together; or perhaps we might not have cared for each other or not realised it. As it is, we hold hands across a river of time. Nigel darling, please remain my dearest of friends.

It is one of the happy things that Stewart likes the people I like. We have a common world to set out in. He is being sent to Antigua. I believe he just couldn't bear to go alone and had to have a wife among his tropical kit. Anyway, I am by way of going out in a few months, and going now to London to see it all through in a deplorable hurry. So it all seems very unreal at the moment. I think, too, it will mean no Greece in January, and I don't mind in the least if you are not to be there. But you *must* come here when next I am back, probably in the summer.

Don't mention anything till you see it officially announced.

Dear love,

FREYA

BERNARD BERENSON
London
22 September 1947

My dearest B.B.,

This long silence has not been forgetfulness: all summer have I been trying to reach you. But it took the Foreign Office six months to decide was it, or was it not, going to keep me travelling about. In September it finally decided not – and then I was plunged into material chaos by masons in my house, and moral chaos by the fact that I am getting married, just any day now, to Stewart Perowne. He asked me by telegram when posted to Antigua – and of course that is how one gets away with these things. I can't help thinking I shall make a very unsatisfactory wife, but one never knows. I had just finished Chapter Thirteen of my book, on Love!

Dearest B.B., I send you this little line as to one of my dearest friends: these things don't go by time.

Your very loving
FREYA

JOHN GREY MURRAY
Asolo
12 October 1947

Dear Jock,

Thank you, dear Jock, for coming to see us off. The last touch to all that went before. I don't suppose we could have got married without you, and certainly not seen so many friends. Tell John we will have a special dressing up so that he can be bridesmaid and carry the train.

Love to you all,

FREYA

JOHN GREY MURRAY
Asolo
17 October 1947

My dearest Jock,

It seems very strange to have been married so long – ten days. I keep on finding it peculiar. But, otherwise, we are passing some very quiet happy days, with just enough of the outer world – the Chavchavadzes to lunch, Stewart lecturing in Venice, to keep us from contemplating the irreparable quality of human actions at any unnecessary length.

We had the most touching welcome here: the house all *filled* with flowers, from everyone around, and all the little people, masons, shopkeepers, the work-girls, etc., coming up to shake hands and quite genuinely pleased. The house, of course, is still a sort of cavern of the winds, with masons, electricians, and plumbers humming and hammering about. But things, like islands or whales, are beginning to appear above the surface.

A sad event occurred in Venice: we thought to economise and go by *vaporetto*, and there was a little spiv who offered to carry. We looked married and innocent, and he just walked off with Stewart's new suitcases into the darkness. And with not even a toothbrush left him. We spent next day largely in the Questura trying to identify the criminals of Venice; they look so very much alike. But I don't much hope to get anything back. Luckily, there were not many presents inside. One is really awfully *separable* from things; one wonders how they ever stick together at all.

I can never thank you, dear Jock, for all you have been in this time. Perhaps you prefer not, knowing that with no one else would I take everything for granted, as with you. But it was great comfort and happiness to have you near.

Always your
FREYA

BERNARD BERENSON
Asolo
19 October 1947

My very dear B.B.,

We are here again, for a short stay in Asolo before Stewart departs for Barbados; but I stay on till after Xmas, so as to clear the house of workmen

24

and to finish the book. I will pack paper and typewriter and do a week of my work at I Tatti if I may, at end of November or early in December, or any time that suits you best. I look forward to this with very great joy as you know, and especially before so far a journey. To work quietly in that lovely atmosphere and talk to you in the intervals is one of those things that make the life one likes to live.

I shall be back in Asolo every six months or so, to keep it from crumbling about us: so that I hope to see you often. If you hear of anyone who would like to rent this house for four or five months, I shall be very glad.

Very dear love to you always,

FREYA

SIR SYDNEY COCKERELL   Asolo
24 October 1947

My darling Sydney,

Such neglect, but you can imagine what a mountain the poor little mouse, my pen, has been eating its way through. Apart from the ordinary business of a honeymoon, and the extras of masons and carpenters, hammering all the wrong places of the house, a garden party on the last of the warmish days, for Asolo and the *provincia* to meet Stewart, and so on. Now his day for leaving is upon us: we go to Venice tomorrow and he starts next day; and I shall follow in January, I hope, and see you perhaps on my way through. I shall be buried in my book for the next two months, in the hopes of getting it done by Xmas.

How happy I am, dear Sydney, that you met Stewart and liked him. The process of getting married was so alarming, and it seems to me so monstrous to undertake such solemn things without in the least knowing whether either of you is going to be able to carry them out, that if it had been at all possible, in that last fortnight, I would have done like an unwilling horse at a jump and taken the nearest gap in the nearest hedge. Many feel like this, I imagine.

Now, however, I am going to miss someone who requires such constant attention, and I am glad I accepted the adventure. It is so hard for human creatures to get near to each other. A relationship that makes this easier is happiness. Even a misanthropist would say that marriage gives one the advantage of having someone to get away from occasionally and increases one's capacity to suffer? Please don't show anyone this letter, or it might be misunderstood. Now we are building up a whole number of things together: books we read, evenings by the fire, the arrangement of the new rooms, and

25

I hope each is making a little bond. And, in spite of being such a middle-aged couple, we do feel very happily alive.

Today is the first day of cloud and cold. The country is so beautiful, just turning to copper and gold.

My dearest love always,

FREYA

GERALD DE GAURY   Asolo
28 October 1947

My dear Gerald,

Not a word from you, not a funeral note, from the day that your friends were both married. I do hope you are not going to let a ripple of this sort disturb the even and pleasant flow of our long correspondence?

Stewart has just left, and I am settling down to a sort of gathering of threads. We managed a peaceful and pleasant honeymoon in spite of a chaos of carpenters, plumbers, masons, and electricians. But the sun shone and day after day was fine; till the last, when it rained in Venice, and the Russians delayed the train, and one felt the closing in of winter. I envied him Barbados, as it will be quite impossible to keep even a room in this house warm till the workmen have done.

Do write, dear Gerald, and tell me all the news.

Your affectionate
FREYA

STEWART PEROWNE   Asolo
31 October 1947

Darling,

You can't think how nice and kind Asolo was to you. It has rained ever since you left; and, the very day after, the electric people came and cut off the kitchen stove because Emma had been using three times her amount of electricity to cook your dinner. Then the marble man arrived, demolished the Gents so as to finish it, and found that a bit was left in Venice. So that it remains for the next fortnight in ruins. Caroly[36] has gone to the hospital and produced a little girl yesterday; and Cici and Franco are going to try to carry

---

[36] Caroly had been F.S.'s mother's secretary. Flora Stark had ceded the *tessoria* to her.

on, but make me quite miserable, as it does seem to me the most gloomy prospect.

As for me, I have done the review, and an article I had accepted months ago for a thing called *Health Horizon*.

Your loving
FREYA

STEWART PEROWNE Asolo
5 November 1947

My darling,

So glad to get yours of the 30th, but what *does* happen in the post to mine?

Perhaps it is just as well you are not here. The *discomforts* of these days! Amadeo's pipes all leaking gently into the walls into which they had been bricked. Even Solomon's roof only leaked *outside* and not *inside* the masonry. But when the sun shines it doesn't matter, the world is so incredibly lovely. I long for you to see the full autumn here: it glows like all Veronese and Giorgione put together, and no painter could help being a colourist in such a land.

I have got into Chapter Fifteen, working like a slave, but mercilessly interrupted. I long to get on with it.

Your
FREYA

LORD AMHERST Asolo
8 November 1947

My dear Jeffery,

I was glad to get your letter. Now that the barbarous ceremonies are over, I feel very happy and contented and am really longing to get out to domestic life as a Colonial Officialess in the Spanish Main. I hope to pass through London; and, if I have a day or two there, will give you a ring. It would be good to have a gossip, and I will tell you about my book, which I am struggling hard to finish by Xmas.

I would love to have a present: something old, ornamental, and not useful. Perhaps you might think of Barbados in the spring. It sounds great fun with a Negro government and the population all divided into parishes and 'fiercely parochial'. And the Governor's name is Blood.

Much love,

FREYA

Asolo

11 November 1947

Darling,

In spite of all the trouble, delay, weariness, and financial agony, I do think it is pleasant to have managed to give all these men the chance to do something that restores their morale so completely. Amadeo has just made a brass towel rail by filling a tube with lead so that it is malleable and melting it out again when bent. So that now we have lovely brass instead of dentist chromium – with hot water running through. Oh my! *What* have you arranged about my voyage out to you? You say not a word, and I have a horrid, but I hope unjustified, suspicion that you haven't done a thing about it. I expect it is monstrous of me to doubt you, and that you have done it all; and, if so, you must just put it down to the fact that I have never had anyone to lift any single burden for me.

Such a day, all azure in the distance and gold in the foreground. I walked up to a little hill top and said goodbye to an elderly man attending to three cows. He said, 'You English? I not born here.' So I found out he was from near Toronto, and came here twenty-five years ago. 'I will be buried in Italy,' he said, and it sounded just as sad as one of those epitaphs in the Greek anthology.

Your

FREYA

STEWART PEROWNE   Villa di Maser[37]

13 November 1947

Darling,

I walked down here, only to find that Marina had mistaken the day and is in Venice; and has just telephoned that she will not be back until ten tonight. I have been sitting very happily reading Napoleon's letters to Marie Louise. He always says exactly the same thing six days running. But they are very touching all the same; and, it seems to me, there is very little to be said for M.L., even remembering she was a Royal Austrian. The only point I would like you to imitate is Napoleon's way of dealing with his wife's journeys, Here is one specimen:

'Amica mia. I desire to see you. You will leave on the 22nd and sleep at Chalons: the 23rd at Metz, and the 24th at Mayence where I will join you.

[37] A Palladian villa near Asolo, famous for its Veronese frescoes, and bought by Contessa Marina Luling-Volpi's father.

You will travel with 4 carriages for the 1st service, 4 for the 2nd, and 4 for the 3rd. You will take the duchess, two ladies [I would dispense with all those], one prefect of the palace, 2 chamberlains, 2 pages, a doctor, and two red and two black ladies [their clothes, not their faces it seems], and your dinner service. Take a coach for yourself. Prepare it all. Adieu, my darling. Yours entirely, Nap.'

Your
FREYA

STEWART PEROWNE   Asolo
15 November 1947

Darling,

I am stupefied with writing so much and long to get it over. I think I must go on regularly writing a *little,* so as not to do it in these paroxysms; and begin another book next year to take us to Greece when the debts of this house are paid?

Tomorrow (Sunday) I am going to take a rest from Chapter Seventeen (Old Age) and write to a whole mountain of people. One very exciting letter from Archie John Wavell who showed a letter I wrote about *Hamlet* to Dover Wilson (with whose book I had dared to disagree), and the *good* man said he thought I was right. True magnanimity, and it pleased me. It is nice that you and I both enjoy being praised a little. It's one of those things that are wrongly, I think, trampled upon. It just comes from modesty and a liking to be reassured (at least that is what I like to think). It's really horrid not to mind what anyone thinks about one.

Yesterday and today are both St. Martin's – gently warm and golden, and roses still out in the garden, and the last yellow leaves fluttering off the poplar trees.

Your
FREYA

STEWART PEROWNE   Asolo
15 November 1947

Darling,

Archie John Wavell has written me a long letter. I would like to send it to you, but am afraid of losing until I know that these letters *do* find you. It is so interesting about his father's plan for India: withdraw gradually, first from the South, while still keeping order in the North. The Cabinet turned it down, probably because it meant legislation. History will do justice one of these days, but what prices we do make people pay for our mental timidity!

Your

FREYA

STEWART PEROWNE   Venice
                                                    20 November 1947

Darling,

I started at seven this morning from Asolo in the bus, with a fantastic sunrise, waves of red cloud over the yellow woods, and the fields on the plain like striped velvet, green and brown. The young corn already shows. Then rushing about here, usual chores, and then I thought I would go and see how your gold case is getting on. The jeweller lives in a flat as clean as a pin, smothered in aspidistras and lace mats, and does his work in his own home in the good old way with a small boy learning from him. I discovered it was he who mended all my Persian pottery for me years ago. He asked if I knew anyone called Stark in Asolo! The case is promised for Xmas, and I will take it out to you.

As I was walking away from the *piazza*, down that wide street, there was a happy sight: an old man with his overcoat buttoned over an immense white beard which burst out here and there like waves, standing in front of his easel and painting S. Moisé. It was the first swallow of a normal pre-war world. That and the fact that one needs no visas at all now to go to England.

Your own

FREYA

STEWART PEROWNE   Milan
                                                    21 November 1947

Darling,

I left by starlight this morning, very cold but beautiful on the Grand Canal with Orion shining on the roofs and chimneys and obelisks of the admirals. You know that rather bare and severe fish market, always empty? It was lit up and bursting with life; booths and baskets and people chattering and the bronze statue looking down. It is evidently only awake in the dark hours.

The trains are not heated, and felt like one of those nice Dakotas in wartime, but they have risen to a restaurant car now. And here the sun is shining, and I walked up M. Napoleone, turning resolutely away from all allurements; there was a Venini wild goose with gold wings which I am thankful you didn't see as it was almost irresistible to me singly and would have done for us together!

Your
FREYA

STEWART PEROWNE   Asolo
26 November 1947

Darling,

I can hardly see the paper out of a headache that you could cut like cheese. A sort of collapse has occurred, believe it or not, from *overwork*. Polizzi came last night and found my blood pressure even lower than the bank balance, in fact well overdrawn, which the Bank of England won't allow with the other. He is going to pump it up with injections, but says I must take six months easy (he has been saying this for two years) so as to make up a reserve. Luckily only two more chapters to go, and I will do those or bust. The revising is not such exhausting work. I only hope the book won't be as bad as I feel it now. Rebecca West told me that she ends every book with an illness. I hope I won't, for your sake.

Love,
FREYA

STEWART PEROWNE   Asolo
28 November 1947

Darling,

I am still in bed, but much better. A horrid day pouring with cold rain. It is good to think of you in sun and warmth by now, just about to sight Jamaica? How I long to hear about it all.

The bathroom, far from being looked upon as a plutocratic folly, is applauded as a public-spirited effort to give people here something they like to do. I do think this is much nicer than the *grudging* spirit in England, which is making everything dull because all must be one level. A sort of Renaissance spirit has come over the house – Emma, Maria, everyone – since the placing

31

of the marble has shown what splendours are coming after all these sordid months of hammering. Emma said, 'I can hardly bear to stay in the kitchen and cook; I would like to be making the house beautiful.'

I do hope you find a Barbadian negress with feelings of this sort. Set up a very *modest* establishment. It will be such a lovely feeling to be inside one's income. I would much rather do the cooking myself than make ends meet when they won't!

Your
FREYA

STEWART PEROWNE Asolo
30 November 1947

Darling,

It rains, and my head still hurts so that I can't work, and everything is very difficult apart from the fact that people are beginning to be murdered in Milan. But the bath is *exciting*. The canopy is stuck up and all ready with a cement cupola, 'a miracle of rare device'.

I have been filling all the little drawers in the new passage with bits of pottery, etc., from the Middle East and a whole collection from Meshed and Hadhramaut, and spices from Aden bazaar. The smell made me feel so homesick, that unmistakeable mixture of heavy scents that brings back all the noise and life and colour. I hope we shall see Aden again one of these days.

Dear love to you.

Your
FREYA

STEWART PEROWNE Asolo
4 December 1947

Darling,

I leave at seven tomorrow for Venice and Florence; I am taking my mss., the Jacopo Bassano, and your wedding photograph to show B.B. and hear what he has to say about you all.

I am nearly dead with tidying. Marina came to dine last night and was delighted with the house (having also known what it was like in the two unheated winters before). We sat and gossiped and she told me about the

Germans during the war, how everyone went to them, as they alone gave the nice parties. And laid themselves out to be agreeable. Prince Bismarck in Rome told a friend of hers how, when he was in command in Russia, he used to ride out all night and return at dawn while his troops were let loose on those poor towns 'because he couldn't bear the sight and sounds of horror'. What *can* one make of people like that? All Marina's friends were so surprised that she refused to go and dance there. When she was hiding from them in this house, she peered out of the bathroom window and saw their troops marching down this poor little street all dark and cowering, singing their songs and filling it from side to side. How hard it is to picture this already.

Your

FREYA

STEWART PEROWNE I Tatti, Settignano
7 December 1947

Darling,

I wish so much you were here. You would be so happy in this house. Everything is just right. There is a garden of cypress, ilex and laurel terraced down the slope, and opposite it is another slope of olive trees whose tops are light like little flames; and beyond, in a grey and silver light and with gentle hills behind it, is Florence with its domes. A beautiful Lorenzo Lotto is over my chest of drawers, and every piece of furniture in the room is a lovely object in itself, but not overpoweringly *rich*. One can't explain that touch in a house where people have chosen things because they loved them. In the morning B.B. takes the people he likes for a little walk under the ilex trees; and Nicky,[38] still lovely with grey hair and blue eyes and pearls, deals with all the others. And conversation is still an art. If you say anything brilliant, B.B. clasps your hand: how civilised and pleasant it is! All the servants have been here at least twenty years. And B.B. himself is always saying enchanting things; and yesterday we sat and talked about Asia Minor and a Greek theatre, intact, that lies somewhere between Halicarnassos and Alexandretta. B.B. is eighty-two, and he told me that up to now life has grown more fascinating for him with every year, and the power of enjoying it greater. What a charming way of growing old!

In Venice I was strolling on to the *piazza* when I suddenly noticed it was full of the British Army, rolling its drums to burst into 'God Save the

[38] sc. Mariano.

King'. A crowd, very silent but not at all unfriendly, looking on. I asked an old man who took his hat off for the National Anthem, what it was all about. 'Sono gli Inglesi, che ci abbandonano,' he said. They marched past beautifully, legs all moving like one, putting their whole souls into them, one felt. It was so exciting to see it, with St. Mark's and its pale gold as a background in the winter sun. The Italian contingent then took over, a little more like a centipede with all its legs different and that air of being bored at having to be all alike, which is really so charming. One could see that the officer was English (it was the Folgore division), and that he was marching along at their head, saying to himself, 'Well, I've done all I can, and I love them, and there it is.'

I left Venice in a deluge before dawn. The water was lapping out from the Grand Canal into all the little *calles*. It took nine hours by coach to Florence, with lunch at Bologna, and a gleam of sun on snow as we crossed the Apennines. Desolate it is, and every house or village pock-marked or blasted by guns, and a monument to the British dead on the height.

Dearest love,

FREYA

STEWART PEROWNE   I Tatti, Settignano
                                                   8 December 1947

Darling,

I have been driven out by the ancient chauffeur to see a villa that has been bought by Lionel Fielden.[39] The villa is very fine: rather a fortress, with only two heavily barred windows on the ground floor, and a garden hung in space on high old walls; and then the land drops and sweeps away, and the hills fold one behind the other, all smoke-coloured with cypress and olive, and houses at intervals. An incredibly sophisticated landscape, refined through so many centuries. B.B.'s garden has a wonderful triple hedge, immense, of cypress, and then ilex, and then cypress again cut broad and flat on either side of a central cascade of steps, and grass. I admired the sunlight which seems to *die* onto the darkness, and he said, 'Yes, they are the nearest vegetable things to metal.' He always has these happy phrases. A woman with dyed hair and lots of bracelets came into tea, and he said to me, 'Ever since I have known her, she has been this *article de commerce*. What I call a woman of clank and flashion.'

[39] Lionel Fielden had come to Italy in 1945 as Director of Public Relations, Allied Control Commission.

I am working like a slave at the book; I have all except the epilogue done, and am half way through the revising. It is extraordinary what a help it is to be in a sympathetic atmosphere for writing. B.B. makes me talk about it, and reads it, and it does help a lot. But I *am* longing to see the last page sent away, and so relieved to think that tomorrow morning, instead of finding adjectives, I am going to buy a hat.

The name of the Greek theatre between Halicarnassos and Alexandretta is Aspendos. Do let us go!

Your
FREYA

STEWART PEROWNE I Tatti, Settignano
9 December 1947

My darling,

B.B. has now approved of our Jacopo Bassano. I brought it down, and he says it is a particularly good one, and on no account are we to sell it, as it will go on increasing in value. He never puts his name to anything, but as I left it in his hands, and as I had pasted a piece of paper at the back, repeating what he said about it last year, he pulled out his pen and put down his signature. This is most angelic of him.

It is so agreeable to be here, sitting with such good talk, as if it were a wide panorama unfolding, literature, and people, and art, and wit, and Nicky surrounding everyone with kindness. Today they were telling me of the wonderful Norman churches in the South, and a shrine at St. Michael of Gargano where Tancred went on pilgrimage from Normandy and, being a strapping young man, was taken on as a soldier. And so the whole Sicilian story began.

Dearest love,

FREYA

STEWART PEROWNE I Tatti, Settignano
13 December 1947

Darling,

The Marchesa Fossi, who is half English and very pleasant, brought me a tiny silver Madonna and child, two inches high, as a present yesterday. I do hope she will see to it that we lose no more of our wedding presents.

I will bring her out and keep her in great honour and comfort on my dressing table. Otherwise, I am sure I shall drop my wedding ring one of these days, as I have just lost Patsy's[40] little ring. It is so *sad*, and B.B. says think of Polycrates who couldn't lose a ring when he tried, as if that were any comfort.

Victor Mallet, the new Ambassador in Rome, came and lunched today. He is an agreeable man, but I sat on B.B.'s other side and listened to him all through lunch saying the wrong things. B.B. very dangerous and urbane. How desperate it is when public servants come to think that just making a noise with their mouths is pleasing to other people! He evidently thought that it made B.B. happy to have the wrong names stuck onto his unique pictures. 'A Baldorinetti, I feel sure. Ah, no? How *could* I have thought it?' And all he had to do was to ask and be interested in hearing *who* it really was, or else talk of something that he knew.

13 December 1948

You never saw anything so like an Old Master as Florence today: a green sunset sky with pink clouds, reflected in the river, and the houses and the ruins all greens and yellows and browns. The ruins are coming to have a Piranesi beauty and B.B. says it is a pity not to leave them, which rather naturally must annoy the poor Florentines. But the Communist Municipality are thinking of an ultra-modern rebuilding which will look very painful with all the old things around.

14 December 1947

We have had a fine day: Florence like a statue with a veil, in her mists in the hollow, and every gentle line and colour of grey and green and rose in the hills that rise about her. Hoping to send off all except the Epilogue to be typed for the third time, tomorrow, before I leave for Asolo. So I do nothing but eat, talk, sleep, write, and take two little walks with B.B., who makes the whole of the last half century live again in his memories. He was telling me about Oscar Wilde. They were great friends, until Lord Alfred was so objectionable that B.B. couldn't bear him, and told Oscar not to make them meet again. Oscar was passing through Florence and visited B.B., and there was this (so he says) dreadful man. And when Oscar came to apologise, B.B. told him that he was courting destruction. Oscar said to him, 'I am like God in every way and must have constant praise.' He brought him the first copy of *Dorian Gray*, and B.B. read it and told him he thought it appalling; and Oscar was almost in tears, and said he

---

[40] sc. Lady Patricia Lennox-Boyd.

knew it himself that it was bad, but they offered him £100 to write it, and he needed the money so badly. And the whole continent of Europe has been reading it ever since, apparently unaware of how bogus it is.

B.B. dreamed that at last he wrote something which delighted him; and, in his dream, said to himself, 'Now this is prose like Freya's' (such a kind thought in a dream), and woke and not a *word* remained. I have often written long poems in my sleep, and would like so much to remember; but one only sees a sort of form disappearing into shadows when one wakes.

Your

FREYA

STEWART PEROWNE

Asolo

17 December 1947

Darling,

I came back here to the good old sound of hammering. It died down as soon as I left, and needs strong words all round to get going again. There *is* no way to get Italians to work in your absence. But, in fact, we *may* be quite finished by Xmas, even with the heating.

The journey over the Appennines yesterday was one of the loveliest imaginable. Starting in darkness in the shadow of the Duomo, just a bit of marble pattern showing by lamplight; and then climbing into a Primitive sunrise, very neat little clouds outlined with gold; and so up through lovely colours to highlands of snow. As one crosses the ridge, the traces of the war are all about, every little house on a hill a ruin; and when one looked down, there was the Bologna plain drowned in white mist and the little ruined villages silhouetted against it, one behind the other in the winding valley, like a surrealist picture – not grim, but fantastic and beautiful. On the last ridge is a British obelisk 'To Our Heroic Dead', and one thinks what a lot of feeling must have gone into the choice of that adjective when they put it up. I nearly froze and never felt myself below the waist all day (and am in bed at this moment, not yet thawed).

I am so glad I made the effort to go. Eighty-two is an age, but I hope we shall find the dear little man when we return – like a thin, fragile flame, all pure light and fire. Even the quite ordinary people become different when he talks to them. He told me that if only he loved people as he loves trees, he would be a Saint.

Love to you,

FREYA

Asolo

18 December 1947

My dearest,

This is purely business, inspired by the fact that you are now grappling with our ugly duckling of a house. Do make your budget ever so carefully and allow for all the dull things one forgets: kitchen things, including cloths, dusters, aprons; floor polishes and brushes; electric iron; fans; some sort of furniture for sitting in the garden (?); two *comfortable* chairs; blankets (?); pillows; cushions; buckets, pails, jugs, and basins, etc. You needn't get all these, I will cope; but you *must allow for them*; and you will find they will swallow most, if not all, our £100. I take it that a frigidaire and cooking stove exist? and baths, and beds? and cupboards with *shelves*? and a means for heating bath water?

I have an idea that we shall be rather hard up. I don't mind, if you don't (am only too accustomed!), but do let us have as small and modest an establishment as possible. It's so much nicer being comfortable in a small way than grand and stingy (at least I hope you feel it so, as I do).

If there is anything you think I could bring from here, send just the word by telegraph. Asolo is sufficient address, as there isn't another in the world.

Dear love,

FREYA

Asolo

Xmas Day, 1947

Darling Stewart,

A happy Xmas to you. It's ten o'clock and I am still in bed, with a rather morning-afterish feeling as it was 4 a.m. before I got home last night. Marina sent the car for me, and there was the Capuchin friar inside who was going down to say Mass. It was after midnight when we got there, and the house party and the servants gathered in the beautiful, but *icy* chapel. Friar *galloped* through his Latin; Father, Son, and Holy Ghost almost in one syllable. I think the way they treat their language is enough to put one off the Catholic Church. At dinner, I sat next Enrico, who told me what a rush he had had in Milan, as he had been a second at a duel a few weeks ago and that makes you *excommunicated*; and he went to get back into the fold, but the usual little confessional wouldn't do. He was sent to the Penitentiary Father-in-Chief up three steps in the Duomo, all in his office hours, and got un-excommunicated *and* cleared of two months' sins at the price of nine Ave Marias. I told him I calculated he worked off about twenty sins per Ave Maria, and it seems very cheap. He says he always goes to a different confessor so they don't realise the total. Once he and his small innocent nephew of nine years old both confessed for the same period of time, and he got off with six Aves and the poor little boy had twelve and four Paternosters!

I wonder how your Xmas is being spent? I hope I shall soon get out now.

Your

FREYA

STEWART PEROWNE   Asolo
                                                31 December 1947

Darling,

The year ends with a most welcome, long-awaited letter from you. It is such very good news that one can ride. I hope you are finding me a nice little animal my size? How *lovely* it will be. I long to hear what it is like and whether soft tracks among the cultivation, like Egypt, or sand like Aden?

I am not happy at all: a fearful cold of the worst kind (so am writing in bed) and twenty-two people are coming to have supper at midnight; Marina insisted on this, which is not my sort of party in the least. They are all bringing their own food and drink, and Emma is making some huge plates of macaroni and salad. How glad I shall be when it is over!

New Year's Day

We went on till 4.30 this morning, and here are the signatures of all the guests; and the blots are not made by drunkenness, but by the effect of fingers on a Biro pen. Twenty-five people came instead of twenty-two, and they brought far too little to drink; but luckily my Mediterranean background led me to expect this and we were prepared. We had three tables in the hall downstairs, and candles, *grappa* and talk till midnight (from about ten o'clock); and then opening of windows, banging of pans like the Arabs with an eclipse; and Esmeralda and one of her young men walked in dressed enchantingly as 1848, and presented nosegays and favours all round. Marina produced champagne; I drank your health and wondered what you were doing. It was all so friendly, genuine, and full of a simple *joie de vivre*, that it was pleasant to see it under our roof. I am recovering today and tomorrow begin to pack.

The island sounds enchanting. Your letter of the 9th has come today, and tells me of your office and the harbour view. But there is so much to hear, and all I know of our house is that it will have electric lights and a frigidaire.

Love,

FREYA

STEWART PEROWNE   Asolo
                                                              4 January 1948

Darling,

You sound awfully cluttered up with domestic problems, and so many more will be bearing down upon you when you are a Married Man with a Household (though I will save you from dealing with the servants); I hope you won't repent and wish yourself a bachelor. It's much easier to think only for oneself, but rather arid; you can always look upon a wife as very good for you (I believe Socrates did). I am finding it rather sad to leave Asolo (Emma in tears at any moment and Caroly, also); and I long to be so far on the way that you are growing a little more real on my horizon!

The bathroom is finished and is such a gem that it is worth being in debt for years. It is not opulence, but it is so beautiful. When I first came back here, I made a five-year plan, and it is now three years done all in one go. So it is not bad, and such a comfort to have all that mess and trouble behind one. And you can go in and shut the door and turn on that beautiful light and forget that the world of Utility exists. I feel as if I had purged away a little of all the ugliness of all those years of war.

I have packed five big straw hats and four parasols (the hats are bigger than the parasols), two fans, and some mittens. All this because you have given me no really intelligent information of what is worn; so it will be all the worse for you if parasols are 'not the custom'. I am feeling so unflatteringly sad at leaving. I wish you were here.

Your

FREYA

STEWART PEROWNE   Train from Milan
                                                              7 January 1948

Darling,

This is a beastly journey. We have been sitting in Milan station all day with rain drip-dripping on the roof and everything clammy and cold, all because of the Yugoslavs doing their sabotage on the Belgrade *wagons-lits*. We are off now, I hope.

9 January 1948

Now I am in London and not quite so tired after a good night, and your dear letters, four of them, brought by Jock to the station. They make me feel that the Stewart I left so sadly in Asolo and the one in Barbados *may* be the same after all!

I hope we shall never become as conjugal as half the people one sees eating in restaurant cars. They sit side by side eating and looking fixedly into space. You think they must be contemplating divorce; until suddenly one makes a remark and it is quite amicable, and you realise that this is just their habit of daily intercourse.

11 a.m.

They have got me a passage, sailing on the 24th to Trinidad; and from then on, no one knows!

Love,

FREYA

STEWART PEROWNE   London

12 January 1948

Darling,

This is an exhausting round, but nice. I went yesterday to Margaret Olivier,[41] who remembers you with *simpatia* all those years ago. And Billy Henderson[42] fetched me there, lunched me at Claridges and then took me to see the cleaned pictures in the National Gallery (*so* much improved), and the Dürer Madonna – a *glory* all in red with another red for her mantle, and hair like gold foam flying, and the most exquisite plants and flowers. I had to tear myself away in sleet and rain to visit Sybil Colefax[43] in bed, clinging onto life with determination, rather pathetic. Then afterwards Lulie and I were taken to dine at the Cadogan Hotel, a marvellously solid place, the

[41] F.S. had stayed with her in London before the war. See *Letters* Volume III, p. 230: 'I went to Margaret Olivier's for lunch yesterday and had Michael Huxley and Mr. Perowne and a young archaeologist who is going to Behan – and we discussed the world all through lunch and the possibility of running international colonies.'

[42] Artist and former A.D.C. to Lord Wavell in India.

[43] Widow of Sir Arthur Colefax. Prominent hostess and founder of the decorating firm of Colefax and Fowler.

upholstered essence of Repose with an Income behind it. Then, pretty tired, to bed.

Billy gave gloomy details of India. People's Muslim servants pursued into their masters' dressing rooms and butchered there. The Muslims hate the Mountbattens, of course, and I wonder if the Love of Congress is worth it?

I have just been reading how the UNO vote for Palestine was packed by the Americans. It will be an *appalling* world if there is nothing but Russian or American to choose from.

Love,

FREYA

STEWART PEROWNE
London
13 January 1948

Darling,

I lunched with Terrell[44] and heard all about the difficulties of getting posted to the Mediterranean. It seems to me that the really *fatal* thing is to be good, in Government service. The F.O. has been begging for a good man for Iraq, and Terrell told me that he was determined not to let one (i.e. you, I presume) go at any cost, and will only part with duds. He told me about his travels in the Crimea, and was most cordial.

Lady Wavell says that some friend told her that 'Freya is really original. She has interrupted her honeymoon to write a book on Love.'

FREYA

STEWART PEROWNE
London
13 January 1948

Darling,

Business. Your melancholy little finance note just came and I *agree* that we ought to contribute to each other's housekeeping. The only extra income that is likely to come to me is a book now and then, and that I *never will* devote to Ordinary Life. It is the stuff one's dreams are made of and, however poor I have been, I have always devoted it to dreams. I think that has allowed me to move quite spaciously in life, with the income most people use on a semi-detached house in a garden city. Please never ask me to spend it on

[44] Richard Terrell, in the Colonial Office. Son of the colourful Sir Courtney Terrell, Chief Justice of Bihar and Orissa 1928–38.

everyday existence, because I won't. For that we must share and share alike, and we shall be poor, and there it is. *Don't* have a chauffeur. I loathe them and love driving; and would, anyway, prefer a Commando scooter to a car.

Your loving

FREYA

STEWART PEROWNE   London
                                                        16 January 1948

Darling,

Two letters from you, and *what* an effect they have. I read one while waiting for a bus in Sloane St., all alone, and lifted my eyes as the bus arrived to see that a long queue had formed *ahead* of me, so that I had to wait again. The second letter I read in the bus, and discovered myself two stops beyond my stopping place. So I had to get a taxi, and went to lunch at the Apéritif with Moore Crosthwaite,[45] who told me tales of Spain. We *must* go and look at that country one of these days. They have a miracle opera at a place called Elches near Alicante where the choirs of angels and the Madonna and Holy Ghost sing suspended in air from the dome of the church; and it is all music of the fifteenth and sixteenth centuries. At the end of the performance, the audience or congregation were fluttered over by little printed leaflets that said: 'Elches believes in the Assumption.'

Your

FREYA

STEWART PEROWNE   London
                                                        23 January 1948

Darling,

I believe this *may* yet catch you and tell you I leave tomorrow. The book *finished* at 2 p.m. Jock and Diana kept me *in bed*, fed with stout and claret, pens and paper; and I revised it all in four days and got up yesterday to lunch.

The evening spent at home with Harold Nicolson and Jeffery Amherst; such a pleasant evening. Harold in his best vein, telling how he went to dine with General König and de Gaulle, on their return from Normandy in '45, and heard how they had driven inland from the beaches and, after three and a half hours, König said, 'We haven't yet spoken to a Frenchman. We must stop the first we see.' So they stopped two gendarmes who came pedalling

[45] Then with the Foreign Office in Madrid. Later Ambassador to the Lebanon (1958–63) and to Sweden (1963–66).

along on bicycles, and sent them ahead to prepare their reception in Beauvais. But, by a mistake, they were shown to the back door of the Mayor's house, instead of his office. His wife led them through, and they came into the office and found the Mayor standing on a chair taking down a picture of Pétain.

An easterly gale is beginning to blow. It *will* be nice on the Atlantic.

Your

FREYA

MR. AND MRS. JOHN GREY MURRAY

S.S. *Ariquain*

3 February 1948

My dearest Jock and Diana,

This is the first day I feel alive again. The hurricane (it was an official hurricane) is over, the sun shines, the portholes are open at last, and a soft, tropical breeze is flapping this paper on deck, and my bread and butter letter would like to say thank you for so much more than bread and butter (and I am not referring even to claret and stout). One makes oneself such various homes in this world. When I left Asolo, I was feeling homesick for that, and I imagine (hope) there will be a growing 'homeness' out here; but I know that I shall always think of you two as one sort of best sort of a home, where one can be oneself and find oneself together.

Malory was on my rack ready to be opened for the birthday, but alas! this poor little boat is very light, having no cargo, and she creaked and rolled. One clung to a perpendicular bunk like a fly on the wall. The waves looked like the stony desert hills, huge and full of barren ridges and shining like mica in pale grey gleams of sun. It felt almost *indecent* to be there, like intruding on a family scene with the winds and waves howling at each other, or jostling like huge herds of grey elephants, and tilting us up and down their great slopes. I felt much too ill to enjoy it; and the stewardess is a good old type and, without even pausing to think, contradicts anything any passenger may say. In the calmness of the Bristol Channel, she went about as glum and disagreeable as a funeral, grudging one even a hot water bottle (and furious if one got it for oneself). Then suddenly she appeared, beaming with cheerfulness and kindness, to tell us that 'The Captain says it's a hurricane' and enjoyed every minute of it, with her tray cloths all sopped down with water to keep the things from slipping, and everyone ill in every cabin. She liked me better after she heard I had had appendicitis on the Atlantic, where she went to and fro in the war, 'getting the bacon and eggs home: it had to be done.' Now she is quite a friend and would love me if another hurricane came to bring us together.

We had a day's lull in the lee of the Azores. I *would* like to stop off there for a week. Nothing can be stranger than to come upon them there in the middle of nothing, with huge cliffs; and, on the top of them, flat lonely pastures, well tended and walled with hedges, but no houses, until you look toward the softer slope of the islands where sparse little white groups are scattered and there must be small hidden coves. Terrific white towers of spray were breaking against their dark red walls, and there was a big distance of sea between the islands and, of course (I was told), a strong disapproval of one for the other. We went right in towards the mouth of the chief harbour (Fayal) and saw a little clean white town, prosperous and quiet.

No more now, except love to all five.

Your
FREYA

NIGEL CLIVE   S.S. *Ariquain*
                                                  5 February 1948

My dearest Nigel,

What a lot of the world is sea. We have been going and going, a week of misery, the wind at hurricane speed, the waves on deck, our cabins with mad chairs and suitcases careening to and fro; and I not caring *what* happened and longing for a solid desert underfoot. Now all has cleared away and little blue transparent flocks of flying fish escort us; and one feels the whole, huge curve of the earth between ourselves and Europe. I don't think I want to be very long away from all the sorrows of our own places; but, for a while, it is very thrilling to come to a new continent. I have been reading about the pirates, the slaves, the islands; it is a Hollywood sort of history, and *still* all here: the huge Barbados negroes walking about the deck, the naval commander who hates the red tape of the New Order and has come with his dog to find an island and build a house. In Trinidad, the Shaws[46] (who were in Palestine) are governing and I am spending a day or two before getting an aeroplane on. The most alluring thing has been a sight of the Azores. After days and days of sea, there they emerge with cliffs and peaks and clouds and little white houses; and perhaps they will go on when all of us have gone, and new nations will wonder where all their strange primitive customs come from?

Your loving
FREYA

[46] Sir John Shaw was Chief Secretary Palestine 1943–46, Governor and C.-in-C. Trinidad and Tobago 1947–50.

BERNARD BERENSON   Bridgetown,
                                                      Barbados
                                                  12 February 1948

My very dear B.B.,

You must not think me forgetful: I have sent you so many thoughts in
this silence. I have just arrived three days ago, and it is the strangest place
for me to be in – full of the things you Do and even more of the things you
Don't do – and oh B.B., what silly things they are. 'In the beginning was the
word': but at least St. John had the decency to put it in the past tense: and
here there seem to be lots of little words and all in the present. It will be
harmless if one can laugh at them together.

How can I ever thank you for those days? They shine like gold with the
little flames of your olive slope and the cypress trees: and what would I give
to have you knocking to me to go out and walk with you in and out among
the little paths? One is loved so often, and so rarely for oneself. At least I
know the value of such affection, immune from space or time, and send you
many thanks in my heart.

This is a pretty green island, sweet-smelling with sugar cane and salt with
the Atlantic, and half white coral rock and half dark lava. No jungles, but
an English neatness which grows smug only when it becomes didactic. We
rode this morning, and that was happiness; the canes waving in the wind,
thinking only of themselves and God, and much happier than the people
who cut them down. There is a sadness of old slavery hanging about in spite
of all.

A dear embrace to Nicky and my love to her and you.

                                                    Your loving
                                                    FREYA

BERNARD BERENSON   Bridgetown
                                                  24 February 1948

My most dear B.B.,

I think of you so often here: sometimes because of likeness and often
because of unlikeness. The lovely Atlantic light, which seems to be a brilliance
in itself independent of the things it clothes; the pale island with its green
waves of sugar cane growing and brown swathes of sugar cane cut; the funny
little houses made like those cardboard toys, with little slats and wooden
painted gables; and the charming black children with curls screwed into

pigtails all over their heads, or little caps with peaks, and a tab of colour on them for their school – all these I wish you could see.

This island is called Little England; it has a charm, like a field in hedges. It has eleven parish churches and tombstones that go back two or even three hundred years. Stewart is very happy here, and I shall be able to leave him with a quiet mind in October when the house and servants and all will be going smoothly I hope. I shall be back in Asolo and hope your visit to Venice may be delayed till I can welcome you. If I can possibly do so I will hop over to Yucatan and tell you of the temples; but it is unimaginable how little interest is taken in the huge continent and all it holds: if anyone goes any-where it is only to another island, and a British one at that. I believe that just as it takes a generation of sinners to produce a saint, so it is the smugness of the stay-at-homes that have roused the English traveller and made him long to wander.

Dear dear love to Nicky and you

FREYA

JOHN GREY MURRAY   Bridgetown
                                                          25 February 1948
My dearest Jock,

I have been here a fortnight and haven't written. Really not lack of time, but a sort of caged feeling; and I felt if I wrote it would be just a wail. I found Stewart turned into the perfect Civil Servant, completely occupied by files and minutes and the *things that are done*; people with cards (three of them) in shoals every afternoon; and days filled with groceries and servants. Don't repeat this, Jock, but I did look down into an abyss and am still very wobbly. However, the household now goes smoothly with a minimum of my time; and the callers are beginning to develop individual faces; and, no doubt, there are casements here and there opening on the foam. I do think there is an element of *darkness* in the Government Service; it makes people think themselves important, a *frightful* thing to do. I will rather sit among the Negroes in their touching little Methodist wooden chapels (called Pilgrim Holiness) than take an official view of my only life in this earth.

I have pulled out the autobiography and will look it over next week.

Dearest love, dear, dear Jock.

Your
FREYA

47

Darling Sydney,

I have pulled out the autobiography, you will be glad to hear, and mean to try to see if any work can be done in this island full of noises. The cocks crowing all night, the wind perpetually moving in fronds of cane or palms, the flowers all papery and rustling, so that it is almost as if the Atlantic continued its movement of ebb and flow across this small piece of solid land.

Peter Fleming[47] is here, and very pleasant, spending a week with us. He is so modest, sane and observant, with a wry way of looking at things, that deflates all except the essentials. I like him very much. It refreshes me from the burden of being vice-governor's wife (H.E.s being away for five days). I never was meant to sit on platforms! We have given three dinner parties, and made an innovation by sitting after on our suburban lawn, with two big trees showing their outline against a soft sky full of stars. The Great Bear sinks and the Southern Cross rises. One gets the swing of the world much more visibly here near the Equator.

Dear love to you,

FREYA

Dearest Jock,

We have Jenny Clifford staying, back from Guatemala and Honduras, and Trinidad, and filled with horror at the backwardness of our colonies; and I foresee that her name will be mud in the West Indies, at least among the Governors. I have been urging on her that we are nearly always quite unjustly blamed for sins of commission in our colonies, while the real blame, much deserved, is for sins of *omission*. One could make things much simpler if this were clearly pointed out. She says that South America is making one big push, and all together, to push the European right out, and that they may succeed. I do think it is rather a pity to greet any mention of jokes like the Argentine navy with shouts of laughter in Parliament or anywhere else. We will find it difficult to laugh it off if they stop their meat supply! Or even if all their little armies and navies band together.

Did I tell you we went in a flying-fish fisherman's boat to see how they

[47] Author, traveller and journalist; married to the actress Celia Johnson. Elder brother of Ian Fleming, the author and originator of James Bond.

are caught? We had a ballast of old iron which had to be shifted with clangs and thuds when one tacked; and three black men who shared the profits; and the boat went up and down on a dark blue sea for six hours in the sun, while the bait (of rotted flying fish) smelt like quite a lot of the perfumes of Arabia. We only got five, but sometimes they catch over 1,000, and then return to the beach with a red pennon flying at their masthead. One of the pleasant things to see here is the colour of the black skin against the sea, which has a brittle sort of glass-like brilliance; and the black has, as it were, a brown heart, a warmth dusted over with black, like those volcanic hills of Southern Arabia. It looks quite lovely in the sun against the shine of the sea, and is a much more useful skin than ours.

I have discovered a Russian on this island (there are two, but one is in the lunatic asylum). She is married to a retired engineer who spent years in the Caucasus, Urals, Roumania, and Kirkuk, and can't bear the thought of old age in England. So they have a little house here under palms by the sea close to where the cinema people are building the *Caravel* for Columbus. (They are all arriving, and came to drinks with us, and explained how they are throwing a love-affair in the Azores into the picture!) I don't think the Russian woman can teach, but she can read with me an hour a week. It is quite a drive to reach her, through up and down streets between the boxes of houses with their overlapping wooden walls and fretwork painted gable ends, all looking like a very modern, invented picture; and then along the coast, with the children from school and the black girls in their big hats (Salvation Army, almost) and with loose dancing-walk going all across the road.

Dear love to you all,

FREYA

FIELD-MARSHAL LORD WAVELL   Bridgetown
Easter Day, 1948

Dearest Chief,

Your lovely letter came a week or so after mine had started, and now I have just heard from Sydney that you are back from South Africa. It is Easter Day so that one *must* be allowed to do what one likes, and I am doing some Russian. If I had more time and this were a less sleepy climate, I might do you credit and speak quite a bit when next you see me; but it is a lotus-eating island and always afternoon. And an hour's work makes one go right off to sleep. Even the cars here are not allowed to go over thirty miles on the loneliest roads. The country is charming and gets wild in a small way at the north end; and one looks down steeply to the rough coast where the long rows of breakers come in. One can wade out there quite happily with water scarcely to the knee, and a backwash comes suddenly – a terrific rush of ten feet deep or more – and carries one out to sea.

There is an Anglican sort of smugness about the island which would make me hate it to live in. I was told the story of a German governess who went off her head and decided to worship the Sun God. So she took off all her clothes and swam into the sunset and was seen miles out at sea. A boat put out to rescue, and came up with her, saw she had no bathing dress, and turned back to shore to fetch one. When the poor thing could be rescued with propriety, she was very nearly drowned.

I am going to be back in Asolo some time in June, I hope. One ought to be delighted to be here out of all the turmoil, but I feel as if I were imprisoned in a dewdrop and long to be a part of the living world again.

Love always,

FREYA

JOHN GREY MURRAY   Bridgetown
                                                          3 April 1948
Darling Jock,

I am earning $100 by doing an article for *Foreign Affairs*, but I am not at all well, sheer harassment, and can hardly make myself do anything at all. By hook or crook, I hope to get three weeks walking in the Dolomites to restore the inward balance. Would you think of it, too? July or August? From hut to hut and a little inn here and there? Oh Jock, how I long for it.

We saw two monkeys on this island playing in the high mahogany trees in the sunset. They leap about with a lovely curve of their long tails. The great little pets are the local sort of sparrow. They come in with the morning tea and then pull themselves together to take a drink from the milk jug. First a wide reconnaissance, then little expeditions nearer and nearer, till they flutter up three or four times just *brushing* the rim with their toes. When they feel quite sure it won't explode, they settle on it and take a long pull, a look right and left, another long pull. When one thinks that all wild animals have to make these momentous decisions every time they eat, one realises that private enterprise is pretty basic, doesn't one?

Love and thanks, dear Jock,

FREYA

JOHN GREY MURRAY   Bridgetown
                                                        19 April 1948

Dearest Jock,

The marriage business is not going at all nicely. I had a miserable time, and now the decision is made and I feel better, like after an operation. Perhaps a summer away may do good. I don't want to quarrel and I won't, but I will just go. And this would be such a dear little island with anyone who was a little bit in love with one. What a letter! Dear Jock, bless you.

                                                              FREYA

JOHN GREY MURRAY   Bridgetown
                                                           1 May 1948

Dearest Jock,

I leave possibly on the 20th; but we appear to be visiting Jamaica, Bermuda, and Tampico, so will probably not reach Tilbury till after June 20th. All the frangipani are in flower, bunches of blossom red, salmon, pink, white, at the end of branches like coral with no leaves. When the leaves begin to appear, they look like the trees in Jacobean embroideries, but before that they might be marine plants, so strangely bare and rich. The sea has turned emerald green because of the Orinoco waters. On Sunday we went with the Cunards[48] for a picnic in one of the gullies that wind and water has worn into the coral rock and we lunched in a grove of nutmegs looking just like Kate Greenaway. There was a clove tree, too. Fascinating to see grocery growing wild. Today we have been riding and Rosemary Grimble fell off and had to be found a car. I couldn't help feeling that we were brought up much tougher and would have ridden back somehow ... not what we were in *my* young days.

Love, dear Jock,

                                                              FREYA

JOHN GREY MURRAY   Trinidad
                                                          19 May 1948

Dearest Jock,

It was strange to see that little island vanishing back into the waves and clouds from which I saw it emerge so few months ago; and filled with such

[48] Victor Cunard and his cousin Nancy. Victor had served throughout the war in the Political Intelligence Department of the Foreign Office. Nancy was the unconventional daughter of Sir Bache Cunard (d. 1925) and his wife Maud (Emerald), the well-known hostess.

a mixture, rather unhappy, of new days. It is like a frame with no intrinsic character of its own, but lovely or melancholy according to the stuff one has in oneself. I hope to flit gently and unnoticed through London, with a little leisure for Godson.

Love, dear Jock,

FREYA

STEWART PEROWNE   King's House,
                                                                    Jamaica
                                                                 24 May 1948

Dearest Stewart,

You would love this island; its hills are not so sudden steep, its jungles not *voracious* like Trinidad. On the flat land are park glades of grass and trees and cows grazing. There are charming smallish trees with round shapes, elegant and compact, with blue flowers like mist and yellow berries simultaneously, and the lovely name of *lignum vitae*.

The people have finer, longer faces than Barbados. The feel of the country is bigger and the Municipal stamp less evident. Spanish Town has a charming square laid out in the sixteenth century by the Spaniards and still keeping a spacious feeling of proportion. A monument to Rodney with porticoes, dome and flanking buildings in eighteenth-century Palladian, and a lovely façade for each side of the square with grassy little gardens in the midst. It was all very solitary and quiet; all around is the nineteenth century in a miasma of tumbledown slums with something drab and solid in school or religion here and there. What *is* it that we do to places? Works without grace, I suppose. The old Spanish feeling comes with strange graciousness through all that has overlaid it.

Lady Woolley and I were switched out of our troopship by a brigadier and brought here to enjoy this house as the occupants are on tour. It is very restful, all to our two selves, but there are no pictures and no books and the drawing room very sumptuous by some decorator who evidently thinks it *risqué* to go in for anything but beige and a few photographs of Royalty. Our Arab room *much* nicer.

Love,
FREYA

King's House,
Jamaica
26 May 1948

Dearest Stewart,

I went out to Port Royal this morning. It is derelict and grass grown, and the brick parapets clustered with trees, and only 300 out of the remaining 800 inhabitants have any work to do. But there is a *feeling* about it. The pleasant naval man who took us round loves it and took me up to 'the words I love best': a tablet to Nelson which says: 'While treading in his footsteps, remember his glory.' Nobody talks of glory now, do they? We are afraid of anything so bright. But the eighteenth and early nineteenth century were not afraid. At Port Royal Nelson still seems to walk up and down the wooden floor of his quarterdeck as a young lieutenant in the sun. The old guns point quite uselessly over scrub of acacias and swamps of mangrove, as the sea has receded. The big earthquake lifted that side while it scooped out the inlet and really created Kingston harbour. The church there has a beautiful carved organ loft of 1743, and the seventeenth-century silver plate that Pirate Morgan offered when he melted down his buccaneering profits and became respectable. We got passes on the Ordinance boat and on every post in the shallow water as we went by a black pelican with a white ruff was sitting and flew away slowly with great fringed wings almost brushing the water, which was plopping with fish. All the mountains were sharp in outline against a soft woolly sky. There are no hard lines as all is vegetation to the top; but the backbone of the island is beautiful and I would like to spend two or three weeks walking and camping in the many little inns, and crossing passes, and getting up into the good air.

Tonight we are back in the desolating efficiency of the troopship, with the megaphone blaring; one's time and thought taken up forcibly in listening to things one doesn't want to hear. And only one life in this world.

I was thinking as I drove through one of these appalling slums that *taste*, far more than philosophy, is what we lack. It should be impossible to go on looking for years on end at anything so hideous; and if everyone tried to make their own surroundings pleasant, all the world would become agreeable. And none of this governessy feeling to it at all.

Lots of love,

FREYA

S.S. *Empire Windrush*
                                                                 31 May 1948
Dearest Stewart,

Four days we have been chugging through the Mexique Bay, cutting its dark flat waters in a swelter of heat and noise. And this morning we saw long, low sand dunes, and thirty or forty chimneys and oil tanks, and empty low lines of scrub to right and left. And that is all we are likely to see of Tampico, for the river and the town must open out beyond a low breakwater on our left, and we are not going in but waiting for the sixty Poles to come to us in boats. It seems wildly extravagant to send a huge ship, 2,000 on board, eight days out of its way for sixty passengers who would have been flown or taken by schooner to Bermuda; and I believe it is just that someone in London was unable to realise the difference made by looking at a small-scale map, and thought this was all on our way. We are short of water and likely to stop in Havana. I hope I may *never* have to travel in a troopship again; regimented from morning to night and blared with hideous noises. And *why* are we so desperate *en masse*; always thinking of what we ought to be thinking instead of what we are thinking? It really is sordid. It is a godsend to have Nancy Cunard. We omit breakfast and lie with very little on in our cabin till lunch, and then sit in hot shade with typewriter or Russian. Heat really exhausting. It was as bad as Delhi last night, the sheets almost scorching; and poor miserable people are down below in decks that descend to E, without a breath of outside air. The Crusade book is a great standby, very stodgy but fascinating. I have also been reading *The Tempest*.

Love,

FREYA

S.S. *Empire Windrush*,
                                                                        Cuba
                                                                   4 June 1948
Dearest Stewart,

We are here since yesterday, not allowed on shore; just frying like the Ancient Mariner on a painted ocean. Meanwhile, two of our naval draft have vanished ashore and not returned. How very understandable.

Cuba, even flashing by as we steamed under its old fort into the harbour, gives a glance of opulence: wide, straight streets; porticoes, and shops; shiny *rich* cars; the waterfront finished off with a low parapet of stone and backed with gardens; domes; and low hills covered with lights of streets and houses.

There must be about a million inhabitants and one has a feeling of a metropolis standing on its own feet. How *maddening* not to be able to land.

Love,

FREYA

STEWART PEROWNE S.S. *Empire Windrush*,
Bermuda
11 June 1948

Dearest Stewart,

I am just on board again. This depressing boat, eleven more days to go. But I got off last night and had a bed up at the Tennants.[49] Beautiful bed and bathroom, and a bathe before breakfast. It was lovely slipping down barefoot over the wet grass and finding the little cove all pure and quiet from the night and swimming out among the white birds in an almost waveless sea.

Nancy says she loathes the British. Every time she sees lots of them together, she loathes them more and more. I don't think this is fair, though I must say they are rather indigestible in chunks. All these solid virtues are the foundation of everything, but foundations should be hidden. A few graces in sight and the solidity supporting it *unseen*.

Love,

FREYA

STEWART PEROWNE S.S. *Empire Windrush*,
Gravesend
21 June 1948

Dearest Stewart,

We are off this ship early tomorrow morning and I am posting you a fat letter by sea mail at the same time as this. Do you know Chaucer's

> 'The lyf so short, the crafte so long to lerne:
> So sharp the essay, so sure the reckoning:
> The fearfull joye that always slit so ierne:
> All this mene I by love . . .'?

[49] Admiral Sir William Tennant was C.-in-C. America and West Indies Station 1946–49.

What changes in all the centuries? Nothing at all in what matters. Solomon and Chaucer and Plato and Shakespeare. Do you know that in all this lending library there was not a single book whose author I knew? It is so cold that the ship's heating is on again, *icy* winds, a green-brown sea, fog on the Goodwin Sands. But then the river slowly gathers between its banks, gently rolling down in fields with clumps of trees, which keep company right to Gravesend and the forest of cranes and black wharves. Little low houses, the ships like towers among them, a few little tugs, and the factory chimneys' smoke; but there is a great repose because of the dock strike, and it gives one a sad feeling of England and her river slipping away into the silence of the past.

Am so looking forward to news.

Love,
FREYA

STEWART PEROWNE   Hampstead
                                                          26 June 1948

Dearest Stewart,

Oh what heaven to be here at last. Roses, cherries, strawberries, little allotment gardens, the elderberry flowers and the dogrose hanging over canals as we drove in from Tilbury last night. Jock, of course, was there with a car to meet at St. Pancras, and then the Edwardian room at the Café Royal, all rich and shabby, and Jock thinking out with proper care the right sort of Barsac to drink. 'I feel my age,' says Jock. 'I like my wine sweeter than I did.' What a *nice* way to look at getting old, making it enjoyable as it should be. From lunch to Elizabeth Arden: they had been primed and were oozing charm in a disgusting way. Just time to read your letters, four, and so very welcome at last. And then dinner at the Cholmondeleys', lovely house with rooms with columns and the trees of the park outside, and the Duke of Palmera on one side and Archie Wavell on the other.

I found an invitation to the Royal Garden Party (addressed to Miss Stark, rather poor A.D.C. work); but can't be here, and would much rather go when you are over.

Love,
FREYA

London

                                                                       27 June 1948

My dearest Stewart,

This is going by sea so as to fill in the blank before you begin to get Asolo letters. I am supposed to leave the day after tomorrow, but an awful germ from the accursed *Windrush* has got me down. Lunch, dinners all cancelled: I have been lying prostrated here at the Lancasters', and am writing from bed. And it really is very sad for one's only week in London.

Esther Wright[51] is coming in October. I would like you to think out and tell me what you would like the F.O. to offer, as I am quite sure they mean to offer something and it might just as well be something you would like? I told Michael my own views of the essentials: anywhere in the Mediterranean basin, where one can lead a civilised life, and that seems to me far more important than anything in the line of hierarchies or incomes. For what is the use of being rich or important in a place where one grows dull inside? But I was very careful to say that this is only my own personal idea, and that I don't even know what you think above it, though I hope that we agree.

                                                            Your loving
                                                                       FREYA

Golden Arrow,
                                                                         Calais

                                                                       28 June 1948

Dearest Stewart,

This is being written under difficulties on my dinner plate after a very comfy crossing. I took a cabin, shut my eyes so as to see *no more sea*, and the kind stewards saw to all the rest. I had a warm and lovely send-off from Victoria: warm and dear affection, it felt sort of pre-war, if you know what I mean. It is good to be back in a world where one is talked to as a human being and valued for what one is, not just 'a black', or 'a woman', or 'a senior', or 'a junior'. How easy and sure it makes all intercourse, clearing away such masses of middle-class accumulated lumber, and making a simple matter of one human creature talking to another. That career-hierarch mind corrupts almost more than anything else. I believe it's better to be a black

---

[50] Wife of (later Sir) Michael Wright, then Assistant Under-Secretary of State at the Foreign Office, and subsequently Ambassador to Norway 1951–54 and to Iraq 1955–58.

market profiteer! There are lots of them on this train. Wonderful to think of being in Venice tomorrow.

Love,
FREYA

JOHN GREY MURRAY   Milan
                                                29 June 1948
Dearest Jock,

I got a lovely cabin and slept without ever *looking* at the horrid sea. Found Pam in Paris; dined with her and Juliette Huxley and May Sarton (quite delightful); and Paris looking its best and their flat one huge window on the river with the Eiffel Tower in the middle distance looking rather like an Angelic Ladder. The *Ancien Monde* personified walked in on us: the old Duchesse de Clermont Tonnerre, with yellow satin ribbons on her hat and a goitre, and quite enchanting, amiable and secure and so victorious over World and Time that she had long ceased to trouble herself about them. It *was* good just to get a whiff of Paris in passing (but you had much better come, for your week, to Asolo from a financial point of view). At Milan Franco walked up, amiable and no less dull, and tells me Cici's baby is due August 20th, which means some rearranging of my Dolomites. Now I am in Padova in a fine huge thunderstorm, lightning's zigzagging in and out all in a good Mediterranean way.

Will write from Asolo, this just to say thank you again and again and again to you and Diana. That little bedroom is a refuge, indeed.

Love,
FREYA

STEWART PEROWNE   Asolo
                                                1 July 1948
Darling Stewart,

So strange and so lovely to be here again. Great waves of Peace come lapping up against one. The roses and lilies are nearly done, but there is a sort of lush wastefulness in the garden. The house is coming to life as I go into one room after another, all polished by Emma and Maria to the nines. And suddenly I feel beautifully happy and optimistic again. I *know* Barbados is not right for us; it seems to make all the wrong things important. The

East is big enough for one to keep one's own scale of values; and, anyway, our values *are* to be found there.

All here are asking after you and so much hoping for your coming soon. A pure *New Yorker* character, Peggy Guggenheim, is in Venice, with a face as amusing as if it were a caricature of herself, and a collection of *modernissimo* pictures which she travels about with and hunts for houses for (and took B.B. to see, with the results you can imagine). Venice is ravishing, but sad: there is no work anywhere.

Bless you,

FREYA

STEWART PEROWNE Asolo
9 July 1948

Dearest Stewart,

I had a pleasant hour yesterday buying, after years and years, a pair of mountain boots! I wonder if I shall still be able to use them? I went down to the factory and you will have to look and get some shoes there; they look so good and are so reasonable. The nice little harassed man who runs it told me his tale of troubles, only too general; it is rather pathetic to see that nice factory with only a poor handful of people working. I saw all the things that happen to a shoe from the moment it leaves the cow or calf to the last brush of polish. Very neat how they flatten down the leather, turned in round toe and heel. A mountain shoe is an event in one's life, as one's happiness depends on it for ten years or so and it makes or mars your days. My dear Mama kept every silly little scrap of evening nonsense in my wardrobe and gave away boots, mountain suit, and ice axe; so uncomprehending are one's nearest and dearest about one's hobbies!

The royal lunch party has gone off very pleasantly, Princess Aspasia arriving in an immense car with GR for Greece and no chauffeur, and Mrs. Guggenheim (who looks just like that and is very ugly, but fun) inside with Alix Cavalieri, Russian, who has bought a tiny house here in the middle of our view, and thinks her dead husband has reincarnated himself in one of her beige poodles. They sat in the garden with vermouth; the sun shone on all the little white pansies by the grassy path, and the last roses above them. Emma gave us a wonderful lunch. They bought a dressing gown, and ordered a silk dress. Peggy Guggenheim is looking for a large Venetian palace to house her surrealist pictures; she showed me the little catalogue and some look very interesting and far more like experiments in allegory of the later Renaissance than anything else. I shall have to go and see them one day and tell you about them; but feel it will be better *after* I have been to B.B., in case I liked them and had to confess it, which might ruin my friendship!

I am longing to hear if Michael Wright's efforts produce a result.[51] Do accept if you possibly can. Not the pension, not the status, but the life we are to live is all that matters.

Love,
FREYA

STEWART PEROWNE   Asolo
11 July 1948

Dearest Stewart,

I have suddenly realised *why* I dislike a complete autobiography. It came to me while reading Dickens. It is because nearly always the end of one's life makes an inartistic anti-climax, a tailing off which leaves the reader depressed after all the promise and fire and achievement of youth. Whereas, if you take it in bits, you can start low down so to speak and always make your climax somehow, like *Samson Agonistes*, or *All Passion Spent*. In fact, every age ought to be an artistic achievement of its own kind; and therefore it's a mistake to put old age, which needs a subdued and gentler sort of lighting, into the same work as the fierce illumination which adds to the excitement of the earlier chapters.

Let me see what you write on Barbados. The *Foreign Affairs* liked my effort so little, they sent it back. I am evidently no good for the U.S.A.!

Your
FREYA

STEWART PEROWNE   Asolo
21 July 1948

Dearest Stewart,

That wicked old dear, Monsignore, came and sat for an hour in the garden, waving his topaz ring at me and saying what he thought of the Russians. He told me how, when the partisans shot a German major at our front gate, he went down to try and intercede for Asolo with the German general at the bottom of the hill, who showed no sign of being mollified and

[51] sc. to find a post for Stewart Perowne in the Foreign Office.

was for burning the houses round (including ours). Monsignore at last said, 'You must remember you have *lost* the war' (this was 1945), and the general got this surprising statement translated, and two huge tears come rolling down his cheeks. Monsignore then said, 'Have you seen what has happened to all your lorries? Send someone to look.' He had just had to take the long way round because the R.A.F. had discovered the lorry park all along the Forestuccio and every one of them was in flames. In a very little while the despatch rider returned with the confirmation of this news, and the general ordered the burning of Asolo to be countermanded. Caroly tells me that my mother had grave doubts as to the morality of providing false bills for the people who asked for them, and so she asked Monsignore, who told her gaily to go ahead, that it is perfectly venial. Such a *sensible* point of view (but I must say I wouldn't ask my father confessor to confirm it!).

Love,
FREYA

JOHN GREY MURRAY   Asolo
                                                    22 July 1948
Darling Jock,
  Do tell me what you think of mss. when it comes, as I am in the usual incapacity of judgement. Will it tack on to the other without too much alteration? It feels very egotistic, but how can one write one's life without being egotistic? It is so strange to contemplate that funny, positive, ardent little monster and to know it was me. All sorts of funny pictures coming popping like rabbits out of holes. It would be fascinating to study how much of one belongs to the first years before one remembers at all.
  Oh Jock, what *happiness* in this garden. A lovely peace; it laps all round me, it is heaven.

Your
FREYA

STEWART PEROWNE   Vallombrosa
                                                    27 July 1948
Dearest Stewart,
  I do so wish you were here. I lay down to sleep last night wishing you could breathe this *life-giving* air, scented with all the damp hill-scents, and filled with a murmur of leaves. Milton's beech woods are sadly diminished and replaced with conifers, horrid little trees really. And the size of the old chestnuts can only be seen by their stumps and the craters left by their roots,

so wide that a cart could drive through. Far away westward and below, surrounded by the most gently noble outline of hills in the world, is the saddle of Fiesole and Florence hid in mists beyond. One's heart recognises that this is *classic* landscape, but why? I should like to sit for days and try to find the answer. A little gleam of Arno river catches the evening light and makes a meaning as it were for all those wooded lines. Long after the sun has set, when all seemed half asleep, the little travelling clouds suddenly lit up to gold as they sailed over these resting valleys. From my window one looks down over woods and the other hillsides to all Tuscany beyond; and a little path goes in a curving zigzag, so happily wilful, up the slope, almost the colour of the fields, so that one loses it and finds it, and thinks how it has probably been walked on since Etruscan days. When I reached Florence, everything was hot down there in full summer, and the palaces very noble in the shadows of their streets. It is such a sombre town in cold weather and needs the warmth to mitigate it.

B.B. is in fine form and Nicky, too. Both hoping you will come too this winter to stay at I Tatti. No one else here. We sat by the fire in the evening, a high stone hearth and B.B. reclining on his chaise longue with a rug, and talked till nearly midnight. So pleasant, like a string of beads from one thing to another. What an art of living! B.B. says I have 'the supreme gift of *living*', but he is the absolute master; and one can say one *has* accomplished it at the age of eighty-three. The two of them took me for a scramble up their steep little paths, as active as goats. Poor Mrs. O.K.[52] in her high heels apparently said to Nicky, 'Does B.B. *like* these stony paths?'

I had a very good journey down of only a few hours (three from Padua) in a quick electric train full of Members of Parliament. I happened to know the Socialist member for Treviso (and, incidentally, got him to promise to do something about our roads) and they were all very pleasant, and gave me sandwiches and beer and peaches, and we talked about the partisans, which is always a pleasant talk to fall back upon.

Love,
FREYA

SIR SYDNEY COCKERELL   Vallombrosa
28 July 1948

Dearest Sydney,

B.B. and I have been speaking of you and he sends his love. He is so well and full of life; it seems to me that the old lady was right who said, 'The

---

[52] Mrs. Otto Kahn, of New York, mother of F.S.'s friend Momo Marriott.

seventies are tricky, it is all right once you get into the eighties. You and B.B. are both examples of it.

I have done four chapters to bring the autobiography up to where the mss. you have starts in Asolo; and have read them to B.B. and he thinks I ought to do it on quite a different plan, not going straight, chronologically, but building it up more artistically to lead up to my own real life of travel and writing. I feel he may be right, but it is an appalling thought. I think I will get it all straight on the present plan and then send it for you and Jock to see and advise on.

I am reading David Cecil's new book on Dorothy Osborne and Gray. Very good, I think, as all that he writes.

Love, dearest Sydney,

FREYA

STEWART PEROWNE   Vallombrosa

28 July 1948

Dearest Stewart,

There is such a peaceful feeling always in a high place that looks *down* on a valley. Monasteries and castles are so attractive, because nearly always in such a sort of position, like this one, where I wake up in the morning and look straight down on the stretch of Arno gleaming so far below.

I wish I could send you all the talk. It is so good, and I come away and it has all melted out of my mind. Such a waste. We were talking about the Hindus and B.B. was saying that the deeply rooted Muslim represents the European, the *life-accepting*, and the Hindu is the ascetic, the *life-denying*, and there is a real abyss between them. He told me he had always been attracted by the *deniers*, but felt like saying, 'Retro me, Satana.' I said I felt the same in a different way in thinking over the Negro and the Indian as I had seen them. The difference of our European (he says Europe goes to the Euphrates) is that we have the spirit of adventure, and that might be called *life-acceptance?*

I must end this with the Chinese aphorism quoted me by Nicky: 'To go to bed in the dark so as to save candle light is a false economy if the result should be twins.'

Love,

FREYA

Vallombrosa
                                                                29 July 1948
Dearest Jock,

I have been reading my first three chapters to B.B., and the poor darling went *fast asleep*, and bore this sad lugubrious symptom out by saying that he thinks this sort of book (plain chronological) not very exciting. I have an awful *feel* he may be right. Of course I really hate writing an autobiography, as it means contemplating myself all the time, which depresses me and is the exact opposite of a travel book which always looks *out*.

It is so peaceful and beautiful here, and we are all alone, with a wood fire in the evening, a tiny brook-gurgle and sound of moving leaves coming from the valleys all about one. There are oaks, beech, chestnuts, and, alas, a growing intrusion of pines. These are not right for Italy, but there is one hillside where they are most beautiful, cut in patterns with dark clefts of clearing between them, and groups where the stems show, like a great organ covering all the hill. The broom is still out, smelling sweet as sunlight. I go back tomorrow and up to Colfosco.

Love, dear Jock. Very despondent over the beastly book.

                                                                Your
                                                                FREYA

Asolo
                                                                31 July 1948
Darling,

Just back and find your letters by air of the 16th and 19th and send this the same way, not to reassure you, for how can one do that, but to get at you a little more quickly and tell you what I plan to do. First of all, I hear that Tito has removed his troops from this frontier to the Albanian, so that should give us a few weeks even if the worst happens. So I will now write to Victor[53] at the Vatican and suggest, if war is declared, driving down with a lorry of things and ask if he can deposit them there with his own? If he can't, I will take them to Cici in Dronero, and then make my way to Rome where either Victor, Vatican, or British Embassy should find me. I will also write to Michael Wright telling him I shall await events in Rome, as I feel sure either the C.O. or F.O. will want us in the Middle East (I will send you a copy of both these letters).

I had a lovely night yesterday at Malcontenta.[54] It *breathes* peace, the very

[53] (Later Sir) Victor Perowne, British Minister to the Holy See.
[54] V lla just outside Venice, owned by the Landsbergs.

absence of anything like a view, just greenness and meadows when you wake. Everything old and faded and has-been, and all beautiful.

I have sent you a long batch of letters from B.B.'s. I spent four lovely quiet days with them in Vallombrosa. We went to the Abbey, but it has been renovated in late seventeenth or early eighteenth century, so is not what Milton saw, though the grand wooded hills must have many things the same. You never saw anything more lovely than coming down the Arno valley with the mist in it like a river and islands of hills just emerging here and there. B.B. full of wisdom about life and the conduct of life. You must come soon and not miss knowing him, for such are very rare. He is so *fragile* now. He just held the door for a minute in the car, and the touch of the handle bruised him.

Love,

FREYA

BERNARD BERENSON AND NICKY MARIANO Colfosco
3 August 1948

My darling B.B. and Nicky,

The morning was a dream, with the mist like a river in the valley, and a sky as clear as one of your pictures, the hills so gently drawn against it – and I came down feeling so full of thankfulness for those happy days and your affection and all it means. These things never lose their quality: one looks back at them shining there in a light of their own, our only real 'possessions'. Thank you, thank you, *ever* so much, always.

Here the mountains have not lost their magic. The stillness full of voices of little tumbling streams; the flowers in little shining colonies everywhere. I shall be out all day long for my one fortnight if only it will not rain and rain as it is doing this morning. If it does, I shall have to work at that tiresome book.

All love to you and Nicky,

FREYA

STEWART PEROWNE Colfosco
3 August 1948

Dearest Stewart,

I do wish you were here. Sheridan Russell turned up the day before yesterday in Asolo, and we got to Belluno by car, and then cramped and clamped into a bus just starting, packed far more tightly than sardines which have at least some oil in between them. We got taken to a little place called Arabba (strange name) and lunched there. A nice old boy with fierce Austrian blue eyes and white moustache was the hotel owner. He told us how democratic these valleys are; and so they are, with the cows drifting by morning and evening to their communal pastures and the people building their houses and burning their fires out of the communal woods.

I had forgotten how deliciously one sleeps in the hills. I think I must be particularly sensitive to air, and read the other day that living creatures can be killed merely by having their air filtered through cotton wool. I am sure that is what begins to happen in 'air-conditioned' rooms which always make me feel ill. Here it is a pure cool stream, and the water is like the air liquefied; and the brightness of the tiny flowers shows how they drink it in.

I am reading *Paradise Lost*. How nobly *spacious* it is, all the pictures of *space* are perfect. I don't think one must look so much for the particular images, as in Dante or Shakespeare, but be receptive to a *cumulative* effect from the whole. I have begun in the fourth book and will do the beginning last; one begins so often at the beginning that the first books are much clearer than any of the others (to me).

Much love,

FREYA

STEWART PEROWNE   Colfosco
                                                            8 August 1948
Darling Stewart,

I am a little drunk, not with the thin little *vin rosé*, but with seven hours in the air and sun. I saw the Landsbergs off this morning and then went up: a cloudless day, cool wind like rustling silk in the pines and playing arpeggios with the grasses; you could see them bend and glitter like water, and longed to catch the fingers that did it all. I climbed for two hours, puffing and hoping it good for the figure, and then there was a wood of scrub pines that had to be circumvented and I went up instead of down and got into difficulties with rocks – huge jags and precipices – and my boots hurting still like fun (what a subtle mind the man had who thought of things 'hurting like fun'). I find that I have not the slightest wish to try rock faces; merely sorry not to have done more when I liked it and could. There were strange, sharp edges pushing into the bluest sky, and the valleys and many outlines below, so beautiful. Bertie and Dorothea Landsberg have been three days; I was delighted to have them as they vetted my new chapter which is so difficult, as my mother is so *improbable*! If I don't explain, it looks very *louche*, and if I do, it is rather brutal. However, they both approved of my effort and I will send it to you from Asolo when I hope to have two more.

It is lovely to read Milton here: the high pastures are so like the Garden of Eden. I came upon Adam and Eve, quite middle-aged and with very little on, taking the sun in a sequestered dell with only the oaks looking down on them, huge mountain faces, and a clear grassy tumbling brook. They seemed so happy and right, and set me on my way. After reading Book IV, one can't think of Milton as the dour old Puritan he is made out. I suppose his wife loved someone else and that was all the sorrow. Do you remember her most poignant letter to Verney, 'While we are both tied in the same faggot of time'?

Love,

FREYA

SIR SYDNEY COCKERELL   Asolo

15 August 1948

Darling Sydney,

I agree with all you say about Communism, but wouldn't dare to say so to B.B., who feels it very strongly. And, perhaps, if we knew more about Lithuania and all that, we might feel more prejudiced. My own feeling is that, in two or three hundred years, a Russian Europe might be less bad than an American. But the intervening centuries would be very unpleasant. We shall not save our own civilisation unless we make it worth saving. But then look at my poor little effort in the cause: my *Perseus*, whom you really dislike in your heart of hearts! Yet he is doing all that I was able to inspire him to do.

I am working hard. When the sun shone I walked and wrote when it rained, and have done seventy-two pages of the autobiography and hope you will approve. You do not think it too private to publish? I find I can alter very little.

With love, dear Sydney,

FREYA

STEWART PEROWNE   Asolo

21 August 1948

Darling Stewart,

I have been sorting out letters from my infancy to 1927 and throwing away a whole basketful. There are two enormous drawers full from '27 to

'47 and it will take three months at least to read them through when the next stage of this autobiography comes to be written. I thought of dedicating that one to you, if you would value such a little monument, and this early one to Sydney who made me write it. What do you think? I feel you would prefer the Middle Eastern years? But either are at your disposal.

Such a pleasant restful three days at Malcontenta with time to work, which is always being snatched from me. Diana Cooper came to lunch, looking miraculous, not only young, but ageless, just Beauty herself (although we know she is fifty-six), dressed in yellow trousers and a pointed Mexican hat on top of a jade-green veil swathed round her face, and high sandals of striped red canvas. She isn't happy retired, and finds Chantilly a disappointment and is not sure of liking the French to live with in non-ambassadorial state. You see how right I am to refuse to take the hierarchic life seriously? It lets you down with a flop. Duff, she says, is perfectly happy anyhow and anywhere because all he needs is books. One must have one's own world inside, in this world. How I feel it just now, with everything shuddering on the edge of war. Venice is almost empty and everyone I meet asks for work. I can't do a thing for them because I am determined to get solvent first, which I know will please you. It should happen by Xmas if all goes well.

Malcontenta was particularly soothing just now. Its things so old, passed through so many catastrophes, and still carrying their faded intrinsic goodness undestroyed. The Landsbergs brought me back in their car, and I gave them dinner at the Sole with a strange little lot of American culture-seekers from the Cinema week in Venice.

Your

FREYA

STEWART PEROWNE

Cici's Clinic, Milan
26 August 1948

Darling Stewart,

I had never assisted at childbirth before, and it really has been a fearful night. Cici started at eleven and I got out to her at one o'clock, finding a late taxi. And a small, extremely hideous little boy was born at eight o'clock this morning. His head was just like one of those cannibal tribes, but it seems that this normalises itself in a few hours. Poor little Cici is recovering now. So lucky, Franco was away for two days, and she was so touchingly pleased to have me near and kept on saying, 'You are my only family' till I could have wept. All the in-laws will be arriving this evening and tomorrow, and she should be out of the home in ten days. I hope it may be happiness to her. Poor mite, to come into this sort of a world! What a mystery it is. How all the inherited things, looks, character, ways and habits come, not from two people only, but from centuries of ancestors, transmitted through two single little cells? I believe this is one of the things still unexplained, just like life itself, and love, and beauty, and everything that matters.

Your

FREYA

STEWART PEROWNE

Eden Hotel
above Strésa
29 August 1948

Dearest Stewart,

You would enjoy this funny little expedition so much. Nigel and I left Milan, sweltering in the train, and got to Baveno, with lots of drama on the way, as a poor Italian had his pocket picked with all the documents.

It was so pleasant on the lake. We told the old railway porter we had no money and he took us to a maternal little hotel run by two plump women and their two elderly amiable aunts; and we dined out on the *trottoir* and saw all the families enjoying their yearly holidays, in little boats, at little tables, or walking up and down. Then got on and spent next morning rowing to the Fisherman's Island and back to lunch in a villa more rich than you would think possible. In the evening we escaped up the little cog-wheel railway to Mottarone (do get *Beauchamp's Career* and read the early morning on Mottarone; it was just like that). Halfway up a terrific storm broke; we sat in darkness for one and a half hours with the electric current taken off and watched the fireworks. A telegraph pole less than 100 feet away was snapped and fell over and I felt a lot of little prickles in my fingers. The nice old train conductor came in to smoke a cigarette and 'sit with the passengers in case they felt frightened' and eventually we got up to the hotel at the top at 10.30, extremely hungry. Such a charming little inn, each room called after a mountain. Nigel had Mont Blanc and I had Grappa, which couldn't be more suitable for me. I lay awake half the night, first the stars like turquoise lamps, then the moon. One could see a far outline of hills and hills; it was like one of the gentler cantos of Dante. At last I got so afraid of missing the sunrise that I went and called Nigel at five, which he strongly resented, and very nearly refused to get up at six with a cloudy sky. But we walked for twenty minutes or so over turf just wakening to the colours of

69

daylight; and the whole of Italy lay at our feet as if we were the Goths or Vandals: lakes, and Lombardy, and eyebrow pencil lines of hills with mists in the valleys between them. I can't tell you what a view: the lakes still asleep, tucked up as it were in their shores, and the sky catching cloud after cloud with a dark glow, and a huge mass of darkness over Monte Rosa and all the Bernese Oberland, while Ortler and Bernina, under the rising sun, and M. Viso in the far west, shone clear. And then the great cloud mass began to grow to dusky rose in the depths of the valleys, and little flocks of cloud gathered from the surface of Maggiore and followed the sun, like Arab sheep their shepherd. A blue sky appeared, and the white shoulder of Monte Rosa, the cloud rolling off as if she were slipping out of her *peignoir*. What a vision: white and burning as truth. One looks and just feels satisfied.

We went back to eggs for breakfast and a sleep, and got down to lunch on Isolabella with terrace gardens full of obelisks, unicorns, clipped trees, and friendly gods, and a *festa* going on with concertinas. Such excellent food, a pink trout just out of the lake. We got back with all the other holiday-makers in time for dinner, and found Cici surrounded with relations and well. I shall be with her tomorrow and then back to Asolo. All this month has been *just* paid for by the tenants' rent, which is a wonderful arrangement, but only easy to do in summer. Do you know, these are the first few days since the war of just pottering with no object at all except to see the world? And to think how it was the normal thing to do for a few months a year always! One is constantly coming up against these contrasts which show you suddenly the decline in the civilised life. It is so *good* for one to sit back awhile and look on.

Love,

FREYA

STEWART PEROWNE Milan
31 August 1948

Darling Stewart,

Nigel left, very sad, and doesn't know what his future is to be, but he will hear next week. I went and watched the small infant sucking away like a steam-piston. What a marvel it is, so full of character always, though it can only hear and not see. Cici loves it already. I don't think there is any happiness for her with Franco. So she must just make her own life in other ways. I went out with his Mama all morning and wished that the mere exercise of virtue gave me more pleasure. It doesn't give me *any*. It does to some, but I don't think they are such very nice people. Anyway, Mrs. Boido[55] bored me to tears. I have been puzzling to think why that small commercial *bourgeoisie* is so deadly, so much more so than peasants, princes, prostitutes, or poets, and I think I have found the answer: they want to *mass-produce* human beings. Everything is made to pattern, every relationship has its special set of platitudes. They came popping out of Mrs. B.'s mouth till I had to go into a pastrycook's and suffocate them with éclairs! And, of course, insisting on being an individual, and saying what you personally think (or even just thinking it) is anathema to them. For one thing, it rouses a terrible dark envy, the envy of the bound for the free. Poor little Cici – what a desert to be ploughing through. She is coming to me for November, and is putting a little money in England so as to get an open door.

Love,

FREYA

STEWART PEROWNE   Asolo

11 September 1948

Darling Stewart,

There was a ballet on at the Fenice and Charles Rankin took me down. I stayed with the Wilsons and he found a room after combing all Venice. It is so full and so cosmopolitan: the *piazza* crammed with all those Cunard types, among whom Victor came sunning himself, just out from England. The Fieldens dined us. They *are* such nice people, English gentry with a modest knowledge and taste in pictures, music and the art of life: We all went to the ballet together and sat in the gallery from which one sees the whole Fenice, orchestra, public, and all; and it was a gala night, everyone in satins and long gowns trailing through the *piazza* afterwards, and the foyer all white shoulders, gossip, and chandeliers. The ballet was poor because they just can't dance, but they didn't try for more than a few pirouettes; and the last one, the Stravinsky *Orpheus*, was most beautiful.

I spent a happy morning with the dressmaker just back from Paris. I have renounced my Schiaparelli (such *virtue*), but even a modest Italian tailor-made (which is all I shall get this year) is 120,000 lire.

Bless you, darling.

Your

FREYA

[55] Cici's mother-in-law.

71

SIR SYDNEY COCKERELL   Asolo
11 September 1948

Dearest Sydney,

It is weeks since I have written, but also even more weeks since I have heard from you; and I hope it is just World and Time and not any tiredness or illness that keeps you silent. I have been overdriven with really *too* many things, including a fortnight in Milan looking after Cici and the birth of a little boy, Paolo. What a strange affair it is, quite tremendous to make such a sudden step, from non-existence to existence. I have often seen the opposite equally shattering one of death, but had never seen birth before and came away very much moved.

Do write, dear Sydney, I wish you were here.

Your loving
FREYA

STEWART PEROWNE   Asolo
15 September 1948

Darling,

I think that, with any luck, this ought to reach you about October 7th, when you will be thinking of our wedding, not with too much regret, I hope, in spite of all. I would like a little message of affection to reach you, and hope the Post Office, blind as Fate, will not intervene. I have been thinking over all this year, full of strangeness, and find rather to my surprise that I do not really love you less! How astonishing! I think you have left something lying between us, untold. Whatever it was, it will not make me think less of you or care less for you; I can't think of a nicer wedding-day message to send you!

Your
FREYA

STEWART PEROWNE   Asolo
22 September 1948

Darling Stewart,

So difficult to get paper and pen and five minutes' quiet; and now we are back in Asolo with the addition of the two young Eustons, the most charming young happy couple.[56] All came crumpled into the Youngs' van,[57] Hugh

---

[56] Hugh and Fortune (Earl and Countess of) Euston. He had been an A.D.C. to Lord Wavell when F.S. stayed with the Viceroy in New Delhi.

[57] The distinguished Arabist Sir Hubert Young and his wife Rose, friends of F.S. since the early '30s.

at the back extinguished under the Venini lampshade (for I may as well confess that that is your Xmas present; I thought we might be enjoying it meanwhile).

We all spent the morning in the Accademia and it *is* the most lovely exhibition now, everything cleaned and shining, and *The Tempest* and that Lotto portrait and all the Bellinis ravishing. On Monday we got a box for a French play with Barrault – very well acted and lovely décor and costumes, but such a dull play – eighteenth-century. As if the Venetians, shut into this parochial country for thirty years, wanted to be told about eighteenth-century imitations of themselves! But it was a very smart evening at the Fenice, and the Italians all wearing exquisite and sumptuous gowns, filling the poor victorious English with envy.

It will be rather nice to have this rush over, and be quiet. There must be something wrong with the sort of social affairs that leave one depressed at the end; or perhaps it is only I who feel that flatness, and prefer a quieter life? Anyway, I find that I go to bed happy after a quiet evening with real friends and good talk, and go to bed with a feeling of *futility* after all the whirl and stir. I feel the same with books. Your Graham Greene novel has just come and is already making me unhappy; whereas nothing but a lovely serenity follows on *Paradise Lost*. I will tell you what I think of it when I get a little further. With most of these writers I think there is a lack of final balance which the classics never emit; I mean that the misery and squalor are obviously real things that exist, but they are not the final sum of things. The great writer never forgets to put his work into the proper perspective even if he is only concerned with some squalid aspect. I believe that is what we have forgotten in our lives, too often, and therefore in our art. One should never specialise so much as to forget that the bad patch is only a *detail*. The beauty of life is that the good and the happy exist, and even if it is we ourselves who miss them, it doesn't *really* matter, does it? If one could feel this strongly enough I believe one would attain happiness, and certainly serenity?

Dear love,

FREYA

STEWART PEROWNE   Asolo
                                                              27 September 1948
My darling,

We went up Grappa on Saturday. I thought so much of you, and looked down that steep zigzag way by which we descended. I hope we will be doing it again when the narcissi are out. This time it was a still autumn day, the black and white cows were grazing on very green grass and the tips of the beech scrub just turning yellow. The road has become appalling, with all the surface off so that it is like one of those anatomical drawings of muscles without skin! We went late and saw the sunset from the top, with the huge mountain shadows slanted across the plain, the windings of Brenta and Piave lost in mist; and then descended to Feltre by a slightly better road, from the sunset rim into darkness. There was an uncertain moment when a huge lorry blocked our way and we thought we were stuck for the night; but the drivers were just having a wayside drink at a cottage hidden below, and we got them to move on.

Love,

FREYA

STEWART PEROWNE   Asolo
30 September 1948

Darling,

I have sent you Robin Maugham's *Nomad*; it is not well written, but is a sincere little book and all our friends in it. Suddenly, when he describes the black tent and the camels browsing through the night, my first Druse evening came back to me as if I were actually there, awake in a little court in the moonlight, with the camels scrunching their feed gently, and all the romance and strangeness. How lucky we are, with so much to remember. If war comes, it comes, and all here will vanish into the different world of dreams. But I have just found this in *Julius Caesar*:

'The gods today stand friendly, that we may,
Lovers in peace, lead on our days to age.'

May God grant it; and, if He doesn't, may we still walk in peace and happiness together.

I have also just finished *Jane Eyre*. How well those old writers last, what *human* worth is in them! All that youth of hardship, those bleak winds, those appalling schools. What stuff it makes when it turns into literature! There is a sort of *steadfastness* which we rarely attain. What I notice, too, is the immense part that the sights and sounds of nature had in their life (even in Jane Austen), ever so much more than in our generation.

The dear young Eustons leave tomorrow. They are the best that England produces: no wonder we hope to get by without a continental revolution – when one compares them to the aristocracy here! They gave a wonderful description of their weekend at Windsor – a quiet one with only the Crippses, and no restful moment. The ladies were plunged into 'letter games' the moment they reached the drawing room, and were surprised to see the servants come in to carry away all the pokers, tongs, shovels, etc. from the numerous fireplaces. Presently the King and gentlemen all came marching in at a goose-step with all those things over their shoulders, saluting the ladies where they sat. Old Lord Spencer doddering along but succeeding in his effort to kick Sir Stafford in the behind. What a life!

Your loving

FREYA

STEWART PEROWNE   Asolo

3 October 1948

Darling Stewart,

I am still lying in bed languid with 'flu, too overcome to do anything about it till today, when my temperature has dropped and I am better.

When you come I shall give you all W.P.'s[58] letters to read. I have just gone through them, and it has been a gentle occupation, bridging even the stream of time and death. His voice just as it used to be, except that I can understand more now of his depth and love – how true and constant it was. I have now tidied all the letters necessary for this first autobiography and hope to be at work again next week, now that the Eustons have gone.

If ever you read my letters, you will realise why I wanted to go to the East: it was the only escape into a tolerably peaceful life. My mother just threw *everything* onto me and I got so exhausted in parental tangles that the only way to survive was to get away. How exhausting it is to read over one's past. How crude and foolish one seems and how little one noticed. And yet was loved so dearly. One can't think that God will look with less kind eyes than all those human beings who were good to us in our youth?

Your loving

FREYA

FIELD-MARSHAL LORD WAVELL   Asolo

6 October 1948

Dearest Chief,

A beautiful letter from you; and the days and weeks have been passing and I haven't written, partly because it's so *difficult* to make up one's mind

[58] W.P. Ker, F.S.'s early mentor.

as to what gifts from a fairy godmother one would prefer – health for the body, I think, though I would choose beauty if I were *braver*; it is such a sharp-edged thing that cuts oneself so deep, so I shall keep plain and contented with health. Then poetry, or perhaps painting: it doesn't matter what it is so long as it opens 'the casement on the foam'. Poetry does it more than anything else to my mind. And for the soul, I think I should choose a feeling like that of the Greeks or even the early Christians, of a sort of divinity all around and inside one. Perhaps that and the poetry are rather alike, so that if *one* of the three has to be given up, I should do without the middle one and jog along contentedly with Good Health and the Grace of God? Now what made you think of these questions? I will be very curious to hear whether you approve of my philosophy when *Perseus* reaches you; he is due out in four weeks.

Momo and her general are coming to lunch today.[59] He is taking a fortnight's leave, so I hope the European crisis is not quite so acute. I am simplifying life by not reading about it; at intervals of a month I look, and it is always either Stalin or Molotov refusing visitors, and what is the good of looking at every swing of the pendulum when you are not consulted about the striking of the hour? So I have been reading Shakespeare's comedies and trying to decide whether Beatrice or Rosalind is my favourite.

Love to you both,

FREYA

STEWART PEROWNE   Asolo

11 October 1948

Darling Stewart,

As these are Charles's last two days, I took him to Marostica and we climbed the castle and looked across the waveless sea with all its farms, villas, and churches shining in the sunset and more little villages, churches, farms, thrown like the scattered beads of a broken necklace about the declivities of Asiago. What a *smiling* land! Living just as it did under the Romans, and I believe it will take even more than the Atom to shake it from its roots.

12 October 1948

Tomorrow is already yesterday. Time seems like a waterfall, pouring over the edge with us inside it. I had begun to recapture a lovely feeling of

---

[59] Major-General (later Sir) John Marriott and his wife Maud, 'Momo' (see note 52, p. 62. He was at this time G.O.C. London District.

stability and immobility and here you are wrecking it for me. How much nicer would your coming have been than my going! What I can hardly bear is the thought that all this might disappear and you would not have seen it, or only in its chaos of last year. I shall barely have time to get all in order when I leave.

Your

FREYA

STEWART PEROWNE   Asolo

18 October 1948

Darling Stewart,

I am trying to get a little order into my papers. In looking over these mountains of letters, I came on one from Herbert Olivier saying that there are two climaxes in an artist's life: one when he is discovered, and the other when he is found out. I hope *Perseus* won't be the second. You and I are to be sent the two earliest copies, any time now.

Very dear love,

FREYA

SIR SYDNEY COCKERELL   Asolo

24 October 1948

Darling Sydney,

All my plans are accelerated by a month by Stewart who has written to beg me to be out by December 1st in Guadeloupe, where he has a conference, and suggests a little holiday among the islands. So I am going. There is no point in disappointing him for only a month. I wish he had been able to come instead; but he can't. Anyway, I am crossing that weary ocean again (but by air this time) and am a little fearful of Barbados.

Dearest love,

FREYA

STEWART PEROWNE   Asolo

25 October 1948

Darling Stewart,

You will be jealous when you see my new luggage. The man in Venice has just made it: a *huge* trunk with five light suitcases (for aeroplane) inside and a tray on top. All one's world like a snail and on the same principle, as the Mother of Suitcases can push the five little ones out or keep them inside according to the requirements. They say nothing so practical has ever been invented and I am bursting with pride. I shall pack it with all the most precious things and leave with Cici till next year, and may we then be taking it to Egypt. I have bought it instead of a new dress, so that you won't have any lovely Schiaperelli to cheer you. I will only be able to have clothes if we are kept in the Mediterranean; £180 each way is really a fearful lot to spend on journeys.

Love to you till next month,

FREYA

STEWART PEROWNE
I Tatti,
Settignano
7 November 1948

Darling Stewart,

I have come here for two days to say goodbye to B.B. I hope he will live till you can come with me. He says he feels he has no business to be here; but he continues to talk drops of wisdom, and never anything banal falls from his lips. What a man. He left Lithuania at the age of ten with Cossack massacres all about him. Yesterday I went with Cici (whom I brought here as a treat and left at the hotel to look at Florence) to the Michelangelo tombs. Those three women figures are so tremendous that they scarce seem created by man at all; more than the greatness in *them*, one feels the greatness of the man who made them. I said this to B.B. and he said, 'They should never have been made. They show the danger of power, in art as in anything else. I sometimes feel that art ceases to be beautiful when the artist is able to attain his object and can do what he wishes to do.' How true that is, don't you think? As soon as one can attain, all hope of the infinite is lost.

At Asolo a frantic five days' wait for me to get packed and away. We had three days completely taken up with a visit from the Madonna of Fatima, which is a place in Portugal where she appeared and is now 'visiting her people' all over Europe. The dioceses send out a statue and from parish to parish it is handed on. Asolo went to receive her at the bridge of Pagnano on a very wet night, about 5,000 people with candles wrapped round with pink or green paper guards, under umbrellas. It was so wet I stayed and watched from La Mura where one could see the little lights and shiny umbrellas pouring like a Chinese print down the church steps while the loudspeaker chanted, 'Vogliamo Iddio: il Nostro Re.' Then there were three days of visiting, the schools, the orphans, the hospital. An irreverent voice in the crowd said, 'How can we keep our wives at home, if the Madonna gads about at night?' The last of it was an evening procession past our house and down to Casella where the parish of S. Apollinare came to fetch her. Every house in Asolo and all those on the hillside were illuminated; it was charming and touching. The baker stacked his bread with green ribands, and the fruitseller piled his apples and grapes with garlands, and people decorated little altars in their doorways and put the children's photographs with the holy pictures to be blessed in passing. Our house looked lovely as Checchi hung paper lanterns in the poplar trees, and candles and the four-beaked Florentine lamps in the windows, and a candle on every spike of the gate; so that Monsignore, when he came leading the procession like a conductor, stepped aside from the vanguard of rather haughty little boys he keeps under his immediate eye, and stepped out to congratulate (very pleased at this Protestant tribute). We joined the procession for a little way so as to see it as it curved down the valley. It was immensely long, the Madonna fluttering blue and white on the people's shoulders, and a cash-box, white, with two gilt angels, carried before her, and a car with huge loudspeaker just in front, with a strong young priest beside it, intoning into the microphone, 'Maria, ave; abbi di noi pietà.' The chants were taken up and the river of lights sparkled all down the valley. The whole way to the plain was lit with little glow-worms of candles along the walls, and the light just showed the black outline of the moving figures. It was so ancient, pagan, heartfelt, and spontaneous that one could not help being deeply moved. How you would have loved it; it seemed to be a thread of history, tying the little town to all its own past, so that the shops and streets and houses were still what they have always been, right back into their earliest foundations.

Your
FREYA

SIR SYDNEY COCKERELL   New York
                                                  25 November 1948

Dearest Sydney,

I hope to have a letter very soon to tell me that your outing did no harm. It was a great joy to see you even for such a glimpse, and I *couldn't* have got out to Kew. My four days passed like a flash, a pleasant flash. So did the crossing of the Atlantic. It is almost a want of respect to treat an Ocean so cavalierly; the only influence of weather is a little delay here and there, so that we left Scotland at 3 a.m. (which *is* an inconvenient time) and break-fasted in Iceland instead of Newfoundland. One sees nothing. A rather sordid waiting room, with a pathetic little counter of hideous objects made by Icelanders for sale; a streak of sunrise behind rounded ranges of deep purple hills; a crisp air that turns every trickle of water into a cord of ice; and then back into the sky, the stars of morning travelling alongside, just a little more swiftly than we do. To this universal accompaniment one has breakfast or lunch, wraps oneself in rugs, is offered the magazines by a stewardess. We manage to turn the Eternities into a sort of chorus for our suburban stage. One hardly glances down to look at the shield of the ocean, the dreary, flat, waterlogged coasts of Newfoundland; and then tea in New York, with life *bursting* in a flood of luxury, bright lights, bright sun, every-thing lavish, numerous, and expensive. I went down to Wall Street to see a banker there, and it seemed like a sort of Babylonian Holy City where the temples of business, the core of New York, all stand with rather solemn, empty streets down in the canyons made by the soaring houses. Beautiful they are – marble basements kept polished and dusted, and columns and decorations in the high sunlight above.

I have at last met Osbert Sitwell. He came to dinner and I liked him, with his heavy eighteenth-century face and slow modest way of speaking. He tells me he gets unhappy after two months or three if he doesn't start a new book (I wish I felt like that).

Love always, dearest Sydney,

FREYA

JOHN GREY MURRAY

Guadeloupe
2 December 1948

Dearest Jock,

This is ever so much more remote than Barbados; the dingiest little dipper of a boat called *Le Montier* plunges in and out from Martinique, and there is as yet no airstrip to land on. The hills come up out of the sea in points and volcanic convolutions, clothed in thick green forest, bananas and mangoes where there is cultivation, and the fine big leaves and fruits of the bread-tree; and huge turbans of cloud wind themselves round them. Showers pour for a few minutes, whitening the air and beating it with thick bars of rain, and the headlands wind out in a silvery moist light into the sea. The Conference here is a meeting called the West India Conference organised every two years by the Caribbean Commission. They had the opening today; the sailors of the *Jeanne D'Arc* stood to arms under the portico of the 'Conseil', and blew a trumpet while the *préfet* walked up, all decorated. The poor *préfet*, everything went wrong at first. We landed at midnight instead of 9 p.m. and the only way of getting off the ferry boat to land was by climbing and hoisting onto a wooden pier in the dark (if it had been a year of tight skirts, it *couldn't* have been done!). We found a delicious dinner ready, however, and I sat between the French chairman and the *préfet*, who chose discriminating wines. The waitresses, with much more *ligne* than Barbados, and more slanting eyes, wore their costume, and the gayest variety of headdress, bright cotton kerchiefs rolled into various patterns and ending in starched panache of the two ends that stick right out. I believe the wearing of it helps to keep the island happy; they seem quite different from Barbados, natural and easy and not straining themselves to conform. The Guadeloupian ladies wore every sort of clothes, from Paris crinoline, black velvet and diamonds of the Banana Queen, to the home-made little gowns taken out of Paris papers. There were flat French bows on top of the hair, and flowers behind the ears. One could admire their gold earrings and brooches, and heavy chains of gold. They make the most charming jewellery – cameos set in tendrils of gold vines, and huge miniatures arranged as brooches. There is a feeling of Josephine and the Napoleonic era about it all; the driver who drives us is called 'Magloire' and our houseboy is 'Saint Hélène'. We are in a tiny and rather squalid little pavilion in a banana plantation, and a row of small Union Jacks has been hung across the entrance to welcome us.

Must send this for Xmas, with love to you all.

Your

FREYA

LADY RUTHVEN   Guadeloupe
                                                    12 December 1948

Darling Pam,

We are here at the end of a fortnight's Conference; and, my dear, it is so much more like Evelyn Waugh than like real life that one feels all the time as if one were removed from the world and inside a Work of Art. This poor little island lives on dreamily in the year 1850 or thereabout; the Napoleonic Age still its criterion, and the evening parties (with bows, chignons, and flowers in the hair) looking like so many scenes painted by Renoir. There is a circular, good road made by the home Government to go almost round the island; and a volcano with mountains and forests in the middle where one has to walk. The forest eats up every small path unless it is cut out fresh every four months or so and the banana plantations are cut out of forest as if it were a solid slab, and the solidity is left all around to keep off the wind that tears the broad banana leaves to tatters.

One hundred and forty West Indian delegates were poured onto this remote provincial peace. The aerodrome to receive them is only half built; so is the model village to house them; and even the stock of wines and perfumes (which is all this island offers from France) is now coming to an end. The islanders have been so hospitable, and turned out of their own houses. Delegates are parked about in villas, bogged with the rain; and the 'Administration', which promised to give them fresh sheets every few days, has not even been able to deal with the laundry problem. The strike of chauffeurs threatened to leave the Conference quite paralysed, scattered about in remote banana groves. And after about five days a U.S.A. medical circular asked us all to abstain from water, ice, salads, fish, fruit, and Coca-Cola. The Coca-Cola agent came down from another island in a fury, and it must have been very good for the Guadeloupe sale of wines, but it gave us all a tinge of gloom. Stewart went down with fever, and I spent a strenuous day plodding down our banana grove in search of a doctor and food.

This is a much nicer island than Barbados. It isn't so municipal; it is just what one reads about, romantic sunsets, solitary bays, remoteness. The people are so charming and greet you with no inferiority complex as you come to their little wooden shanties in the hills. They speak a formal, forgotten sort of French, and are pleased and proud of their traditions and not the rootless sort of creatures that sadden one in Barbados. The officials have made all sorts of efforts to entertain us, with evening parties and day excursions, all a little difficult because no one thinks it matters to be one or two hours late. On the first Sunday, we were driving along and saw a cock fight proceeding, so stopped and insisted on going into a sort of small wooden amphitheatre, with a sandy pit and two lines in the sand about three feet apart where the fights were started. The cocks were held and made to peck each other so as to make them aggressive enough, just like the poor little nations when a war is preparing; then they were put down and, after glaring and stretching towards each other with horrid cold looks, they wrestled, each trying to get his beak under the wing of the other and round to the back of his neck where he pecked and killed. It wasn't particularly unpleasant, but also not very exciting to anyone unversed in the finesse of the game. The interest was in the faces of the audience and I wish I could have got a picture of all those black and mulatto faces straining down from the sides. A cock costs 6,000

82

francs and takes a month or two to train; and it is the sport of all the country people here, they say.

Yesterday we went by sea across ten miles or so that separate us from Les Saints, where a great volcano crater must lie submerged, leaving a little archipelago of islands. Rodney won a naval battle there, and a little square tower on a round hill is still there, built by the British in their hot red uniforms when they landed and occupied the island. Their roads are still here, with square solid blocks of paving stone cutting through the jungle. But no history could last very long; it is just *eaten up* by the trees. Even the most ancient East would be submerged and lose that magic of the past if the bare plains were not so free of vegetation.

A happy Xmas, dearest Pam,

FREYA

SIR SYDNEY COCKERELL   Government House,
                                                  Belize, British Honduras

My darling Sydney,

We left Guadeloupe on the 15th and yesterday flew from Antigua to Jamaica, over the islands (St. Kitts and Nevis and many little ones, and San Domingo and Haiti). San Domingo is a fine rich plain rising to wild hills, full of small homesteads, a few roads, and a river or two winding; while Haiti looks very lonely, covered with short thick forest that, from the aeroplane, looks just as woolly as a Negro head. The sandy beaches make thin white lines like those firm beautiful outlines on oriental paintings. There is something so majestic about the Atlantic floor, when you see it in the sun, smooth under tiny ripples, with the little high white clouds throwing their shadows upon it as if it were a mirror far below. We stayed at the Governor's in Jamaica and came on here yesterday. The coast is a firm straight line on the map, but, in reality, it is an outer shell of reef where the sea waves nibble round long shallow pans of lagoon, brilliant as a butterfly's wings, and swampy islands.

Your
FREYA

JOHN GREY MURRAY   Belize
                                                  20 December 1948

Dearest Jock,

Such fun, the Guatemala frontier today. You go for two hours of swamp, mangroves, a tangle of roots like heresy, crawling and sucking, and little

83

barren palmettos; and then eventually rise and go for another two hours through forest, not oozing wet like Guadeloupe, but with sun filtering in, though only the tall strong trunks carry up into the light. It isn't like a cathedral, as I had imagined, but matted, bound, and gagged with creepers and orchids, and only to be hacked through with an axe. A Maya ruin emerged from the trees on a little hill, but they said it would take three hours to break a way up, and the forest is full of ticks. So we didn't, though there are toucans, pumas, jaguars, anteaters, and (if you are *very* lucky) wild green turkeys to be met. Also snakes. So we stuck to road and car, the only good road that goes any distance, and climbs to Cayo, which is all spick-and-span little wooden painted houses by a deep smooth river as green and dark as the woods. These all look as if they were really made of *metal*, dark at heart and only outwardly green; and we lunched with the water flowing and this huge still mystery of impenetrability just opposite. It feels like a Conrad story, a mounting emotion out of sight which might break out into anything at any moment.

There are small Maya villages, people with flat faces and straight hair looking not interesting, but very aboriginal. And then the road turns to a track, and you might be in England, with grass and trees and horses grazing; and another series of wooded undulations opens out and a cottage or two thatched with maize and wattled, as it might be England of the Britons or Saxons. One is technically liable to be put in jail, but the soldiers take it all very gently. One of them strolled up, dressed in blue cotton slacks (all the uniform he gets except for a rusty bayonet) and worn-out shoes of his own, and a straw sombrero; and, as he was tall and good-looking and moved with a good rolling mountain stride, he just *made* the Guatemala frontier. Five, he said, are there, and eight guard the next opening (the contraband, I take it, goes by little forest tracks unknown). We shook hands, nothing could be more friendly. We did all this today; so glad to have seen the good bit of Honduras. The coast is one long reef, and sheets of water, blue-green like turquoise, but glittering and filled with light, and catching every colour of sky; and then this soppy country which sucks in everything you put there. Even the tombstones are askew and the roads are slowly swallowed, and the poor planters get mildewed and rotted out of all their ventures. But you would like the little capital; it is 1824: a town hall with iron fretwork and painted wooden houses with balconies and Government House (where my bedroom was the ballroom) has walls and ceiling of white painted sheets of metal in the designs that inspired linoleum. A wonderful mahogany stair and banister, about a foot wide ending in a pedestal carved in one piece. We think of buying some of the lovely woods here, and mahogany to make writing desk and bookshelves, etc. . . . Lots of people crate their belongings in it so as to have it afterwards.

We cross to Yucatan tomorrow, to Merida. Christmas loves to you all, dear Jock. I wish you were about to think of a Maya stocking.

Your loving

FREYA

SIR SYDNEY COCKERELL

Puebla,
Mexico
29 December 1948

My darling Sydney,

Did you ever see a bull fight? We went on Sunday last. Mexico has the largest arena in the world (43,000 people) and it is a tremendous sight: the deep *well* of human beings, with the little openings disgorging people, like the Colosseum, and the round red sanded palisade below. The instruments and trumpets are above one's head and their sound seems beaten back from the sky, so that it comes with a sort of far solemnity, sweet too, suitable for such a game of death. At every moment of the ritual, the bull can, by one movement, destroy his fate; but he has never met men before, and he doesn't *know*. Like us all, he gets his chance but with no allowance for rehearsal. He improvises and feels strong and secure, and is killed. He is given his bits of success at the beginning when the picador waits on his horse to prod and weaken the great muscle of his neck; he gets at the horse (now padded thickly so that none was killed or maimed) and three or four times a picador was thrown. I have never seen anything so beautiful since the Diaghilev ballets and in the same way – everything depending on the perfection of judgement, agility, and time. And here, of course, the contrast of this delicacy and the danger that surrounds it gave the sort of beauty that an ice slope has in the mountains where any tiny carelessness is death. The human sympathy is for skill against force, so that one's heart is with the matador; for the power he defies is so obviously great. Our hotel concièrge, who took us, said that it was not a good fight as the matadors 'were all frightened'; and it must be very remarkable not to be so after a toss.

We had three days in Mexico City and yesterday came here over the shoulder of Popocatapetl and his sister, a thin smoke rising like a mist from the round crater. The lines of the land are beautiful, very like Persia here, but round Mexico City the plain has long cactus rows and pepper trees that give it a look of Modern Art. The city is a poor mixture of Spanish baroque and modern U.S.A. and not at all endearing but here we are in something authentic again, a market town for a big agricultural district, all straight streets with more coloured lights and signs than you would think possible; and many houses' façades with a pattern of brick and coloured tiles. It was built in 1581 as a rest camp on the way to Mexico.

Love always,

Your

FREYA

JOHN GREY MURRAY   Bridgetown
                                                      10 January 1949
Darling Jock,

I have just got back and sorted the mail bag, and there are forty letters to be answered and you are coming first: I hope that is documentary proof of your place in my heart. I wish you had been in Mexico. I wonder if you would be as passionate for bull fights as Stewart and I? But there are so many other things. Volcanoes for instance: three have snow; one, Orisava, is on the edge of the plateau, with his feet down below in forests on one side (as if he were sitting at table). One looks at him from a luxury hotel owned by the ex-Minister of Economy at a loss, and one can look up at his (Orisava's) elegant pointed profile through a screen of palms and hibiscus while floating in a swimming pool stocked daily with a floating carpet of gardenias. We didn't spend more than two days with this volcano (counting the dollars); the other two are *on* the plateau and Cortes descended on Mexico between them. They rise up as if they were sitting on thrones based on the plain, which is grey with long rows of agave (to make two drinks called *pulche* and *tekuila*) and the thin clear Mexican sky tints them in the morning – one can see the pink catching the white summit and the blue climbing up like a dust of butterfly wings as the sun grows. I do love those high *pellucid* skies, too rarefied to produce more than one little bar or two of gold even in the afternoon. A little wisp of vapour comes out of the snowy cone of one volcano (Popocatapetl), but that is all that happens, as it's dormant. It took six days to get from the plateau here, just twice the time of a journey to London: one can only do hops in the morning. We had all our tickets, and after reaching Vera Cruz hopped back to Merida; ate all the exotic foods of Yucatan – venison, peacock, armadillo, turtle, oysters, and the shrimps that are the export of the mangrove forests; and we saw a second city of ruins at Uxmal – a sort of Oxford of the Stone Age with a quad surrounded on three sides

86

by stepped buildings with carved façades. They used no metals, but the stone it seems is soft when quarried, like Roman tufa, so they chiselled it out into all the patterns we know, and other things – thatched huts, snakes, tortoises – from the life they lived. The pyramid-observatory is close by with four shells, one built every so many years outside the other: they seem to have been slaves to the calendar. How strange it is to have been there – a *continent* sprung out of nothingness into one's real world.

Love,
FREYA

SIR SYDNEY COCKERELL   Bridgetown
10 January 1949

Darling Sydney,

We got back two days ago, island hopping: there must have been a long curving range and the volcano tips, and sometimes just small flat bits of plateau, stuck out like a split necklace from the sea. It must be a fine sight down below where the fishes go in and out of the submerged slopes and chasms. Jamaica is the island I would choose for 'tropical island' films: the mountains have a blue bloom, like fruit only much more brilliant, or like Limoges enamel, only soft; it gives a radiance to the hills and makes them look like peacocks' tails with the varied green of their forests below. How lovely the bamboos are, like cathedral columns with their shafts gathered in sheaves and the round ribs of the stems arching in great curves: the sun shines *through* the pointed leaves and makes them paler and more brilliant than anything else in the jungle. The mangoes, rich and dark, look like Rossetti backgrounds; and in the damp dark places, where the streams trickle down in perpetual shadow, the begonias grow wild, and a white-green datura hangs pale little lanterns.

Dear love, darling Sydney. I hope for London in May.

FREYA

GERALD DE GAURY   Bridgetown
14 January 1949

Dearest Gerald,

Euphrates pulls at my heartstrings. I can't make plans at all, everything seems very uncertain in my world and you mustn't try to make me think of anything except the summer coming and May in London before that. I do hope for that and think no further ahead just now.

This is such a flabby climate. I long to get at my work and can't. Steven Runciman has done his first volume on the Crusades and I long to see it. I long to lead a more settled life: a quiet pendulum between exploring and books with a month of friend-visiting here and there.

Love,

FREYA

BERNARD BERENSON   Bridgetown

14 January 1949

My dearest B.B.,

We're out of Mexico again. What a lot has been seen: too much to write, but I will tell you – perhaps in June in Asolo or later in Vallombrosa. The best things were Maya in the jungle or bull-fights in Mexico and Puebla: one has to be lucky (and we were) so that the grace and the style, the elegance of danger, the wonder of colour and that tremendous ballet of the strength of the animal and the intelligence of man – come to one without being spoilt by some fearful sight of death. We had a young *torero* of eighteen making his début, and 23,000 people waving their handkerchiefs, showering their bags, hats, flowers, shawls in delirium. The little boys, *toreros* of the future, carried him out on their shoulders to his hotel. It is such a *ritual* thing, I imagine the human sacrifices were looked at much in the same way, except that one looked up the pyramid steps and not down – and there was no fight. The audience must have looked much the same: the very curious Mexican face, exactly like the portraits of the friezes.

Your book is here waiting for me and I am in it already, and hear you speak in it, and will write soon to tell you my enjoyment.

Dear love to you both,

FREYA

JOHN GREY MURRAY   Bridgetown

3 February 1949

Dearest Jock,

It is nice to hear of Harold Ingrams in England.[60] Do tell him I hope to

[60] Originally in the Secretariat in Aden, later Adviser in the Hadhramaut and Resident in Mukalla.

see him. My, what a six weeks it will be! Do you know anyone who has a ticket for the Flower Show to give away? If you can, do find two tickets and let us go and choose new lilies, and pray it may be fine. I will try and do that article and one just asked for by *Spectator* before I leave, but we have Harry Luke[61] staying and Molly Huggins[62] coming over for a week from Jamaica panting to talk to Women's Welfare. Such *strange* tastes people have. I give away cups, I see my frightful pictures in the paper, and long for Asolo and London. A woman asked how I like this 'life of grandeur' and I told her I feel more and more that I was born for the gutter. My best companions are two little finches; they come in about 6 a.m. and get more and more impatient for seven o'clock when the tea comes. I have got them to perch on the milk jug and drink while my hand is round the base of it, but with a terrific expenditure of emotions. They seem not to mind eating every meal of their life with fear and watchfulness.

I long to hear what you think of the book and to know it has all reached you. Am remembering lots of additional little bits to insert.

Love,
FREYA

SIR SYDNEY COCKERELL Bridgetown
28 February 1949

Dearest Sydney,

I have just sent ten more chapters to Jock and am taking a day off for the mountain of my accumulated letters.

I found Berenson's book very stimulating in spite of his use of difficult words; and now I have the history of Frederick II. What a saga and what a man. I had no idea that he practically founded Prussia by placing the Teutonic Knights there. I wish there were world enough and time to study much more history; I hope to have done with autobiography by the end of next year and to be able to sit down and study for another journey.

Yesterday Stewart and I went for a long ride in a bevy of planters, nice people on good horses, all across the island: four hours' riding and a lorry-drive from the last house down to lunch by the sea, on the north coast where the Atlantic boils and foams against the coral.

Your loving
FREYA

[61] Sir Harry Luke, colonial administrator and author.
[62] Wife of Sir John Huggins, Governor of Jamaica 1943–50.

Bridgetown
19 March 1949

My dearest Jock,

The last of the book has gone to you. I hope you will like it now.

I am coming over earlier, so you should see me in London on, say, April 26th. Is that going to be inconvenient for Diana and you? And, dear Jock, will you get my appointment with Miss Kelsey at Hartnell's[63] made earlier, as early as possible? A little black corduroy is in the air! In return for all this, I will send you a picture in today's *Advocate* of myself planting a tree, looking almost worse than in any picture ever before and that is saying a lot, as you know.

Love,
FREYA

STEWART PEROWNE Wishaw House,
Wishaw, Scotland
25 April 1949

Dearest Stewart,

It was absolute heaven to land in Scotland on a cold spring morning smelling of rain and moors, wind-blown daffodils and the beech leaves just breaking from their pointed sheaths, and primroses in the grass. Then, of course, I immediately crumpled up with a bad chill; one just isn't *meant* to be tossed from hemisphere to hemisphere in a matter of hours. I spent yesterday in bed, reading Ham's[64] story of the Legion; he has been working on it, and I like it because there is imagination and a real knowledge of what the desert marches are. I hope it may go. His stories of the Aden tribes are very good value. Did you know of Jamila, whose brother was killed and father died, so (aged fourteen) she refused to be a woman but took on the blood feud and lived with twelve slaves in her tower? Ham met her when he was organising some small siege, and she had the most dangerous of the outposts and carried out the operation better than any of the others. And he was then told she was a woman, and knew her quite well till she was killed at sixteen and thrown in a sack over the wall of the *khosh* of her tower. What a country.

There is a fascinating portrait here of Mary Queen of Scots, the only one I

[63] The couturier.
[64] Master of Belhaven (succeeded as thirteenth Lord Belhaven 1961). Had been with the Colonial Service in Aden when F.S. and Stewart Perowne were there in 1939–40.

have seen which makes one able to picture her charm. The house is a jumble of pictures and furniture gathered slowly at many different periods. Less a house than a Way of Life, with so many centuries behind it, a nice *decent* way of life where every dog and child, and tree and even inanimate chair or table, is cared for and respected for itself. A sort of sublimation, quintessence of freedom.

Jock telephoned and is meeting me tomorrow night and says the ms. is 'splendid'. Such a relief.

Love,
FREYA

STEWART PEROWNE

London
27 April 1949

Darling,

Yesterday I reached London, seeing the spring grow as I came down; so incredibly green, the buds on the trees like jewels, the little leaves like enamel, the cows bright as if painted. A wonderful atmosphere of normal, good, *kind* life full of very simple things. Dear, dear England: the sight of her fills one with tenderness. One should not be too long away.

Jock met me (Ham having put me into the train for Birmingham, but I go out and into mine at Carlisle; Ham musn't be allowed to guide till we reach *camels*) and we dined at Prunier's and the head waiter came to shake hands and ask if I was writing a new book. Here I found Cici till Friday and we go to a play tonight. Wavell rang up and we look in this afternoon. I long to hear from you.

Love,
FREYA

STEWART PEROWNE

Merrimoles,
Nettlebed[65]
2 May 1949

Darling,

I wish so much you were here. You would shiver in the May wind, NNE, but the sun is out in a blue sky, a film of white over it, and the buds of the beeches and all the young leaves looking as if they were drinking it up in

[65] Home of Peter and Celia Fleming.

ecstasy. The place is so peaceful: a single gentle slope of grass closed in by trees, ridge after ridge, all low and easy, to a far gap of horizon. And I had forgotten how blue the bluebells are, faintly scenting all their woods with hyacinth. How lovely England is; one loses it, because it isn't a beauty of sight – the *feel* and scent and everything make it up.

English intercourse in the country is very like the Arabs, isn't it? The same casual talk with no worry about long intervals of silence; and the same real hospitality, letting the guest wander about and do as he likes.

Love,

FREYA

STEWART PEROWNE London

3 May 1949

Darling,

Your letter of the 21st, so glad to get it, all about packing. I am sure you are right and when I want to write about anything I never think about it as writing, but only try to *feel* it, and then the writing sorts itself afterwards, in exact proportion to the depth of feeling. I just open all the windows as it were, to take it in. I believe life in general is like that, too, and the art of living the same. I went and did my little B.B.C. talk this morning with nice Mr. Lewin. You may hear it. It will be so bad, but I had four and a half hours to put in with the dentist and it leaves one shattered. I was going to Kew today but it poured, so I went with Charles Rankin to the Munich and Vienna pictures. What a feast, the latter especially. The four Velasquez, whole rooms of Titian, Van Dyck, and then unknown names like Cuello and wonderful Italian portraits. The old Pope Paul III Farnese, the wicked old villain, is surely among the ten or twenty greatest portraits of the world.

Your

FREYA

STEWART PEROWNE London

13 May 1949

Darling,

I have such lots to tell you, but first of all – Hatfield![66] I am just back from lunch there, what a place! There is a purely English art in these old

[66] Hatfield House, Hertfordshire, belonging to Lord Salisbury.

houses of making time seem at once static and alive. The trees are already like summer, heavy clumps of chestnut, lilac, pink and white may. They roll and coil in great swathes over the landscape, and there among them are the brick walls mellow with so many years. The old house where Elizabeth spent her girlhood, her yellow stocking knitted in lozenge pattern and her straw garden hat are there. And the window where Mary called her father and he refused to turn round and hear. And in the great house are the long galleries and rows of panelled rooms, the Tudor embroidered bedspreads, the bedrooms decorated for Queen Victoria and Albert (with an 'A' carved on the mantelpiece); the innumerable portraits of Burghley (who must have been very vain); the ancestress who beat her little boy to death because he was bad in Latin; and Mary of Scots as a young girl, quite uninteresting, and then as a plain middle-aged woman ready for the scaffold with a touch of magic still in her eyes and mouth. There are a number of portraits of Elizabeth and that tremendous character comes through in all. And after lunch we went down and saw the muniment rooms and the actual letters. How I wished you were there! Elizabeth as a girl fighting for her life, writing to Somerset against her accusers, in a beautiful script, 'I know that I have a soul to save the same as other fokes have', asking to be allowed to appear at court, 'to show myself as I am.' The Casket letters, and Mary of Scots writing to her cousin in a less strong, French hand. Elizabeth's letter to Burghley to order that Essex have a fair trial with three judges (evidently afraid that Burghley be prejudiced against him), and addressed casually by his pet name 'Ye Elfe'. Burghley's diary, 'The great Navy of Spain forced into ye North Seas and so with great wrack homewards about Scotland and Ireland.' Another two entries, 'Pain in my foot from paring of my nails', 'Emperor Ferdinando died.' These diaries have never been published, or even looked at by more than a few dozen people. There is a letter from Francis I signed in a bold Renaissance hand and countersigned by Bayard. And the signature of Catherine de Medici, just like her, illegible but ter- rifically strong. I said it would be a good idea to have letters and signatures beside their portraits in as many as possible of the National Portrait Gallery pictures.

It was one of the pleasantest days I have ever spent, and am going there for the weekend of the 21st. Betty had been dusting the books all the morning. It is all beautifully kept with the ancient silk curtains dripping in rags, but lovely. It is like the whole history of England alive and moving in these old rooms and avenues.

Your

FREYA

Darling,

I think I must have reached my highlight in weekends: lunch at Hatfield, Friday night at Magdalen with Tom[68] and the David Cecils, and nice Italian d'Entrèves, Saturday night at Cliveden, and now on the way to spend the day at Sissinghurst.[69] It does gather the cream of England, though it would be nicer to do it more slowly. Nancy[70] insisted on this one night, and I said, weakly thinking it impossible, that I could only do it if fetched from Oxford. She mobilised the whole Rhodes Scholar department (the only ones who have petrol) and two charming young men and a wife came along and drove me across the fat peaceful land, oozing with serenity and peace, till one feels that nothing in this world can break it, neither invasion nor conquest. Albert Haurani came to see me and said he would be interested to see what happened if England were occupied by the Germans. Tom and I agreed that something would happen, but it would be to the Germans. The comfortable land would slowly swallow and digest them and stamp them with its character as it has done before. The gardens of Magdalen were all a foam of hawthorn and chestnut, the old walls deep in wistaria, forget-me-nots and tulips and narcissus in the long grass. And the young men and girls punting along through the sunset. I am avoiding Cambridge out of a *delicatezza* and I hope you approve, for I thought you might like to be the one to show me round there.

The best talk I had was with Waldorf Astor, who told me how he got Drake's drum to be brought by its owner to meet the *Exeter*[71] when she limped home to Plymouth. They should have struck it, but they didn't. *Nothing*, I believe, will beat this people or really change them. They were saying that Bevin would have gone in with Churchill if Churchill hadn't insisted on clinging to Beaverbrook. Someone was asked why this friendship continued when Bevin was known to be working against Churchill, and was told that he was like a 'mistress who has been going on a long time: he knows she betrays him, but he has got accustomed to her.' Cliveden was so beautiful, the azaleas yellow in the woods and the red masses of rhododendron just beginning in that sort of valley as you go up the main drive.

[67] Home of Lord and Lady Astor.

[68] T.S.R. Boase, President of Magdalen College, Oxford.

[69] Home of Harold and Vita Nicolson.

[70] sc. Lady Astor.

[71] English cruiser, survivor of the celebrated encounter with the German pocket battleship *Graf Spee* in December 1939. (Nancy Astor was M.P. for the Sutton Division of Plymouth 1919–45.)

I crept out early this morning while all were asleep and am now rattling mistily through Kent.

Dear love,

FREYA

STEWART PEROWNE

Train to Bradford-on-Avon,
Wiltshire
16 May 1949

Darling,

Sissinghurst yesterday was beautiful, a sort of labyrinth garden, all mellow walls and rare flowers, kept rather sparingly and cut down and carefully chosen. Vita showed me how to get roses low down by pegging creeping branches along the ground. I shall learn so much for Asolo before I leave. The visit was rather spoilt by Rose Macaulay[72] being there. She is rather old, virginal, and embittered, until she smiles, very sweetly. She has strange goat's eyes and pale suffering lips, and I was quite surprised to see how self-centred authors can be for she kept the whole party discussing her review for about twenty minutes till Harold came and asked me if I was an egotist. I said I didn't feel anything particularly mine once it was out and done with. I was more interested in living than writing, and he agreed. Vita roamed about with her slow big stride in plum-coloured trousers and a corduroy jacket and coral earrings; she has lovely young lips, full and generous, and slow eyes, understanding and unhurried; and she wanders off on domestic errands which she forgets as she goes by some rosebush in the garden, and then Harold comes along and copes, almost quite amateurishly but with more concentration. The son, Nigel, was there and has the charm of both. Vita told me they had always been very happy on a basis of complete liberty both for themselves and their children, and there is now a charming mellowness in themselves and everything about them. The Weald of Kent stretched away in a dream of blossom; it lay like a mist over all the hills.

Love,

FREYA

STEWART PEROWNE

South Wraxall Lodge,
Bradford-on-Avon
18 May 1949

Darling Stewart,

It is pleasant in this kind, easy, Young household. Hubert does all the chores, Simon (who is the *image* of his uncle Mark) seems to be perpetually

---

[72] Novelist and travel writer.

95

sent out to feed the goslings and ducklings, and Rose thinks out new flower-beds.

We drove over to Len Woolley,[73] who looked much plumper and less worried: he seemed to think of a month or two on the incense route with great interest. He says that the Sumerians trace their civilisation from the south west; the Egyptians from the south east; the Phoenicians from the south; and that the answer must be somewhere in Arabia, wherever a certain kind of prehistoric stone pots can be located. The R.G.S. would be interested and would finance us. I said it cannot be till your next leave, i.e. in two years or so. But what fun it would be and need not take very long.

Love,

FREYA

STEWART PEROWNE   Bradford-on-Avon
                                              21 May 1949
Darling,

My week with the Youngs is nearly over, such a pleasant time, though today the best of all as I have been sitting quietly in the garden writing letters in the sun. Yesterday they went to the Lascelles wedding and Billy Henderson took me to Wells. That chapter room and staircase! Like water flowing, and done, one can see, in the simplest way, probably by the local mason. There are two recumbent tombs still painted with rich red, and I think more beautiful than the unpainted stone or marble. It is so pleasant motoring gently through the early summer, the Mendips swelling like breasts, one hardly thinks of them as hills. Billy took me back to Bath and we drove through its great circles and crescents; and saw the museum and a house even more beautiful, a little manor with Ionic columns, a dream to live in.

Some of the houses are now rebuilt, and the new stone is shining white, so one sees what Jane Austen meant by Bath being 'dazzling'.

Love,

FREYA

STEWART PEROWNE   London
                                              24 May 1949
Darling,

I was so pleased with your telegram, though it is almost as extravagant as a hat and more so than *kalima latifolia*, which is one of the dreams I saw

[73] Sir Leonard Woolley, the archaeologist. He has supervised the excavations at Ur 1922–34.

yesterday at the Flower Show. It was just the gentle English equivalent of the bull-fight; everyone wholehearted, taking active part, the growers standing round benevolent and pleased, like God 'seeing that it was good', the onlookers with their little bits of paper, asking if north-east aspect would *do*, some wealthy, looking at the new iris (£2.10s.), some evidently saving up two pence a time to buy their little bit of joy for the rockery. It was pleasant and touching, and the flowers just as gorgeous and far more agreeable than the Rosary Chapel of Puebla. I have got a huge list, but so far only committed myself to a parcel of small rock plants for Jock to bring next month (he and his sister are coming for ten days in early July); the other things are providentially only available in autumn.

I have sad news. Mrs. O.K. died at Claridges as her maid was packing for a stay in Paris. She knew nothing of it, but fainted at her desk and never came round. I am so sad to lose her; she was one of the people who really meant something, sterling and a true friend, and a character quite independent of all her wealth.

Love,

FREYA

STEWART PEROWNE   London
                                                        28 May 1949

Darling,

Yesterday Jock took Diana, me, and a charming literary lawyer called John Sparrow[74] to *The School for Scandal*. What wit, what elegance, what a lovely setting of clothes and scenes. Not a dull second and all the actors (except Joseph) first rate, and Vivien Leigh ravishing. It is such a *nice* play, too; I mean it has that sort of sanity and charity which sweetens English literature from Chaucer, Spenser, Shakespeare, Milton, right through, an innate decency. What other nation would end the play with happiness for old Sir Peter and Lady Teazle? Laurence Olivier was excellent, and walked about with a stiff leg, which he told us is real gout and a cartilage broken in the knee. We went to the Green Room and he was so pleasant. He is just like Herbert Olivier when he makes himself up as an elderly man, and has the same boyish delight, and manages to share it with the audience. He seems to do so little, and with tiny gestures, intonations, lets the audience guess all the tenderness and gentleness, the very opposite of the words – such beautiful

[74] Later Warden of All Souls.

acting. Jock had got us all a dark carnation and gave us lobster at Scott's and supper at the Coquille, and we sent you a *saluto* and wished you were there.

Love,

FREYA

STEWART PEROWNE

Ditchley,[75]
Oxfordshire
5 June 1949

Darling,

I suppose this is one of the loveliest houses in England. Such a façade of old grey-yellow stone, with the old panes of glass shining with *mauve* lights as they catch the sun. Such a courage of simplicity about it, relying on space and value for its beauty. I have sent you a card, from us all.

Ronnie Tree's two boys are here, very gay with the world at their feet, all going to parties and dances. And Michael Wright told me how Evelyn Waugh had been describing Peter Quennell 'looking as if he had just ordered himself from Asprey's'. 'He is in bed,' he said, 'trying to grow a club foot like Lord Byron.' He *is* witty, but how horrid, and everyone listens and despises him for amusing them.

There is a lake in the dip in front of the terrace, and a little temple, and many trees, and a great peace. Yet how glad I am not to have the burden of owning so much. It seems to me quite perfect to be poor enough always to want something and not to need too much time for looking after what you have, with just enough to make it possible to come and enjoy the life of your friends. I think one can improve on the gospels by being 'of the world and not in it' instead of the other way about.

Dearest love,

FREYA

STEWART PEROWNE

London
7 June 1949

Darling,

I shall miss this swift post when I get to Asolo.

I went along to meet the (C.O.) Martins yesterday, a charming young and sensible couple. He asked if I liked Barbados, and I said, 'So little that it

[75] Ditchley Park, Enstone, then home of Ronnie and Marietta Tree.

looks as if the C.O. is becoming responsible for a divorce.' 'We *must* prevent that,' said he, and then we had a long talk about North Africa and I told him about Sayyid Edris and visiting him years ago in Egypt, and about the Volpi villa in Tripoli, and asked him why they treated Cyprus as a home for convalescent governors. He finally said you were being too good and making yourself indispensable in Barbados; and when he went away, he said to John Colville at the door, 'Those two *must* be moved.' So I hope I have done my little bit. I also put the financial difficulty of the yearly Atlantic.

I left Ditchley in heavenly weather yesterday p.m. after a morning visiting Blenheim (the outside). David Cecil was at lunch and described it as a civilised building built by a savage, and I suggested 'a Parthian version of the Greek'. It is heavy, and Vanbrugh, like Lutyens, doesn't enjoy himself. There are two beautiful formal gardens and one (the water garden) was made only in 1920 at a cost of £200,000, *worth* it, and how pleasant to see that it is still possible to produce such beauty now when the means are given.

Dear love,

FREYA

STEWART PEROWNE
London
10 June 1949

Darling,

A few minutes' peace while Pam is frantically packing in her little mews and will take me in her car to Cliveden for the night. I have just given such a nice lunch to the Wavells and Wrights, all old friends, in the new place in Piccadilly, where the Milanese proprietor nearly fell over himself. Our lunch was so pleasant and Archie says he is collecting his discourses and going to call them 'Silence is Golden'. He says he pleased a university audience by proving the superiority of youth by saying that it takes two cats to produce a kitten but only one kitten to produce a cat. In coming away we happened to find ourselves just behind the Wavells as they walked along Piccadilly, and there was something strangely touching in the two backs, a little bent and weatherworn now, and *sagging*, but so gently, unassumingly gallant, asking nothing and always giving all. I think they liked being with us who love them for themselves.

11 June 1949

This is Cliveden now. We left two hours late and Pam forgot Lady Gowrie's hat in which she is going to Ireland today, and in the middle of

Piccadilly the back door of the van flew open and shouts were heard and a white-haired old man plunged through the stream with my Hartnell coat, new burberry, and little case with all my jewels. Very like the little Brothers of Freedom. I have the Rose Room here and can sit up among the pillows and see the view, the incarnation of Peace, the Thames without a ripple and all the catmint in purple among its little walls of box. Nancy is an *angel*. She saw I must be dead and asked if I wouldn't have dinner and a quiet evening in bed. Now what other hostess would do that? I feel renovated this morning. She is really good, and genuine and kind. I am so glad I like her and she me.

Pam and I gave a young man a lift to Hermione's.[76] He told Pam afterwards that he usually liked 'actresses and very glamorous people', but that he had never in his life met a nicer woman than me! Now isn't that a rather touching compliment from a young tough?

Love,

FREYA

STEWART PEROWNE London
12 June 1949

Darling,

The summer has come with a rush. I pulled out my crumpled yellow dress and straw hat and went to see Sydney in Kew, looked at his facsimile of the Folio Shakespeare (we *must* get it when both our debts are cleared, it only costs £4 or so) and then strolled with him in the gardens. What a pleasure for 1d. They make £7,000 a year out of pennies and spend £70,000. There were the *mecanopsi*, and the single peonies, and cascades of saxifrages and dianthus down the rocks. And then we called on Sir Edward Salisbury, the director, and were shown the oldest tree but one (80 million years old the Americans say), a little seedling growing there as cheerfully as if it had no pedigree at all. Sydney thought I had been going away without seeing him, and was so touchingly pleased and told me he would constantly be remembering this morning. It gives one a little twist at the heart to see this enjoyment of small things by the very old, like the enjoyment one has in the last autumn sun.

This may reach you for your birthday and brings you my love, then and always.

Your

FREYA

[76] sc. Countess of Ranfurly, a friend from wartime Cairo days.

STEWART PEROWNE   Hotel Metropolitan,
                                                                   Paris
                                                            15 June 1949

Darling,

Everyone seems to be recovering, sun shining, taxis waiting, the shops absolute ruin. Perhaps it's lucky you aren't there. Mlle. Suzanne says she knows me so well she can always send me a hat *wherever* I may be. Isn't that dangerous? Two ravishers are being made for the winter: a little brown felt to go with the ermine, and a black taffeta for cocktail hours. And today and tomorrow I spend all my time looking at clothes. Sybil Cholmondeley has sent me to her Maison and a draped jersey, black and slightly classical, is being made for cocktail. It is such fun, and *so* difficult not to buy something mad and bright and unsuitable for people with debts. How we shall let ourselves go when those are paid off! The British Council has got in touch and it may be possible for me to come here in late autumn and meet you. It would entail one lecture and broadcast and we could meet and return together?

                                                            Love,
                                                            FREYA

STEWART PEROWNE   Paris
                                                            18 June 1949

Darling,

The Parisian has studied the Art of Living to a hair's breadth, but you have to go further, to the Mediterranean, for the Joy of Living. Perhaps it is the sun. What a *feminine* town Paris is: women move in it as if they knew it for their own, and what a good business they make of it. All the serious things, the style, clothes, food, social life, small commerce, art; all seem to be run by their capable selves or else in such a way to please them. While in London one feels that the woman is incidental, and all the city life throbs to things happening in China and Peru.

Love and many happy returns,

                                                            FREYA

STEWART PEROWNE   Chantilly
                                                            19 June 1949

Darling,

I am at Chantilly with the Duff Coopers. Such a pleasant house on a green slope in the park, with two lakes in front of it, surrounded by miles of trees, and statues in clearings here and there.

Diana was asked at lunch about the new ambassador here and said, 'I loathe them, to make it quite clear.' There was a whole party at lunch, at two tables, and I sat next to Mr. Acheson, the American Secretary of State, also one for saying what he really thinks, straight out, though in a more detached way. He says he hoped never again to have to attend one of these conferences. I asked him about the Italian colonies and he said, 'The people seem so insistent on getting what they *know* is not going to do them any good when they have it.' I said it was a pity some alternative way could not be found for raising their prestige, which is all they want; and suggested that they are always out to bargain because of a preconceived idea they have of being more intelligent than other people – and they aren't more intelligent. He agreed and went on to tell me that Sforza[77] said to him, 'I ought to have refused to enter the Atlantic pact till the colonies were settled.' 'Well,' said Mr. Acheson, 'if you only *knew* what a difficulty we had in getting the Americans to *allow* the Italians into the Atlantic pact at all. It was only because the French insisted that we got them in.' He has rather worried, but very direct, blue eyes, and a look of quiet security about him, and is supposed to be the best-dressed man in America. All very unobtrusive, with a nice but tired wife, wrinkled but elegant in a non-exuberant way.

Love,

FREYA

STEWART PEROWNE

Chantilly
20 June 1949

Darling,

I have discovered that Mr. Acheson, with his good direct look and open ways and penetrating good judgement, had an English father and Canadian mother! Perhaps we shall end by Anglicising the U.S.A. in time?

Diana drove me to the Abbaye de Royaumont, built by S. Louis IX, and now turned into a sort of hostel where artists who are poor and want quiet and beauty can take a cell and live in comfort. They were giving a concert, and the stone hall with its beautiful simple pillars and arches was filled with the voices of the 'Cantor Veronesi', a choir of little Italians all in their rather touching fussy home-made dresses, conducted by a grey-haired Signora Agostini and singing Monteverdi, Frescobaldi, Scarlatti, and Palestrina. The Comtesse de Ségur, to whom it all belongs, was there in high collar supported by whalebone, marabou stole and roses in her hat. And when we had

[77] The Italian Foreign Minister.

102

watched all this, we called on the other 'squire' of the place, and found him practising walking on a tightrope. A wonderful afternoon with S. Louis as a background.

I sat between Cecil Beaton and Duff at dinner. I can't think why people are so very nice to me; when everyone who comes is either young, brilliant, or beautiful, and I feel like the ugly duckling. But they *are* nice, and Duff asked me to stay on over lunch today. One gets to like him more and more. He is spontaneous and human and ready to give and take. He has first editions of Scott, Jane Austen, Dizzy and Peacock, and much more, and loves them. He was describing Diana as a schoolgirl weeping and throwing flowers on Meredith's grave (she was called after Diana of the Crossways); 'drowned in emotion, as she is so often', he added in an undertone, which made everyone laugh. Cecil is agreeable to talk to. What a *medieval* face he has: with a velvet cap on one side he would make a Dürer or Clouet, with those sad eyes and frustrated mouth, and small artistic impotent hands. He told me that photography is not what satisfied him and the setting for *The School for Scandal* gave him far greater pleasure. He wants to come to Asolo.

I don't know how the Duffs can go on with such a stream every day. Diana says it is becoming too much for her. It would keep me from ever wanting a house so near Paris.

Your own
FREYA

STEWART PEROWNE   Paris
21 June 1949

Darling,

Last day in Paris is nearly over. Tomorrow I should be in Venice and next day Asolo, and find there a batch of your letters, I hope. I always remember W.P. one day, when I said that it was sad to be separating, looking surprised and saying, 'What does separation matter? It makes no difference.' Still, there are the little things of every day. I got a message from Lilia Ralli, who was in Cairo and is running the boutique for Dessés (all these places seem to be run by Society women); so I called in on her this morning and there she was in a sort of Rex Whistler background, full of printed scarves and costume jewellery. One is very soon glad to get away from the chi-chi of it all after a few days. These frightful old harridans on the doorstep of the Ritz, if they wore their things with gaiety one wouldn't mind, but it gives no pleasure even to themselves. The only human faces are those of the tired little people who do the work, and they are so nice. Mlle. Suzanne sold me an extra little hat (a black butterfly on a straw brim, such fun and not *too* gay) for less than £4 out of pure love, and I wonder if you would send a parcel of sugar to her and to Mlle. Claude. They live such hard, sober lives amid all the luxury of other people.

Today all the shops in the Rue St. Honoré put the Fables of La Fontaine in their windows. You never saw more charming shop-dressing. The sweet-shop with a white stream of *glacés* pouring out of the Laitière's broken pot; the Fly buzzing over a marriage coach of 1830 or so with all the people in blue hats and white bonnets and a ground covered with sugar almonds; the watchmaker, with small snails each carrying a watch and the quotation, 'L'important c'est d'arriver à point'; and, best of all, Hermès with all little bundles of expensive luggage, umbrellas, and gloves, and on every bundle two little doves under a nuptial veil. I walked by the Tuileries and along the Seine in the sunset and thought what a lovely city it is. But not to live in very long. I think one needs cities less and less as one gets older. My next will be from Asolo.

Your

FREYA

STEWART PEROWNE

Train to Verona
22 June 1949

Darling,

Everything looks a little shabbier than when I left it seven months ago. The ruined edges of the towns, and dusty fields, and ragged paper monies; but now the hard Lombard plain is past and the gentle Venetian background is taking me to its heart; it is like someone not beautiful or grand, but very dear and known in every wrinkle. I am filled with a sort of sadness, for it is silly that you are not here; not physically, with the C.O. as it is, but in your heart, so that it might be the sacrament between us and not drunk off like table wine. I wonder if it will ever be so, or if you meant it to be so? I think often of St. Margaret's and all the mystery we undertook there, and would still like to keep my pledge if I could. I will have faith and wait for your heart to find its way. Perhaps it is silly of me to write like this, but I have been thinking of you and must say what I feel when it comes.

It is very strange that, with all the belovedness of this countryside, I never feel quite that twist of the heart that is given by the English fields. And I have lived here so much more. What is it, do you think? Is it being fundamentally Protestant? I love this always as if it were outside me, while any English hedgerow gives a sort of passionate feeling of being a part of me.

Your loving

FREYA

STEWART PEROWNE Asolo

26 June 1949

Darling,

The Vespa arrived yesterday and is a lovely toy and I came home alone in it from half way up the hill. It feels just like the flying horse in the *Arabian Nights*. The only one who is really overjoyed is Checchi; he is learning how to clean it and I shall have to let him ride it now and then. I think you will enjoy it; really much more fun than a car. The new bathroom, too, is lovely, a shining floor of apricot marble, like gold, and Venini has made yellow lamps scattered with white glass daisies. I think I shall just be able to pay for all. I had hoped to have a balance at last and wanted to offer a little for your debts; but, of course, everything is about one third more than estimated and we shall only just squeeze through. But it really has been worth it, the house is so *livable* now.

Your

FREYA

STEWART PEROWNE Asolo

27 June 1949

Darling,

The nightingales have returned to the garden; they shout in it all night. I have been reading Claudel, rather like Blake and the Bible, and he describes a lark singing in the sky as 'ce furieux peloton de plumes'.

Yesterday Jock and his sister Evelyn arrived, all sending you messages. So good to see them, and specially because Jock is so worn out, I think he needs this sort of a resting place. I wish it weren't quite such a hectic week with B.B. Jock brought out twenty-three little rock plants, and *watered them every six hours*. Now which of my friends other than him would do that? I doubt if even you would! The result is that they are the only plants ever to arrive fresh and ought to grow beautifully. I have been counting the casualties among lilies and, alas, fifteen out of forty-eight have vanished, but some may still be thinking things over underground.

Yesterday we practised the Vespa. Jock is very expert and he has a Corgi;

but this, he says, is almost a motor car (with three gears) and beautiful for him, but not for me. I am far too accustomed to these attempts, and listen to all the imploring of friends without turning a hair, and yesterday succeeded in making second gear without being lost in neutral (as is too easy).

Your loving

FREYA

STEWART PEROWNE   Asolo

30 June 1949

Darling,

B.B. and Nicky arrived in the sunset yesterday, B.B. furious because his old Welsh chauffeur had lost the key of the car and so made him miss two hours' sightseeing in Treviso. He is rather tired, but quite indomitable, and had a long talk with Gerald de Gaury about pre-Islamic Arabic, a long talk with Jock about Americans of the '90s, and was the heart and soul of all general conversation, which he immediately raises to an art. He was pointing out, for instance, in that picture of Bellini where three little boy angels are holding up the dead Christ, how they are *playing* at grief; they are too young to feel it, and will soon scamper happily away. He told me he had seen more loveliness in Venice this time than ever before and that this greater capacity for enjoyment continues as he gets older. I have put him in the pink room as the new bath, which one steps *down* into, seemed to me dangerous for a tottery old man. (It looks beautiful, with a floor that looks like running gold water; even Jock is reconciled to the bathrooms.)

1 July 1949

B.B. is just off. We went yesterday to Possagno and saw the Canovas in that sea-green atmosphere, like ghosts of themselves, and B.B. said (as you did, I remember) how he is not to be despised, 'the last artist to create an atmosphere in his sculpture in which it is desirable to live', for Rodin, equally great as a craftsman, leaves one tired with a sense of strain. B.B. suggests taking off the heads with their Victorian simper, to realise how great Canova is. This morning we all drove to Bassano but found the museum shut. 'It had five bombs on it,' said the little man who came out. 'Five bombs is *nothing* to anyone from London,' said B.B., with blazing eyes. So we drove back through the valleys of the Grappa, all lush and green, and over the bridge of Crespano. B.B. told me that after d'Annunzio deserted her, Duse came to him and would have liked him to love her, but he 'was a coward and drew back'. I asked why, and he said it was because, though tremendously sincere as an actress, she was not so as a human being; and that he thought this often happens to actors who are therefore considered as belonging to a servile art. What a person he is to talk to; every moment he opens up some immense vista, like an avenue in a forest leading on and on.

Love,

FREYA

STEWART PEROWNE   Asolo

6 July 1949

Darling,

I have had my first tumble off the Vespa; I do hope the next will be on the other side as I am scraped by gravel all up one thigh and elbow. It seems such a slow process, one sees a ditch, one knows one is going in, and a sort of paralysis descends so that one takes no action at all. I was trying to turn round and forgot the clutch but not the accelerator. It is a blessing to have had Jock just now to give lessons. He runs alongside and it is wonderful exercise for him, and I am getting quite clever with the gears. If I can only learn without getting killed, it will be a marvellous thing.

Love,

FREYA

STEWART PEROWNE   Asolo

7 July 1949

Darling,

I am alone for the first time for months and months; it *is* rather peaceful and nice. I sent nine chapters with Jock, and all the illustrations are settled, including a photograph of Pen Browning discovered among Herbert's negatives, looking like a tough farmer in a check suit standing in front of a cow.[78] B.B. says he did look like a yeoman farmer. Old Cantoni came to call and told us how Pen and he went down to a fair at Casella at the bottom of the hill, and there was a girl with three pythons, and Pen said he would love to have one. Cantoni went to ask, but they were not for sale. A few days later, the people had made very little and were in need of money, and he bought the biggest python for 300 lire and Browning used it to drape round his models, of whom he had two, one for her face and one for her figure. Jock was delighted with all this.

[78] Herbert Young, artist and long-standing family friend. He had given his house in Asolo to F.S. to make a home for herself and her mother. Pen Browning, son of the poet Robert Browning, also lived in Asolo.

I think when you come we shall have to please Monsignore by going to his church now and then. It is evidently such a genuine, kindly pleasure to feel us 'in the family', and with no wish to convert.

Your

FREYA

STEWART PEROWNE
Asolo
9 July 1949

Darling,

I think your matrimonial quotation charming, especially the *groaning* wife; how touching. How evocative the Elizabethans are in their language, the whole fifty years come up in a flash with the image. It is so generous and sweet of you to say that you owe everything to me. It would please me more than any separate success of my own, I can honestly say that. Do you know that all my life I have lived in a sort of Eden, with no sense of personal insecurity (moral I mean) or danger? Now since marrying you I have suddenly become aware of how precious it all is.

Your

FREYA

STEWART PEROWNE
Asolo
16 July 1949

Darling,

I wrote last night with a headache, due to the thunder that broke at last and rattled round the Euganean hills; it is strange to feel the headache rolling away as if it were a glove, as soon as the storm has broken. Now I am adding the things I forgot before this goes and I settle to the book; how I long to finish and for a few months not to get up every day with that task before me. I wonder if any non-writers realise what a drain it is: always that sheet of foolscap, behind the sunniest morning, that awful strain to drag the butter-flies of your fancy out of *nothing* and pin them down. I suppose I am an artist, but what I really care for is just to be a human being, as complete and contented as possible. It is so dull, as soon as one has a label. Did you notice in Santayana how he says that men were made not to understand the world, but to live in it; one can go on thinking about that quite a time. B.B. said to me that he thought human happiness belonged chiefly to the Neolithic Age; that is the state which most humans most enjoy. Perhaps that is why it does one good to revert and do gardening, camping, fishing, etc., and not be too intellectual?

What, however, I wanted to write about are our books. I thought I might get a few bound when I go to Venice and would like to know your idea of bindings, whether you like them all various, or uniform for certain subjects, e.g. the French novelists, history, poetry? And if you prefer all canvas or with those printed papers with canvas backs and corners, and what colours? I rather like natural grey canvas for the Middle East reference books, for instance? I can get a few done at a time as I feel rich.

The Milanese chemist has at last found the answer for our dyes: one has to precipitate the lime in the water before dyeing. So he left yesterday and asked to take away a bunch of our gladioli; such pleasant commercial relations!

Your loving

FREYA

SIR SYDNEY COCKERELL   Asolo

16 July 1949

Darling Sydney,

I have treated you badly, but I am revising the book and hurrying to get it done, and all letters are piling unanswered into a mountain. But yours has come today, and every day I have been thinking of you and wanting to write. B.B.'s two-day visit went off beautifully. How happy if you had been there, too. He told me he had not felt himself in so enchanting a place since he was a young man. There is here a wonderful atmosphere of peace, and Jock will have told you all about it. I wish he could have stayed longer to get really well again. Now I am quite alone and work all day long except when I can't look at paper and ink any longer and then I sit in the garden and weed. I hope to finish next week and then have ten days to look after the house, my clothes, and a day or two in Venice before going off to the Dolomites.

Very dear love,

Your

FREYA

STEWART PEROWNE   Asolo

17 July 1949

Darling,

That Fatima Madonna, who never sits still in one place, was up here again, and there was a terrific *festa* for her, about 6,000 people, I should say, from all the parishes round, and the Bishop of Treviso all in magenta watered silk standing above the Piazza at a microphone. What is so much nicer about *festas* here than in Barbados is that *everyone* takes part; there are no little coteries with tambourines on their own. Everyone wore their newest, and as it was nearly all peasants, the colours were *so* gay: pale blue dresses with cherry cardigans, or orange with a scarlet headdress. The Medunas (who sell us our coal) gave me a drink at the café and took me to a window, and we looked down on the top square (under the Rocca) crammed with people, the balconies hung with all the best tablecloths and bedspreads, and a circle of coloured paper with 'Vergine Maria' written up letter by letter on the trees. It was all so well done, and must have been what the Greek ceremonies were really like, a part of the very life of the town. The Madonna came lurching along to where an altar and platform were ready, the Bishop's throne old gold, and about fifty banners, with wide satin ribbons and inscriptions fluttering around, each carried by a delegate. The procession was headed by two *firemen* in tin helmets, then small angelic children in white, then Bishop with Monsignore (looking far more grand and ecclesiastical) and a Monsignore from Montebelluna on either side, then four carabiniers guarding the Madonna. There had been singing and intoning while the crowd waited, but a rousing clapping of hands greeted her arrival, and then the priest who conducted the microphone suggested *tre viva per la Madonna*, so she got three rousing cheers and one expected 'and she's a jolly good fellow' at the end. It was enchanting, and funny, and touching. The Bishop gave a monstrous speech, all feeling and bombast, and then everyone knelt while he blessed them, and then a greeting was offered to Madonna, Jesus Christ, the Pope, and the Bishop, and given by acclamation with increasing cordiality. The Madonna leaves tonight for Treviso, her tour is ended. 'How does she travel?' I asked. 'Why, by lorry' . . . what a silly question! When she left, a terrific farewell was given her by everyone waving his or her handkerchief. There was a fearful moment when it looked as if she and the platform were going to collapse; various priests and acolytes suddenly seemed to be vanishing into the ground. But she remained, a trifle lop-sided but with her simper unaffected, holding out a rosary in a pale plaster hand, and a bouquet was brought and placed at her feet just as if she were straight from Hollywood. You *would* have enjoyed it.

Your

FREYA

19 July 1949

Darling,

It is so wonderful to have been quite alone for ten days, so good for one. At first it seems a blank: one has to live with oneself and face one's thoughts, and it is like suddenly taking away drugs or wine I suppose. Then a really sane quiet sort of feeling creeps in; the time, and one's own thoughts, get fuller and fuller; and now I am quite contented but with a pleasant relish at the thought of seeing people again, which is quite different from that over-stimulated feeling.

I have had a sad morning with Checchi, doing autopsies on the lilies, all those that showed no leaf, and most had just become disembodied, but a few showed gnawed remains and horrid wiry worms, a sort of Marvell ode in action. I am now going to write a long letter for advice to the growers, and, alas, a very expensive order for more.

If only you get three months here you may see them next spring.

Your

FREYA

STEWART PEROWNE   Asolo
24 July 1949

Darling,

Last night about seven a wind and black cloud came down from Grappa and the leaves of the trees were all turned upside down, and Emma and Maria rushed round closing windows, and the rain came and the church bell tolled, and the hail came in lumps like grapes, and lay white in heaps on the ground, and not a flower is left in the garden. Masses of torn leaves poor Checchi is sweeping up. The fruit for autumn and the maize are spoilt. Luckily it is a small area, from Possagno to the first villages south in the plain, but in this little area all the year's labour has gone. We shall have few grapes and tomatoes, but the autumn flowers were too small to be hurt and as I am leaving in a week, it does not matter so much. But it was strange to see what a sadness was spread over everyone this Sunday, as if a death had come in the family. No wonder the peasants stand up better than others to wars and go on ploughing under the guns; they are used to that sort of brutality.

I am going to try to have the house clear of people for at least a month, or more, so that we may settle down to get completely bored together. I am sure we *must* have a little time to get started with only one another to think about; and after that, if our affairs allow, we can have a jaunt to Rome?

How lovely it would be to be in Tripoli next year, or Cyprus, or anywhere on those Mediterranean shores; if we can be happy together, I don't much care about other things.

Your

FREYA

STEWART PEROWNE   Asolo

29 July 1949

Darling,

I must tell you some gossip this morning. What happened was that, having a week on hand and the book sent off, I thought I would begin to clear the decks for the next by tidying all the drawers of negatives, and you can't think what it means. I have done about 1,500, and got fearful headaches looking at them into the light, but rather fascinating. Syria in 1928, and the Caspian passes and Luristan brigands. It was really I in those strange places? Then there are *hundreds* of Herbert's, and they are the most beautiful negatives and make a complete picture of life in Venetia and Piedmont fifty years ago. I would make a charming picture book and I think if Jock doesn't like the idea, we might have one done privately by subscription for Marina, etc., all the people about here?

You ask about my ankles: they are not elegant, but no longer *monstrous*, but whether or not they can be cured by walking will appear next week in the mountains. That funny dead feeling still exists, but I have done very little walking here what with heat and one thing and another. I think of you in this sticky heat and wish so much you were coming up into the cool hills.

Such a strange pathetic old boy arrived from Venice to take the photographs of the portraits for the book. He had a red nose, and a mouth shut tight on lots of sad squalid little worries, and his head, very sparsely covered with hair, was *painted black*. What awful transition from the gaiety of youth brought him to this? Perhaps just poverty and the necessity to try to look young for a job. He spent a day taking his pictures, and next day there he was again, his camera had fallen off the bus and all was spoilt and he hadn't dared tell his employer; so we gave him lunch and he set to again, and then the sun went off and he hadn't taken the chief picture (alas, nearly always some good reason to explain these sad elderly failures), so he went away and had to come *again*! He explained to me how dreadful it was for him to make a mistake because he is so 'sensible', with his hand on his poor old fossilised heart, and it cost him 2,000 lire to replace the glass in his camera. This awful *respectable* poverty gives one a twinge, and the world so full of it just now. Thank God to be settled in a place like this, small enough for a little general help and charity to go round.

I have B.B.'s book, but it isn't as good as the first. The fact is he doesn't know how to use words; he complains of their inexactitude, but no one complains because a picture doesn't give the exact texture and matter of a face or landscape; and words are the same, mere tokens with which you build your picture as the artist builds his with paints. It is a fatal trap to think of words as exact in themselves; the *things they evoke* have to be exact. At least that is my theory.

You will be glad to hear that I have ordered eight tons of coal and 250 litres of wine to last through the winter. I am also going in for the extravagance of a car to the Dolomites to take the Venini who have been so kind, and Caroly for the day.

Your

FREYA

SIR SYDNEY COCKERELL

Albergo Costalunga,
near the Karersee
2 August 1949

Darling Sydney,

We came up here yesterday; it is a good stone-built hotel on a meadowy pass 1,800 metres high, and all surrounded by waves and spikes of Dolomites. There is that incredible mountain peace all about it, deep grass with flowers, sleeping in the sun, and motionless pines as still almost as the rocks against which they lean. Only the cars go whizzing by over the pass in their restless human way, but this world is so big and steadfast that it swallows and forgets them.

The two young girls and their father, Paolo Venini, with whom I came up yesterday, are still in bed (ten o'clock); but the sun shone into my room and the outside looked so good, that I came down and breakfasted on the terrace. A few English are here, they have become so modest and quiet in the world, so touchingly happy in their rare and hardly attained holidays that one is drawn to them.

I have brought *Piers Plowman* to read here, and the *Odes* of Horace, but I shall probably do very little but sit in sun.

Dearest love, dear Sydney, and may there be many more birthdays yet, for your friends' sake.

Your most loving

FREYA

STEWART PEROWNE   Passo di Costalunga
                                                        4 August 1949

Darling,

I am having breakfast in the sun, another glorious day; fancy welcoming the sun with joy, as an event, every morning. One side of the hotel it is baking hot and the other, where the wind comes over the pass, one needs a thick coat.

I hope I have made your arrival for Xmas quite safe by promising a candle to St. Anthony. I said it would be valid for all December, but the earlier in December, the bigger the candle; and if you come with a transfer in your pocket, I have promised a second one from you.

I liked the quotations, especially the one from Santayana. It is strange how that feeling of dessication comes through, isn't it, and sad because I do think he is the best writer of English I know now, except Max Beerbohm. Did I tell you, by the way, that Iris Origo went to see Jock, and wrote to a friend of mine that Jock told her he was publishing the 'best autobiography he had ever read'? I am pleased, and hope it's true. It is funny how I can get no idea of what it is like any longer.

The Venini family are recovering and we played an Argentine card game in Laura's bedroom last night. Rather like the Palio,[79] such cheating and shrieking, such ups and downs with victory or defeat. No Dunkirk feelings at all. What a people they are, no sort of *padding* between their feelings and actions.

I am off to take the ankles for a small exercise.

5 August 1949

It was a tough but lovely walk, about two hours up towards one of the Rosengarten 'refuges', and the whole basin of the Adige, the meadows and woods, and tributary valleys, and uplands round Bolzano, and out of the way to Trent, and beyond that the piled-up ridges and snows of Stelvio and Ortler, all lay below under a clear pale sky. And I thought what fun it would be to be a count or marquis when you really owned your fiefs, and could

[79] The horse race in Siena.

114

look over it all, and see the castles of your vassals dotted here and there, and the main road where the travellers paid toll, and your peasants making hay on the long slopes. It is a country meant for the medieval way of life.

I am enjoying *Piers Plowman*. It is such a mixture of what you still meet in England, as far as the character goes, and in the East as to the way of living. One meets the atmosphere of any wickedly governed little oriental town. It is full of humour and the characters are alive in spite of being allegories, and all such fun. There is a 'ribber', a player on the *rebabe* evidently. I wonder if it came from the East or West there with the Crusades. It would be fun to make a little book of Crusading vignettes taken from modern life in the Middle East? One could find a great many, hawking near Latakia, and in the desert, and all the life of the *suq*, and the bath, the barber, all the odds and ends of life.

6 August 1949

I am so tired in the legs when I get home I can't use my head either! Walked *five hours* today, all by myself with my lunch. It really was heavenly, the Rosengarten like a huge fortress above and I going along through woods and meadows. I thought of your quotation about tradition while following the little paths, such a *help* to have a path. Yesterday we all went under the other great fortress of rock, the Latemar, to the Karer lake, a rather shoddy affair of unnaturally blue water full of tourists, and there surrounded by a posse of detectives keeping all away, was Mr. Churchill painting! I got the detectives to take a little paper to give him later and wrote, 'Dear Mr. Churchill, I hope you will have a pleasant holiday' and signed it! From above one could look down on his immense *sombrero Mexicano* and quite appallingly hideous picture of the lake. I daren't write more as no one knows what an extra sheet costs, and I fear it won't arrive. No letters from you yet. I hope for tomorrow. Such lovely names there are in these hills, Latemar, Tiris, Lake Antermoia, Sorapis, one feels the intrusion of a different language neither Italian nor German, like a sort of Arab breaking in.

Love,
FREYA

STEWART PEROWNE   Passo di Costalunga

8 August 1949

Darling,

We had one of the best views in the Dolomites today, I imagine, circling round the outside of the sort of fortress of the Rosengarten, where the straight top cliff takes off; and all, from Stelvio beyond Botzen in the west to Sasso Lungo in the north, gradually unrolls like one of those Chinese river pictures. The little path was very narrow and sometimes slanting down a very steep hillside of small gravel. We reached a refuge and found quite a crowd including small children of about four who are being taken along these rocky edges.

Laura Venini told me of an old man she met in these hills two years ago who said he had not been down to the valleys as he did not know whether the war was over. Wouldn't it be rather nice to tuck ourselves away like that for the next one? I miss a little talk here. Italians, I think, are really bad conversationalists; they never listen, and often make noises only to express feelings, which gets boring.

It does look as if, all debts cleared, there might be £100 or so in hand to play about with at Xmas. What shall we do with it, if so? A porch and double door to keep the hall warm and/or a little visit to Rome (or Austria for which the British Council would pay half)? Or it could pay for a frigidaire which we badly need, or a bit of your overdraft if that isn't fading away as it should. But it would be much pleasanter to do something enjoyable with it if we can.

I have been reading *Piers Plowman* under one of those unwieldy German eiderdowns. So full of good sense. He says, about Noah's ark, how fine it was for all the beasts that were saved, but the carpenters and shipwrights who did all the work, *they* were just drowned; and that, he says, is what happens to the bad priests who save other people by the good gospels they repeat, but get it in the neck themselves. No one else, so far as I know, ever thought about the people who hammered away at the ark?

Love,
FREYA

STEWART PEROWNE   Passo di Carezza
                                                    13 August 1949
Darling,

I have kept this letter a day to tell you, now that it is over, of my little expedition to the top of Latemar. I got a guide and we went up at six and were back at 12.40. Not really a climb at all, but the very steepest of walks, 3,500 feet slap up from here and down again with no let-up at all. The poor ankles are hating it now, and I have laid them flat under the eiderdown, but going up they behaved beautifully; and it was only my breathlessness which made me feel like dying. It was snowing on us and all the little runnels of water were frozen and opaque. One goes up from the back where the grass and sheep reach to the top, and then the whole thing breaks away at your feet in towers and turrets and chasms and cliffs, and the sun and clouds chased each other over one of the most stupendous views in the Dolomites: all the southern hills to the Brenta group in far far distance, and the Ortler glaciers and the Swiss and Austrian snows, and all the western mountains jagged and powdered with fresh snow. It was icy cold, and we came down to the first little bit of flat grass about 3,000 feet below, and slept, and now I am back in my bed, rather surprised at having been able to do it. What a vision it was, brilliant like one of those blue and green enamels, the light so dazzling, the shadow so sharp, and the shadows as if a great fugue of music were thrown across the land. The guide spoke German and had been on the Greek and Murmansk fronts and taken prisoner in Norway by us, and said he was well treated, 'but one is no longer a man when one is a prisoner.'

I am reading a fascinating article on Japanese poetry. It seems they have a term of contempt for the writer who *says all he has to say*; they think it bad not to leave a sort of echo into the unsaid, to evoke all that lies behind the simplicity of any event.

> 'Perhaps a freak of the wind, yet perhaps a
> sign of remembrance,
> This fall of a single leaf on the water I
> pour for the dead.'

One charming quotation:

> 'Lo! on the topmost pine, a solitary cicada
> Vainly attempts to clasp one last red beam of sun.'

How lovely to meet you at Mestre.

Your

FREYA

STEWART PEROWNE   Dolomites
                                              14 August 1949
Darling,

Everyone here sends their love. They are so gentle, affectionate, and kind, but there is a fatal gravitation to sitting in the hotel, which seems such a dreary thing to *pay* to do. I am always surprised by how little people are prepared to ask of life (without knowing they are doing so), when they could have all the kingdom of earth and angels of Heaven. It is rather melancholy in my own letters, how worried I was about all the little miseries of Baghdad when I could have forgotten them and enjoyed every moment of Asia. However, I managed to get away from them a good deal.

Do, *do* come for Xmas.

Your

FREYA

STEWART PEROWNE   Dolomites
15 August 1949

Darling,

I have walked about in the hills for five hours today, leaving the others. I found a rather narrow path on the edge of a slope and came through a little neck or pass into steep country where only the flocks and cattle go, browsing as if on their hind legs, because of the slope. I zigzagged up to the skyline and there was another huge steep grass and rock basin slung between outcrops of Latemar, like the fold in a tent standing on the far valley floor. There were five cows and they never moved, but went on chewing, their eyes half closed, looking at me now and then through their pale beige eyelids as if they were goddesses indifferent and callous to my mortal intrusion; but they had a bull, who stood a little above, and began to snort and paw the ground, so I retreated to a steep place behind a rock and wondered if my haversack would make a muleta.

I don't think I shall mind not ever climbing any more; I feel frightened by the high mountains, a sort of panic fear. I was quite glad to be down in the safe pasture-land, where a herd of goats came up as I was eating. I gave a piece of bread to the old patriarch with lovely horns, and the whole lot of them started to treat me as if I were pasture: just walking up onto me and trying bits of my clothes, haversack, etc. I really got quite frightened and had to get up and walk on, with Methuselah and all his tribe (about sixteen of them) following, till I came onto a meadow where the most beautiful young shepherd I have ever seen was standing, leaning on his stick, and surprised to see *me* with all his goats.

The weather has broken *so* cold, and no look of a change. We are going down on Wednesday, day after tomorrow; after all, there is dear, comfortable Asolo, and no sense in sitting here in *rain*.

Dear love,

FREYA

Asolo
                                                        21 August 1949
Dearest Jock,

I am now reading all the letters written *to* me and arranging them year by year, destroying a good many and keeping what may be useful. The book is shaping itself in my mind: a long chapter of letters for each year, with a commentary or introduction by my present self and an addition of letters *to* me at the end. I think it ought to go right on to 1947, the end of the war and re-settling in Asolo. Much of it will still have to be scrapped, but even so there is a lot (and all the war years still to come). Really, reading it, it makes a lively story. I have a good quotation for it from Sir Thomas Browne: 'Now for my life, it is a miracle of thirty years, which to relate were not a history but a piece of poetry, and would sound to common ears like a fable; for the world, . . . I use it but like my globe, and turn it round sometimes for my recreation.' A little arrogant, but why not?

Much much love,

FREYA

STEWART PEROWNE   Asolo
                                                       26 August 1949
Darling,

Two lovely letters, August 11th and 14th. I was so glad to get them, thinking that if we had not been fortunate in both of us being alike, able to put ourselves into our letters, if we had been tied up and inarticulate, these months of separation might really cause a total separation? As it is, they do the opposite, for we do talk of the things we really need to say. What a blessing!

Yesterday I took the day off at Maser and went on Vespa. How terrified I am of the little beast. When you put her into second or bottom gear, she goes up hill *shrieking*, as if she were a Maenad. I was pleased with myself, though it is still a matter of pure chance which gadget I turn on. At Maser, in front of an admiring staff, I forgot to turn the engine off, so she started going towards the largest statue, luckily not too fast to be caught and stopped.

I have just been reading in More's book how philanthropy flourishes in non-religious ages, because it is fundamentally an enlargement of the self; while in real religion, there is no need for it and it comes unnoticed as a consequence of deeper things. I was delighted, as you know how I loathe philanthropy!

Your
FREYA

Dearest Sydney,

Such a long time without news of you – I hope it is enjoyments and not ill-health. I have meant to write, but I am over the ears in the tremendous job of reading nineteen years of letters: it has to be done before the next bit of autobiography can be planned, and it is like stirring ashes with all sorts of sparks in them. Such lovely letters of yours – how one's whole life comes, still living, out of these old things! It is going to be a very difficult book to write: I don't mind putting my private record there, in fact I like getting at the truth apart from its connection with me; but most of the people whose letters are here are still living, and *they* may not like it: only about three, but they have all the drama of the story. What do you advise?

We came down from the mountains after a good fortnight because it turned bitterly cold. Now it has gone very hot again, and our water is rationed and the garden grass all burnt: rather a wicked heat, with white mists wrapping up the landscape, and no air to breathe. People come from Venice: Princess Aspasia of Greece, the charming Princess Marina Galitzine, the Duff Coopers, all the Venice Season; I have no wish to be in it, am so delighted to have this interval of quiet, but it is pleasant to see those who take the trouble to come. How I wish you were here, dear Sydney.

FREYA

Darling,

The Galitzines are here, wide-eyed innocents. They have spent three and a half years producing a book about Noël, all by themselves, writing, miniatures, and printing by hand, and are trying to sell 115 copies at 50,000 francs each. Poor dears. They are just made to be taken in right and left, they have no money at all. The prince does the marketing and cooking for his beloved princess in their lonely little farm, and she wears an old black woollen dress with her royal rings, and they look worn away but with a something about them that one can only call happiness. She left yesterday in the crowded bus, and I asked the conductor to find a seat somehow, putting it down to her heart, but slipping in the royalty casually, so as not to be like Princess Aspasia who asked Harry in his Bar to get an American to take his hat off, and Harry said, 'This is a public house in a republic, so I can't.'

I hope you will bring the water goggles. I once looked through them and it is terrifying; it suddenly transforms the nice flat quiet sea in sunlight to a place full of mysteries and life, and makes quite a difference to one's feeling when swimming.

Your

FREYA

Asolo

JOHN GREY MURRAY

29 August 1949

Darling Jock,

I am reading such lots of your old letters, such nice ones. Thank you again for them all. What an *old* friendship ours is already, going on for years and years that go in a flash. We stand, you say in one, between love and friendship. What a sensible place to stand in! As I have been reading, I think of you rather like Will o' the Mill.[80] Do you remember it? One of my favourite of all stories; it realises the butterfly wings of things that are best seen flying about and not touched.

My collection of letters is very warming to the heart. All Miss Caton Thompson's[81] and such are long ago in the waste paper basket and I seem only to have kept what gives me pleasure. How wise! I shall make you a lovely book out of the distilled essence.

This is not business, but only affection.

FREYA

Asolo

STEWART PEROWNE

1 September 1949

Darling,

What a nice day yesterday, Diana arriving looking like a vision. She is getting to have a sort of unearthly beauty as she gets older, and a great white straw hat absolutely plain and one of those simple little cotton dresses only produced round about the Place Vendôme. Duff, smiling, and the son, John Julius, one of the nicest young naval things, writing poetry in his spare time, all of it the quintessence of England. And no *Tatler* atmosphere. Lunch

[80] From the story by R. L. Stevenson.
[81] The archaeologist Gertrude Caton Thompson. In 1936 F.S. had been on a not entirely harmonious expedition with her in the Hadhramaut.

under the wistaria (making the wasps drunk with vermouth imprisoned in those little glasses), and siesta, Duff with Benvenuto Cellini on the lawn. 'He loves a book more than he does *any* of us,' says Diana; and then after tea she drove us all to Possagno and we looked at Canova in that sea-green atmosphere and the enchanting landscapes one sees through the columns of the Temple, just like Veronese. I thought how pleasant it is to see what amounts to a Greek portico *in use*. We ran out of petrol on way home, and J.J. had to pour some in from a tin, and poor Duff went through tortures while Diana backed at a smart pace all down the zigzags of the Asolo hills jerking at the reluctant engine till at last it went. How you would have sympathised!

I feel you will need a rather more restful leave this time, breathing the air of Europe. I have been having insomnia, too, and am quite sure it is only fatigue. I get it when my life is unbalanced, too much mental, and too little just ticking over, and cure it either by walking, embroidery, or weeding. I wonder which of these you would adopt? Weeding would please Checchi most. I have nearly done him the whole of the grass path up to Bacchus, and the great advantage of it as an occupation is that, having reached the end, you begin again at the beginning.

Your
FREYA

STEWART PEROWNE   Venice

4 September 1949

Darling,

Venice gay and bright and hot, too full, and the percentage of people good to look at too small. I have put my work away till I get back in two weeks; have read thirteen years of letters, about three to six hours a day, and it is almost as tiring as writing. But the book is emerging.

I only hope the struggle with the bank may be over. Beasts! They have kept my £1,200 for over *two months* so as to try and change it when the £ drops, and this is the *Government of Italy*. I have got (a) the British Embassy, (b) my own bank in London, (c) bank in Asolo, and (d) Marina, a converging and simultaneous offensive, Marina being by far the most potent. She said, 'And I did not hesitate to write what I thought.' Meanwhile I haven't been able to pay even the grocer. I did write to say that these expenses were all those that Italy was to have paid as war damage and hasn't done so.

The Moynes dined last night and have invited us to either Ireland and stout or Wiltshire and Arab ponies from Lady Wentworth's stables, and I said we might be in England on the way to a new post. He has promised to talk strongly to Lord Listowel,[82] but won't see him till after November (and says he is a bit 'gentle' anyway for doing anything). It is good to think of three months' leave; it gives time for quite a lot, and Siena, Florence, etc. Sounds lovely, a leisurely early spring wandering down Italy – Heaven! and you will see our tulips, too, and so shall I, for the first time.

5 September 1949

It is so pleasant to get back from Venice, a day or two goes a long way there, but Georges'[83] concert was fun in the painted hall Rezzonico with everyone dressed to *allure* (only the heat made it difficult). Georges played Chopin and was doing well by the time we were leaving, very nervous I think at first and *no* artist can really live in the atmosphere of the Polignac palace. So it was all rather eighteenth century, not profound but pleasant; and there was poor Georges, who lives in that rather dingy stew purified by Art and looks emaciated by it all. I got into the church of the Miracoli and it's like a goldsmith's work inside, too, not like a church, but most beautiful; and all Venetian brides prefer it because it has steps to the high altar, very becoming to the train.

Dear love,

FREYA

STEWART PEROWNE   Armentarolo

9 September 1949

Darling,

We came up with a lovely perfect day, blue and still, and stopped half way to lunch under pines, with the huge rocks of Civetta tumbled at the end of the valley; and this is an enchanting restful little place, the inn all by itself in woods and meadows. But no sooner did we get in than clouds came like vultures, gathering round us, hail, thunder, and it looks as if the autumn were closing down. Lulie had no shoes (but we discovered in time and made her buy a pair in Asolo), also no rain coat and only one thin cotton dress, so that I shall not be surprised if my next letter is from Asolo. It is a charming little inn and nice Austrian people. We have spent five hours walking up and down a grassy hill and eaten a gargantuan meal in the refuge-hostel at the top, with whipped cream in mountains to finish off with.

[82] Then Minister of State for Colonial Affairs.
[83] sc. Chavchavadze.

Your letter of the 28th arrived as I left Asolo; it will be interesting to see the plans of the new buildings and I hope you will have those put through before the new Governor arrives. The question of whether the artist or the man who pays the artist is to have the last word is always very difficult. When the patron is intelligent and has taste, it is always possible to compromise. Perhaps the success of Italian modern buildings comes from the fact of the artist feeling supreme in his own sphere? It certainly went rapidly down under the Fascists, when the supremacy swung back to Authority. I remember an old friend of my parents, a sculptor called Reynolds Stevens, who designed a fountain held up by four angels whose wingtips touched each other; and his fury when the committee passed a resolution to ask him to substitute four bishops for the angels!

I wonder if you will take to walking in these hills ever; it gives me a great peace and pleasure, and it was nice to see after our exertions how everyone was glowing with that good feeling of being *well*. Even Lulie, who has been and still is on the edge of a breakdown, trying to pull herself too far from her Eastern roots. There must be a terrible conflict. She is touchingly glad to be here with an atmosphere of affection around her.

Your own
FREYA

STEWART PEROWNE   Dolomites
                                                13 September 1949
Darling,

This is a tiny village called Alba and we walked to it all yesterday. I have never seen anything more beautiful anywhere: along steep pastures and across the valley as if it were a dark ravine between us and the huge Marmolada with glacier in the sun. We turned a corner and there was a flat sort of hanging valley, and little lake, and few houses, all out of the world, and a *rifugio* where we sat on a terrace and drank tea. You must hurry for they are going to build a reservoir there and it will be spoilt, though the lovely walk will remain.

We are settled now in a *rifugio* at 2,000 metres. We toiled up for two hours and are here near the head of a stream with only rock and pines and round shoulders of short mountains about us. So lovely and the next resting place four hours away, so we have decided to stop here. We think you would like it if a porter carried up the knapsack filled with books. There is a noise of little waterfalls all around falling into the green amphitheatre from the huge tumbled rocky walls. I, too, would rather not walk with a pack; I believe the beastly thing is too much for me, but will tell you in two days' time. I have brought *Eothen* and read him on the grass beside the path that comes down from the glacier. How well he fits in with this world both wild and old and civilised; the goodness of it is largely in all the things he *leaves out*.

Your

FREYA

LADY RUTHVEN

Up in the Dolomites

14 September 1949

Darling Pam,

What a one you are for not writing – and without the excuse of two books in hand, which has been holding me up all these months. Now I am taking a little holiday; Lulie and Charles Rankin are in Asolo, having come up to the mountains but turned away in revolt after three days' rain. As they want Culture in Venice, they are getting that over while I walk back with my other guest[84] over the passes. We have had two perfect days, and got up here, 7,000 feet up below Marmolada, a little Alpine refuge with nothing but cowbells and waterfalls about. And here the mists have come down, and wind and rain. It is rather fun to be marooned, a lovely feeling that no one knows where we are; and I have a nice long morning with nothing to do, a wonderful chance for letters. It would be fun to have a large party and fill the little hotel and bring books and all one needed in case of rainy days; but one has to book in *February* for July or August. Perhaps we could drive up if you come at Easter (if I *am* in Asolo then). Who knows what will happen to us. Stewart is due for Christmas, and meanwhile I leave my life suspended like Muhammad's coffin in mid air.

One book, up to 1927 when I first went East, is off my hands and getting into proof, and I am now reading all my letters and those written to me for the twenty years following. What a panorama! I am now reading 1940 onwards; what a time, what a rush, what a number of lives we were living all at once. I think it will always be the sort of climax and centre, whatever else may still come into our lives. And the best of our friendships remain wound up in it.

It's clearing. I think we shall be starting. I feel rather old for a knapsack, but otherwise tough enough.

Love,

FREYA

84 Maili Whyatt.

125

SIR SYDNEY COCKERELL   Asolo
                                                    16 September 1949

Darling Sydney,

How sorry I am for this trouble[85] – I find your letter here on my descent
from the Dolomites, and am only glad that you have your wife in a nursing
home, and not with you. It would be impossible and far too great a burden
to have her to care for; and even so I can't bear to think of your sad little
journey every day. There is nothing so helpless and despairing as to look on
at illness for which so little can be done. I am so grieved dearest Sydney, and
hope she may slide gently away, for her sake and yours. How I wish I had
you here; the house now is so comfortable and we can keep it warm, and if
one could really eliminate space how pleasant it would be. I came down
from the Dolomites today and have not settled to the pile of things that lie
waiting, but wanted to write to you first.

How beautiful the high mountains were. We were shut up one whole day
and night by rain at 7,000 feet – a little refuge under the Marmolada (the
only Dolomite glacier) called Contrin: all night the sound of waterfalls,
cowbells and raindrops made a sort of orchestra: the mists blanketed us up to
the very windows: and it was a very *snug* feeling to be there with time
loosely coiled about us and empty, and no one to know where we were nor
how to be got at.

Dearest Sydney, I wish I could do more – I am so very sorry.

                                                    Your loving
                                                       FREYA

STEWART PEROWNE   Asolo
                                                    18 September 1949

Darling,

What an evening last night, or this morning, for it ended about 4 a.m. at
Maser. The Italian Government (having all our £'s to play with) gave Asolo
one and a half million lire to commemorate La Duse. So we had *La Città
Morta*, the very worst sort of d'Annunzio, in the court of Queen Cornaro's
castle, with the tower and the Rocca and its hill all floodlit, a charming sight.
It looked like an old dark tapestry embroidered in light silk, the castle and
winding wall. But the *play* – all about incest, and the woman who wasn't
engaged in incest was blind, and the five people all spent their time in making
ponderous poetical remarks about the weather; and the men wore such

[85] Lady Cockerell had had a stroke.

126

appalling clothes that, incest or no incest, one couldn't help feeling there was something to be said for being blind. And then finally the brother, having killed his sister, says, 'Ora sono tutto puro', and that is that. Monsignore was upset about the play, and how right he was, though it couldn't lead anyone anywhere except in the opposite direction. When it was over, near midnight, and we all very cold, we went to Maser where they had a splendid supper in honour of the actors, and all the rooms lighted up. Everyone wore evening clothes and there was champagne, and all the *élégance* of the province was there. I enjoyed myself talking to Georges, and Lulie had a great success all round, and Marina wore a lovely gown. And we got back after four. I don't like these parties more than about twice a year, and only because at Maser they *look* so well.

Lulie is getting much better and Charles says I do her good and I do hope so, poor child. She is so brave; I think she has suddenly grown up and doesn't yet know how to manage it. I am making her feel proud of being Eastern, an awful inferiority complex has got hold of her. Also I think she had been so accustomed to being admired that the first little lull put her off her stride; so it may be a blessing in disguise, for one can't go on relying on people's admiration without coming to some appalling dead-end some day. I feel, however, that she needs to be with her wise old mother for a while, and forget all about Freud.

Tonight we go for charades to De Lords and Georges. I wish you were here. I always come away from these promiscuous things with a feeling of great loneliness. The curtains are being drawn at night, too, now; and all gives a feeling that one ought to be cosily enclosed in one's own belongings.

Love,
FREYA

JOHN GREY MURRAY   Asolo

20 September 1949

Dearest Jock,

There are too many people about in Asolo – and two nights running in bed after 2 a.m. Tonight they have all gone to Venice to see Jouvet at the Fenice: I should have enjoyed it, but had such a need for solitude that I refused and am having a quiet early evening with milk soup and soufflé.

I haven't got a complete Flecker here and can't find the quotation: I can only remember the last line of the poem which said:

'And know what we want you to know.'

(or very nearly that.) It was a people who created the beautiful statue, and did not care if Time doomed them to be forgotten, for one day this Thing would be dug up out of the forgotten sands and the new and alien generations would 'know what we want you to know'. What a memory I have: only shreds and patches.

Charles took the Vespa to Venice. She now stops and spits with a machine-gun noise but otherwise is in fine form: but I haven't yet started going about on my own.

I have been reading Osbert Sitwell's last:[86] beautiful bits of writing but I can't help thinking that as a story of a life mine is better. Now is this mere arrogance and conceit? It seems to me he is not faithful enough about himself?

Love dear Jock,

FREYA

STEWART PEROWNE   Asolo
                                                        22 September 1949

Darling,

Three letters, just as I was feeling wan and forlorn. I do miss them very much when the days go without them, and it is very like a talk with you when they come. I am getting to be fretful and frustrated merely from seeing too many people. The trouble here is that they, none of them, have anything to do and come for a (well-earned no doubt) holiday, while what I like is a little company and relaxation after a busy day. Yesterday a charming person came, John Sparrow, a friend of Jock's and a barrister, most pleasant and sensitive to talk to and he's coming again for a whole day. Then we had an old and illustrious American couple, the Blisses; he was a poppet and went mad in the *tessoria* ordering six shirts, and two coats, she painfully cultured, but no doubt human somewhere down below. She apologised for going to the loo by saying, 'Nature has its own requirements!' Anyway, they bought 86,000 lire of silk and paid in dollars, which is a blessing just at the moment.

The pound has rolled off its pedestal and it now remains to be seen what the Bank of Italy does about my £1,200. I have said *firmly* that I expect the rate of July, when they received the sum; but if they pinch it, one can't go to them, and it will just be one more robbery on the lines of Machiavelli and we shall be about £400 the poorer. I shall be so relieved to have it settled one way or the other and be able to know how we stand. All Asolo is very upset

[86] *Laughter in the Next Room* (1949), the fourth volume of autobiography.

about the £, as all the servant maids sitting by the waters of Thames see their earnings reduced by one third. I think, however, that the lira will certainly topple, too.

23 September 1949

I am nearly through *Piers Plowman*. I read a little every morning and it is like a friendly small wayside brook, rippling by the high road, not very deep, but fresh and pleasant and entering into all the little events and gossips of the way. It is full of life in spite of the allegory. The haughty person is described as if he had 'Pepir in his nose'. It is all the reading I get.

The lira is still floating loose in air and the bank manager fears the worst and advises a lawyer's letter if they try to impose any exchange later than that of July, when they received the money. I will send the lawyer's letter, but if that doesn't succeed, think better to resign ourselves to the loss rather than have a lawsuit against the Italian Government, and just call them all Swine in private and public, too!

The little local banks, dealing with small sums, are all being very decent and paying their past sums at past prices, but no one trusts a Government concern.

Your loving
FREYA

STEWART PEROWNE   Asolo
26 September 1949

Darling,

I am so boiling with rage, just as if I hadn't all along expected the beastly Bank of Italy to write today and offer to pay my cheque at 500 lire less to to the £. I am writing to Carnelutti who is the best lawyer in Italy to refuse to accept. But fancy the Government blackening its own reputation for these mingy (to them and not to us) sums! This difference in exchange makes just the difference between paying all debts and being fairly affluent, or having another six months or more to do.

Another tumble off the Vespa when all was going so well. I have been out twice, pillion, with Charles who is an expert motorcyclist, and practised going up and down along the flat, changing gears, etc. I got so skilful that I took him pillion up the Asolo hill, did two curves till I tried to get in bottom gear, and something happened: the little brute just *pranced*, and there we were. No great hurt. Today I stayed pillion and we went by those little backways to near Bassano and up the Val Sugana; and ate at a little pub by the green river. The Brenta comes down clear and green as glass and running strong.

28 September 1949

Lulie has gone, rather pathetic, for she looks on me as an island for affection and advice in her little sea of conflicts. She really seems to have found her feet again. I believe all in England did her harm, by taking it for granted that she was to become all English and ignore the Eastern roots. I have been doing the opposite, and always speak of the East in her as a richness and a real foundation not to be ignored but to be treasured. And I could *see* that this did good.

You can't think what I discovered yesterday in the cemetery here. I took Lulie and John Sparrow to the Duse tomb and there is a flat, family tombstone near, evidently an Italian who married an English wife. One of their children died and there is her name halfway down the tomb and a large black inscription: 'Darling, Mama's Coming'; and at the bottom of the tombstone, another inscription: 'Darling, Mama's Here'. John Sparrow quoted someone who said that nowhere is so much real feeling coupled with so much bad taste as in a country churchyard.

Dear love,

FREYA

STEWART PEROWNE Asolo
29 September 1949

Darling,

Do write to Sydney Cockerell. He has lost his wife, she died after a stroke, with little pain, and he feels it. It is rather one's own bell tolling, at eighty-five. Dear old man. He tells me he has 270 letters of mine, 'and 200 of them Literature' and would like them to be made a book of.

Jime Rose[87] has sent me Ham's book to review and asks if I will do reviews for them, only for books I *like*. This is rather pleasant (and v. well paid). I think it is a good idea for us to cultivate reviewing. You haven't much time now, but you would like it when you retire, and I then can hand it all over to you, and weed the garden. Poor Checchi! He put scarlet geraniums in with the delphiniums, all on his own, and I have made him remove them.

Love,
FREYA

[87] Then literary editor of *The Observer*.

Asolo

29 September 1949

Darling Sydney,

Your letter was a relief to me. I was so unhappy at the thought of a winter before you, with the sorrow of watching a familiar life with all its memories, all the deep strings wound in with your own, ebbing away. I remember so well with my sister, so dearly loved, how I longed for her to die and the pain and illness to end – and was shocked at this wish, which I now know was so right. One goes into such a twilight in illness, and would not wish to go through with it more than once, unless one can come out of it unimpaired in the essential things – and that could not be hoped for after a shock of this kind. What a noble tribute in *The Times* (and how few can it be said of) that they did things incomparable in a century or two! That is certainly so: those beautiful books – I can see their delicate, luminous work in my mind, so complete and so sincere. I have often wondered at the sorrow that must have come when such a creative joy had to be relinquished and what was the comfort she found? Bless you darling Sydney, I think of you with very dear love. I wish you could see these autumn days, blue and shining after the drought and mists of summer, the garden full of peace, with a feeling that it has done all the work it could and now can relax and just enjoy its latest flowers with nothing more to *prepare*.

I still hope to ride my Vespa, but it has given me another tumble, and I feel rather frightened of it. One has to reach the stage of doing the right thing automatically, and no way except falling off to learn it by.

It is impressive to think that I have written you 270 letters. It will be kind to let Jock type a copy. Many cover things of which I have no record, as my letters to my mother were few and often lost during the war, and of course after 1942 there was no one to whom I wrote almost daily as I did to her – so that I really need them to *remember* what happened.

Darling Sydney, I am sitting under a canopy of jobs undone and waiting: I must close this, but send you love and constant thoughts.

Your

FREYA

Asolo

1 October 1949

Darling,

I am amused by the Savannah Club. These poor little islands, they concentrate on Respectability as if it were a raft, the only thing to keep them afloat so far away and alone on the Atlantic.

Here the better part of yesterday went in a true Mediterranean way. The local bank manager, who is deeply distressed over my £1,200, came to say that the wife of the Bank of Italy's Treviso manager was sketching at the Castello, and if I went up and talked to her, her husband would probably turn up and I could tell him what I thought of his bank. So I went, found a statuesque and rather Roman beauty dealing with paints, easel, four little yapping pomeranians, and paralysis of the feet, under the arcade of the castle. I went and sat beside her, talked about Art and presently heard that her husband was Director of the Bank of Italy. 'That bank is my enemy,' said I, and I told the sad story, and presently the rather nice little manager came along, a Sardinian, with a worn harassed mouth and kindly eyes, and *adoring* his imperious spouse. So I told him all about it. Caroly was there to write the data down for him, while I reverted to Art, and we eventually had them both to drinks and to show the house. I'm sure they will do what they can, but you see how Oriental it all is (only there is a *sharaf*[88] in Arabia to appeal to, and here only friendly feelings, far less secure). Anyway, I am sending the lawyer's letter as well. It appears that 380 British sufferers are being treated in the same way. I wonder if a gunboat aiming at the main bank in Genoa would not have an excellent effect? It certainly has done all it could to wreck my summer, and will cramp our style this winter unless Jock can get the Bank of England to accept some advance royalties into my account.

The two Miss Wavells (Archie's sisters) and a Scottish friend came to lunch, three weatherbeaten women with nice eyes and quite undefeated by Time and Infirmity. What pleasant people really *nice* old maids are: I think having faced problems and responsibilities and not shirked them makes them so. They bought £20 of silks. I believe I could make the *tessoria* pay £300 or a little more a year to Caroly and us with any luck if only I could prevent her letting it slide back when I leave. One never knows, the little industry might be quite a standby in a crisis. But as you say, we are among the lucky ones who have our own selves to rely on.

2 October 1949

Always being interrupted, and by such nagging silly things. This morning, as I lay half asleep, a wind began to blow outside. It was that thin whistling wind and brought me the brightness of the desert, and that empty gay wind under the sun.

I took Sheridan Russell to lunch at Maser, but there were rows of females, manicured, elderly, empty, rich, and depressing, with a once pretty smile

[88] sc. honour.

and going on with it indefinitely. And poor Sheridan came back overcome with the splendour and nicely happy to sit and gossip through the evening.

Jock writes insisting on 'Minor Prelude'. I like 'Primavera', except that it makes me feel I ought to be like Botticelli, and I never could!

So much love,

FREYA

JOHN GREY MURRAY   Asolo
3 October 1949

My dearest Jock,

I am answering at once and also breaking it to you that Charles took a penultimate package to you; the very very last – and a small one – is gathering itself together on my table. I have just finished dealing with 1946: two more packages, and this letter-sorting labour is ended, and whoever has to wrestle when I am dead should be very grateful. It is rather fascinating to have the panorama of one's life all tucked away in yearly envelopes, and it can now be spread out quite easily and contemplated. But I am quite sick with the sight of handwriting: just realised that I have been three months reading letters and letters almost every day.

Ought I by the way to have a contract for the new book? I only mention this because I have just discovered the one for *Letters from Syria* and see, with sorrow, that I *then* began with 17½%: so don't *please* let me start at the same place now that I am three books on (four with Mama's diary): 20% – where *Perseus* leaves off! How is he going, by the way?

Love, dear Jock,

FREYA

STEWART PEROWNE   Asolo
4 October 1949

Darling,

A sudden decision about Canada has been forced on me.[89] Poor old Tom can't carry on I fear. He is breaking up and says he can't do another year. At the same time an offer of $25,000 is made, $10,000 now and 4% on the rest till it is paid. This makes $27,500 with the other bit of land, and I have written to John Stanton to accept. I suppose it will give us about $24,000

[89] F.S.'s father had left her his farm at Creston, British Columbia. Tom Leaman, who had worked there for Robert Stark, had stayed on to look after the property.

133

altogether when Tom's 10% and all expenses are paid. Perhaps one may have to build him a little cottage, which he would have for life and we would have afterwards. I don't suppose he will live very long, poor old boy, and I would like his last years to be comfortable and happy. Anyway, there will be quite a lot of dollars and I have written to J.S. to think of what to do with them. Would you approve of an annuity on both our lives if we can get one over there (in dollars, that is)? I told J.S. that we aren't a bit interested in *leaving* any of it behind us! There seems so much money all around us this year, and none to pay the grocer's bills.

I have now read twenty years of letters, ending with yours and our wedding. Your letters now are so different, it really is comforting to read the contrast. Oh dearest, do you think we can make a success of it after all?

Your loving
FREYA

STEWART PEROWNE   Asolo
                                                              6 October 1949
Darling,

Two letters at last; and you say you like walking which opens up lovely vistas. One just can't live in Asolo if one doesn't, as it is the only local outdoor amusement (except the Vespa, which might pall in our old age). I think, however, that as we get feebler, a little pageboy to carry the knapsacks will be a good idea?

The bank deadlock continues, but the £ has risen a bit. The bank manager's wife left me an opulent bunch of tuberoses that scented all the house through; like the perfumes of Arabia, it did nothing to cover up the Italian guilt. They are very dishonest, but when feeling very Puritan, one remembers that the Parthenon was built entirely with stolen money.

Sheridan left at seven this morning, nice and brown from sitting nearly naked in the garden. What a little dear he is, but so unhappy, for all his love is going away from him. He still hopes it may not, but I feel sure the corner is turned. These things are never stationary, always growing or dwindling. It does wring one's heart when people who ask of life only the most gentle, immaterial, *decent* things, fail to get them. He will have to get his happiness only by giving, and is lucky to have learned that art.

How I hope this little corner of quiet may be spared to us. You are so right about this ready-made mess of a world, and we have the fortune to be able to get into a backwater where personal values still count. Everyone notices it who comes, a sort of garment of peace. Far too many people come, however, and Sheridan has been telling me that one must be brutal, so I have clamped down on the morning and refuse to be visible at all.

Wedding Day 7 October 1949

Love to you darling and many thoughts, particularly today. I hope our third anniversary will bring us nearer and nearer, in every way including the geographical.

Your

FREYA

STEWART PEROWNE   Asolo
                                                   8 October 1949

Darling,

Your telegram with remembrance, thank you, so warming to the heart. They must have crossed each other on that beastly ocean and I hope made it a little less unpleasant for all passengers as they passed. If you had been here today, it would have been one of the pleasantest days. I realised that this is just the sort of day I like: a fine morning, all alone, walk with Checchi round the garden, post arrives, and then three hours spent over the writing of English (the article is done and goes by surface). A little meditation after lunch under the wistaria, looking at the Japanese anemones now like a white and pink halo round the pool, and then a heavenly walk all by myself for one and one half hours in and out of the slopes of the Rocca that drop quite steeply on the north. It was a day sweet and heavy like honey, a white sky, and all the country sounds, voices and laughter, animals, the crackling noise of carts in the plain below. I sat for a little while enjoying it all, and found another stony little climbing path home. Caroly came in for tea: I wrote to Jock and Peggy Drower (who has a girl); and then Rory Cameron came over to find refuge from what he calls 'the hard glitter of Italian hospitality' and sat for one and one half hours talking about India and Moguls and Hickey, very agreeably. And then a bath and a little chat to you, and soon dinner. If you were here, don't you think that is the sort of day to have? I hope for it so much, just beauty around one, pleasant relations, a little work, a little exercise, decent food, and letters to one's friends?

It is awful however to open my first paper for weeks and see that Russia has the Atom Bomb, but perhaps just as well to *know*? And it does seem to have exploded at the wrong moment.

I am reading Churchill, Vol. II, and thinking of those days as we saw them from Aden. What a proud epic! How glad one must be to have had a part. What frightful sinister people, Laval and Pétain – how Milton could have described that marriage of corruption and stupidity; and poor Mandel, and Reynaud, and what that all cost! I still think if we had attacked Italy on 3 September 1939 most of the tragedy could have been averted; France might have held on the Alps, and the whole of North Africa been saved? Churchill isn't great, but he is very *big*, and he isn't modest, but one feels that it is the greatness of the events that makes him proud and not egotism. He is always in the front, but one never loses sight of the whole of England behind him.

Dear love,

FREYA

STEWART PEROWNE   Asolo
                                                              10 October 1949
Darling,

To add the last touch (I hope) to chores and commission for you, do you think you could add to your luggage in Barbados twelve tablets of soap, a little bottle of vanilla essence, and a packet of nutmegs, cloves, and ginger? I brought these last year and they were a godsend and not to be got here. Another parcel of coffee, too, would be very welcome and keep us right through your leave. I hope this isn't too much; you will arrive like a sort of cornucopia. If you have any old clothes, *don't* throw them away on anyone but Checchi. I hear that he laments to Emma that I never give him anything, but, after all, he couldn't wear my pink crêpe de chine!

I am in the middle of my Italian article which is taking a long time and seems very poor to me. One feels so clumsy with another language, as if going round every pebble instead of stepping over. We shall have to find something we enjoy doing that is not reading or writing. I am sure that it is the excess of this which gives you insomnia. I have been getting it too, and it goes like magic when I stop work and spend days in the hills, or even just lying in the sun looking at the view.

The time does go; it is nearly six months since I left in April, and now in less than two months you will be on the sea. Tell me the exact dates, and name of ship, and where and when in London, and exactly when you sleeper from Paris. I shall be happy to be meeting you.

Your loving
FREYA

Asolo
11 October 1949

Darling,

I am almost in tears about it, I can *never* be alone! I had to go to see a woman who writes bad poetry and is still inconsolable because her husband died happily sleeping in his chair at the age of eighty-one 'in the full flood of life' she says (I wonder if you will feel that about me? I hope not, and anyway have chosen seventy-seven as a nice age to die). So my day was wrecked and I went to lunch in a furious temper with two tiresome young people who let me in for most of it; and started on purpose to talk about bull fights as I knew they would say 'The poor horses!', and they did, and I gave myself a holiday from being tactful and wiped away all arguments on every subject as fast as they cropped up, every single sentimental woolly cliché, and came away like a razor that has tried to sharpen itself on cotton wool.

12 October 1949

The Ronald Storrses[90] arrived here for *breakfast* this morning, a nice sunny old couple, shabby and weatherbeaten, full of good talk. A sudden rest and relief to find people civilised, more interested in the Chinese prints, the Middle East books, than in timetables and market prices. It gives a *physical* sort of relaxation. We sat under the wistaria over coffee, eggs and grapes, and talked of this and that, and Ronald sent his love to you. I told him of the Italian destroyer captain watching the muddle over the manoeuvre when they were taking the Italian fleet to Malta, and turning to the English officer on the bridge beside him, and saying, 'We can't even surrender properly.' Ronald was pleased and capped it with the cry of honesty from the dying Oscar Wilde when the doctor came to him, 'I've always lived, and now I'm dying, beyond my income.' What is so pleasant is Ronald's quickness in noticing the similarity of those two stories, isn't it? Another nice little point, we were talking of Italians writing things on their monuments, scratching with pencils, and I told him of the statue of Cavour standing rather pompously in bronze, and before the last election some Paduan student had put a large question mark in white chalk just over the opening of his trousers. Ronald laughed and said, 'How classic'; of course it is just that, the same old things that made the Romans laugh! I wish you were here, and I have been five days without a word.

Your

FREYA

[90] Oriental Secretary in Cairo from 1909 to 1917, Storrs had been Military Governor in Jerusalem (1917–20), Governor of Jerusalem and Judea (1920–26), Governor of Cyprus (1926–32) and of Northern Rhodesia (1932–34).

JOHN GREY MURRAY   Asolo
                                               12 October 1949

My dearest Jock,

Here is the contract, but I am not really happy about it – only I will never
fall out with you over finance D.V. – and, with that in mind, would you set
my mind at rest over the following?

Is 17½% the summit of what an author attains to as a first royalty? Is it,
for instance, what Osbert Sitwell gets?

Because: I have now written ten books, and every one a success: so that
I am so to say at my apex. I don't see why you should ever give me a higher
royalty than now, and soon you will be saying that I am like that Bishop who
was read in his lifetime and forgotten when dead, – and therefore there may
at any moment be a decline? If 17½ is the ceiling, so to speak, – that is an
end, and I am quite content: but if other authors attain to more, then I think
that this is the moment (after ten successes and four stationary royalties) that
I ought to reach the level of *the best*, of which I consider myself to be
(modesty apart). Now will you please give me a clear answer to this?

Would you also cast your eye over my total net royalties since you published the *Valleys* and tell me how much they amount to? I want to see if,
divided by fifteen, they average out to a living income. One *ought* to make
a living out of being the author of a good book every eighteen months for
fifteen years, – but I really have no idea whether I have done so or no.

The only other point is that I need £200 (desperately) in October, *and*
November, *and* December – by which time I hope my unequal struggle with
the Bank of Italy may be decided one way or the other. My whole summer
has been harassed by this Italian Machiavellianism!

The only other financial news is that I have had to decide to sell Canada –
so that should give me some dollars: but I would rather find an annuity than
spend it.

                                                    Your
                                               FREYA

STEWART PEROWNE   Asolo
                                               12 October 1949

Darling,

We had a pleasant evening, a stroll through the town, with sunset behind
the castle and the heights already lit; and after dinner Ronald read Tennyson's
'Ode to Vergil', and then my favourite bit in the Georgics, about Italy, the
little towers high up and the rivers 'circumlabentia mura', what music! How
nice it is to have Ronald, whatever he may have been as a pro-consul. He

                                   138

told me that in his busiest years he used to read for an hour in the early morning, Shakespeare, Dante, Bible, or Homer, over and over again, to which 'much must be forgiven'? I do like him; he is self-indulgent but not selfish, the *only* one of my guests who thinks of expense to me in petrol when anything is suggested; and so sweet to his rather dull but pleasant wife: he never leaves her out, and turns to her after his *bons mots*, and strolls about taking her arm in the garden. He speaks so nicely of you and laments your absence. It really is the secret of life to like the *best* things, isn't it? There he is, old and happy as a sandboy, because he loves and doesn't hate, and cares, really cares, more about carpets, classics, Carpaccios, Carpano and cooking than about the ups and downs of fortune or the state of his career. And he is such a good conversationalist, because he is never thinking of himself in the picture. He had one good little story of Dizzy walking home with his wife from some party and saying, 'What delightful people they were. My dear, I have an unusual feeling which, if it is not indigestion, must be gratitude.'

Apropos of classics, I have just been reading over *Othello*. I have always been puzzled over the apparently uncalled-for wickedness of Iago; the motives are not only inadequate, but Iago himself gives first one and then the other so there is no feeling of a fate from beyond the person himself pushing him down. But now, reading his speeches one after the other carefully, I think that Shakespeare was drawing a creature quite normal and extremely intelligent, but incapable of any form of love – neither Emilia, nor Roderigo, nor his fellow Cassio, nor his chief, nor Desdemona; there is not a glimmer of affection anywhere, not even *comprehension* of it. Whenever he meets it, he attributes some other base or lustful motive. I think he is not like the other villains *positively* wicked, but *negatively* so, and this makes him by far the worst of all, since there is no hope for something which is just non-existent. Do read it over again and tell me if you think me right? I have been also trying to think *how* Shakespeare did these unerring portraits. I'm sure he never said to himself, 'I will now portray "a man deprived of the power of loving" or Macbeth "a weak man tempted by ambition".' I believe it was much more direct observation. He saw and recognised the nucleus of good or evil from which the action springs, but it was the actual vision of it working and not a reasoned drawing out of consequences which gave us the plays. We will talk about it some day soon and, hurrah, letters have come 26th, 28th, 30th, and 3rd, *wicked* the posts are. They evidently do with mine what they do with yours. Isn't it peculiar how dead we feel when they don't come – we must be fond of each other after all!

So much love,

FREYA

Asolo

13 October 1949

My dearest Sydney,

Your dear letter is here and this is just a short note about our mutual letters – the idea of a joint volume pleases me very much. I would not like to have it published (and I think you will agree) till this autobiography is launched and well away and something different, I hope the Euphrates journey, already contemplated. But why should we not get it ready and keep it till the good moment comes?

It would please me far more not to have *anyone* except you and me entering in this little venture: we could write a little foreword each, you on me and me on you? It would be fun – and we would divide the profits 50/50? I should love to do this dear Sydney as a little monument to our friendship.

Dear love to you,

FREYA

Asolo

15 October 1949

Darling,

Your wedding day letter has come, consoling me for gloomy news from the Banking World. Your aphorism about an unmarried man being like a car without petrol pleased Ronald and even more so Lady Storrs!

Ronald is such good value; I feel restored instead of being tired by their visit. (It is so dreadful that boredom lays a sort of blight on me, I just sink and get ill with it.) We have talked about everything and it is a constant pleasure, like those Chinese pictures of rivers. The Leigh Fermors asked to come, and I said they could stay the night if they took us for a drive in their car, so we started out yesterday, first to Cison (where you remember we lunched with Brandolins), where we went into the cellars of the Contessa Vendramin Marcello to taste wine. It is rather poor wine, but they say it hasn't settled, so I got 100 litres and will hope to find more and better in Tuscany. Then we drove up the S. Ubaldo pass, a fascinating road bang into a cul-de-sac of valley ending in a cliff wall. The road laces it just like those corsages are laced that you see in pictures of Neapolitan peasants or on the Verdi stage. When the walls of the valley get *too* close, the road develops a tunnel at each hairpin and so reaches the top; then one sails gently down into the wide valley of Belluno where we lunched at the Albergo Cappello, and then strolled about the *piazzas* and porticoes. The main *piazza* has a 'calendar of vegetation', red and green foliage grown in the shape of a number (the number is green and the surroundings red) and the date of the day is put out in its square box for every summer day. We came back by Feltre and so home, stopping for a café in that enchanted *piazza*; it and its long sloping street of decayed palaces makes one feel as if one were inside a Nathaniel Hawthorne story.

16 October 1949

Was interrupted, and the rest of the day taken up with Ronald's lecture, *so* good. He has promised to send you a copy. The most excellent conclusion too, saying 'the most important thing in life is not only to desire the best, but to recognise it when you see it' (so curious that it is just what I wrote to you about *him*, isn't it? Then in the p.m. we went to Maser and on to Fanzolo for tea. A young American there who joined the 8th Army and was all through the desert and had become so un-American that one felt it quite possible to think of a United World if only people were allowed to travel.

This thought of restrictions reminds me of that villainous bank. The lawyer writes from Milan that there is nothing to be done, they have the power and there it is, £500 pocketed to console the poor little Italians for Sir Stafford[91] and his currency. Luckily, my patent way of living *below* income and spending all that remains on *superfluities* does come in on these occasions; most of the deficit should be made up by the end of the year, and if Canada goes through, I suggest taking a bit out of that so as to be clear of all debts and have a little over. After all it isn't a moral law to reinvest all one's capital! I had thought of selling that beautiful big carpet for which £400 has been offered, but Ronald says it is worth lots more than that. Anyway, we shall be more or less through when you come and by hook or crook have enough to take us happily pottering down to Rome as well. You will want a quiet month here first, won't you? So that we would spend February going about, and that is lovely in Rome they say. Do bring *warm clothes* though.

I hope you will be happy here; happy I mean by just being here and living an *ordinary* life. We can pretend we are retired! How nice it would be if we were. When one looks at the Storrses, it is a wonderful advertisement for retirement, though I do wonder why the *épanoui* husband so often has a harassed wife. It doesn't seem to work the other way round at all.

You tell me that you feel the *safety* coming; that is what it is, I believe, and then one can be quiet and let the days come trickling by and even let

---

[91] Sir Stafford Cripps, Chancellor of the Exchequer at the time of the £'s devaluation.

them be dull now and then, knowing that the reality we live by is there to carry us, 'the everlasting arms' – what an image!

Bless you and very dear love.

FREYA

P.S. Have just finished *Othello* again and feel more and more that Iago is just like the criminal in the Camus I sent you, *L'Etranger*, a man with *sensibility* left out. That stony obduracy at the end; and 'don't weep, don't weep' to Desdemona; the feeling, the things that make people divine, are just an annoyance to him. And when once you read him so, every single word he speaks is in character. I'm sure Shakespeare never reckoned the thing out but by vision just got inside. I hardly ever read *Othello* because it upsets me so much!

STEWART PEROWNE   Asolo
17 October 1949
Darling,

This enormous list holds, I hope, all my Christmas cards and a large part of yours. I must pay my share, because it will be quite a lot, but if you don't mind seeing it through and letting me know afterwards? As you see, it is very comprehensive and I have also attended to Baghdad for the first time since I left. If we do Euphrates, we mustn't drop all our friends there!

The Storrses have just left and I can't tell you what a nice visit it was. I have always liked him and now I see why, and why his wife is so devoted to him, in spite of many weaknesses no doubt; but he is gay and affectionate and more interested in other things than in himself. People have always told me he married for money but I discovered that he puts a little photograph of his wife into every one of the books he always reads. He was showing me his Dante, and there she was, pasted in not at the beginning over the *Inferno*, but on the title-page of *Paradiso*! How unnecessarily horrid people are in their judgements.

Ronald was agreeing very emphatically when I mentioned your classical reading and said what a good scholar you are. It always gives me a warm feeling when people say nice things about you, a quite different and *nicer* feeling than when they do it about me. He suggested a book we *must* get, by Victor Bérard, *Les Phéniciens et l'Odyssée* (early 1900s); the author went in a small boat and followed Odysseus, and by looking at his descriptions from

the same sort of low, small craft, was able to recognise, and located a great
deal. It sounds fascinating.

Love,

FREYA

LADY RUTHVEN Asolo

17 October 1949

My darling Pam,

Your letter such a joy. I too think and think, but the desk is never clear
and always so many other things waiting. I too am faced with that problem,
how to do the important things and not the others? I have eliminated newspapers, telephones, and Emma keeps away most stray callers so that I expect
I am getting a horrid name for grumpiness, but it does clear the days a bit.
And when one has a day or two of semi-solitude, and can just breathe and
look at the world and let it sink in quietly, one *knows* that this is the right
way to live and feels lighter and better.

Stewart arrives on December 23rd and I shan't go to London to meet him
(being reduced to real poverty by devaluation). Anyway, one has a very
detached feeling about one's possessions since the war. All one has seems an
Extra. I hope to recover by the New Year, but meanwhile am rather in
straits! Also think it will be better to meet Stewart here in an atmosphere of
peace.

I long to see those children and long for summer walks with a knapsack
with them and picnics in the hills. Oh Pam, dear, let us manage it somehow
next year!

FREYA

JOHN GREY MURRAY Asolo

22 October 1949

My dearest Jock,

Thank you for that formidable letter and for the gesture about the 20%,
which is appreciated, though there would have been no falling out even
without it. (It isn't *economical* anyway to fall out about finance after the age
of fifty!) What I infer, picking my way among your delicate innuendos, is

that I must sell at least 250,000 copies to equal the Sitwells of this world. I wonder if I ever shall.

Dear Jock, I would fly over to you in spite of having nothing in the house except £5 and debts, but I think it would just crock me up. I have been feeling rather on a razor edge (sheer nerves, but with some excuse these two last years) and feel I must give them a restful time these two months; even if I see too many people in a day, I feel tied in knots and can't sleep, and it is nothing but strain, I know. This last week, with hardly anyone about, early bed, gentle walks in the lovely autumn land – *alone*! – and quiet time to work in the morning, have been acting like a charm and I shall be all right if only it can continue.

Tell Diana that some sugar should be arriving from Barbados for the Godson's jam.

Love to you all,

FREYA

STEWART PEROWNE   Asolo

24 October 1949

Darling,

Victor Cunard has come for two days from Venice, looking very flourishing; he always looks more 'English in Venice' than anyone else from Lord Byron's time onwards; and tells me he is just reading Goldoni's memoirs. He lives in Venice in her right way, enjoying it past and present and combining it with a sort of Shakespearean Englishness. Also I have had a huge packet of letters from Jock, among them all those written to Gerald over many years, which really makes me feel rather horrid to have let him drop himself away altogether.

26 October 1949

I am not pained but pleased about Harry.[92] I believe that what shocks you is not the divorce but the state of affairs which precedes it; *that* surely is the failure. If one hasn't been able to make a reality of marriage for years and years, why should one mind making the outward appearance correspond to the truth? I don't think I could ever go on for very long living something outwardly that doesn't correspond to what goes on inside; and if one fails in making the two harmonise, why, one has lost the game, but it's not good

[92] Sir Harry Luke's marriage was ending in divorce.

144

pretending that one hasn't. I believe Harry will find some nice little person to be cosy and happy with one of these days.

Victor has been telling me, rather surprisingly, that he is just a bundle of neurotics and has been to a doctor about it, and that he feels it is the absence of religion that makes it all. I wasn't surprised, except at his talking so frankly and intimately. He is rather a dear but a sad and gloomy vista ahead of him for old age. What a lot of them there are!

Your

FREYA

STEWART PEROWNE   Asolo
6 November 1949

Darling,

We are all feeling a little reduced, as a sort of 'flu is wandering about, all the babies are wailing everywhere and everyone who has reached an age to do so is blowing their nose. You will be so pleased with the painted staircase, at least I hope you will. It looks like a Verdi décor, and anyone who comes down it is made interesting at once. Fancy a little man with a sad look and nothing but a pot of paint, brush and a ruler making it all out of his head with no difficulty at all. He sat and worked it out while we watched, suggesting a curve here and shadow there – it is fun! One of the ancient things bought in Venice will make a wonderful sort of tapestry curtain to hang behind it.

I am nearly going mad with finance. Three letters this time, one to say that the Canadian Government won't allow the results of a sale to leave the country; the next from London to say that they must now send all my money through the Italian bank which pinches it; the third from the Consul in Venice to whom I sent a small fee at the new rate, who says that 'for official purposes, H.M.G. still expects to be paid at the rate of 2,000 lire to the £' (though it's H.M.G. that did the devaluing itself). I am so angry that I mean to cheat every government I can, including my own, whenever there is a chance. Why should they have morals quite different from every other human species merely because they are governments? I am now going to write direct to the Instituto Cambi and send a note from both the Sindaco and Monsignore, to ask whether they won't consider making it possible to go on living in this country and helping its little towns, or whether they mean to *force* us to emigrate?

You would have enjoyed our Lebanese carpet man. He came up and, after much persuasion, stayed to lunch, and went away borrowing Abu Nawas, whom he had never read and promising to bring the Lebanese minister to see us. What is so pleasant is that underlying '*fierté*' of the Arab, quite irrespective of his work or walk in life. As soon as you treat him like an equal, he takes it quietly for granted and *is* one.

Your
FREYA

STEWART PEROWNE   Asolo
                                                8 November 1949

Darling,

For some reason it seems less easy to write to you now that I think of you as coming so soon. It makes a feeling of absence. I suppose that huge, awful ocean is in my mind, and the thought of you on the far side of it. I am also wondering how you will like me when you come, feeling rather like Anne of Cleves with Henry VIII!

Cici is going back next week when I go to see B.B. and I feel sad about her. She is going to settle I think, but with all of her life that matters shut away from Franco. They never talk of anything intimate, and she only sees him now and then. I would rather cut off my legs or arms, one would feel less mutilated; and it must be very hard for him, as he did care about her. But there it is, and we have quite enough to do to steer our own little boat without thinking about other people's.

Your loving
FREYA

STEWART PEROWNE   Asolo
                                                8 November 1949

My darling,

Your letter of 27th just come; I long to hear if you are coming oversea by air or ship, and when you leave.

You will be fascinated by the Byron letters. Apart from the frightful caddishness of his letters about it all to England, those written to Teresa show him in a far more sympathetic light. I am quite sure he was genuine in his feelings, and there is something extraordinarily touching about these intimate days so exposed, like those houses in London ripped open by the Blitz with all their little daily things exposed.

A wonderful letter has just come from the Sindaco to send to Rome telling the Bank that Asolo will just simply *collapse* if we go. And a note from Monsignore with a huge purple stamp at the bottom of mine. Monsignore whispers that if all else fails, he might do something through the Vatican!

Love,

FREYA

JOHN GREY MURRAY   Asolo

12 November 1949

My dearest Jock,

I am writing from bed with a sort of 'flu, sinus, earache, and general feeling of old age, but supported by the Byron book, which I find absorbing. It seems to me that all except those objectionable Leigh Hunts come out of it better than they went in. Yet it leaves one rather sad. Four years, and all the rest of life to live! There is a bell tolling all through, the transitoriness of it all. How *conventional* Byron really was. I have always felt that, but it comes out again – and I suppose his heart of hearts always remained really in England?

This is really to return you the book plate – I think very attractive, and why not use it for the autobiography too? I liked the mountain one: I believe I liked it best as I think a book plate should be an escape into the high, remote, and solitary: but Stewart likes the exact opposite, so this is what he obviously must have.

Love to you, dear Jock,

FREYA

JOHN GREY MURRAY   Asolo

17 November 1949

Darling Jock,

These letters! I have now got all I have for 1928 to 1931 arranged consecutively and do you know that I think a few are *still* missing – to Herbert or Mama in November 1928? I happen to remember a description of the journey across Canada and it isn't there. These really are signs of incipient dementia in the typist: for instance when she makes me say that Mrs. Ker is 'very very shy but *folucte* and *shelaibar*': what *can* it be? (It doesn't matter because it can't be as interesting as she makes it sound.) But I merely feel that it, and her lighthearted mixing of dates makes it quite probable that 1929–30 letters are there scattered among the rest. Anyway, my dear Jock, don't please give them any more agony, but let me have them all to sort out when I get a chance: if for instance we were to go to Borneo, it might be quite a godsend.

My fever has at last gone today, and I lie as weak as a wet moth but otherwise normal again – and Gerald has telegraphed announcing his arrival, just simply like that. How easy it makes life to see it all in the first person singular: I don't like to slam the door in his face, so he will sit and sup down below while I lie here in bed.

Love dear Jock,

FREYA

JOHN GREY MURRAY   Asolo
                                                          24 November 1949
My dearest Jock,

I am just sitting up in bed after temperature of 103 and some sort of tummy infection: all very disappointing – Florence given up as I shan't be up out of bed for a week – and this I fear is the climax to the three dead typists, and stops the book until providence sends along a few weeks of quiet next year, I hope, in which to get it started. I am so sorry, and I know you are too, and so sorry all your efforts to get it through in time have to be wasted. I would have liked to get even one chapter done, and shall if only my head stops going round and round – but even so there will not be time in a fortnight to do anything worthwhile. I think perhaps it will therefore be better for you to keep the letters now till March when I hope to be over?

Love,

FREYA

COSTANZA BOIDO   Asolo
                                                          24 November 1949
My darling Cici,

I have been thinking so much of you, dear child, worried over what seems to me a wrong direction in your path. I don't like talking about people's paths

148

unless they, themselves, wish it, and you do not, at least with me; but I may be away a long time this next year, and you needn't pay any attention to my ideas. It would be a grief to me to see you getting into the *habit* of feeling someone is against you: don't let yourself imagine wrongs; it is such a sterile waste to wander in. It gave me a terrible shock to realise that you could think such things, and also to hear that you had an 'inferiority complex'. I don't believe I said anything helpful to you, for it took me so by surprise; but I have lived for years with inferiority complexes of all kinds, as one must in the East, and I know one thing, that they cannot exist with a true feeling of religion. Perhaps that is why they are so bad a thing to have, for they show something wrong in the most fundamental scale of values. Therefore get rid of it quickly or it will make you not only unhappy, but aggressive and 'permalosa' and all sorts of awful things. And why should you feel inferior or superior? The difference between the biggest and smallest of human beings is so small, and you have all you can need to make you happy now, and so much more than most. And what does it matter where you stand in the ladder of human beings so long as you can enjoy the world? You have so much now, friends you are fond of and the chance of making as many more as you want, the work you like and the means to get on with it, the baby you love, the home you love, and a husband whom you are still friends with, which is not what it should be, but is still a picture with enough brightness in it to make a very good composition in gentle hands. There is nothing, dear, to feel 'inferior' about.

I hope you will forgive my saying this. I felt I must, for I would hate you to feel alone if I could help it. I mustn't write more as the fever has only stopped today and my head very wobbly.

Your loving
FREYA

CHARLES RANKIN   Asolo
                                                  26 November 1949

My dearest Charles,

I have been quite ill for a whole month – in bed I mean with temperatures and thermometers. It has made me realise how lucky I am to have a house where it is quite comfortable to be ill in, but still it does seem a waste after all that health and muscle collected in the Dolomites. A letter from Lulie came while I lay there and told me she had not heard from me: I wrote her such a nice long letter full of useless advice, and feel depressed to think that the capacity for getting lost should have reached even the things that are coming to her in the post.

My book is not yet started: first the typing of my letters seemed to be lethal to all the typists, and now they are pouring in and I am too weak to look at them, and in less than four weeks Stewart will be here. Then, by God, I mean to do no work for three months: everyone else thinks a husband enough to justify one's existence with no further trial, so why shouldn't I take this view for one quarter of a year? I think we may potter down Italy in February, by Florence, Siena, Rome – to see those little pink tulips putting out their spikes under the olive trees. I wish I could hope to be here through the spring: you can't think what a Paradise Asolo is from March to June – but I suppose we may be anywhere. I have a hope it may not be Barbados, but that is all so far.

Love and happiness in 1950,

FREYA

BERNARD BERENSON   Asolo
3 December 1949
My darling B.B.,

There is nothing to be done about my visit: I am out of bed now and walking out for an hour or so in the sun, but they have to inflict a cure of fifteen days which means a visit every morning to the hospital – and that will bring me to the 18th and Stewart arrives on the 21st. It is one of the saddest little cups dashed from my lips for a long time, but we shall be travelling down towards Rome at the end of January or early February, and hope you may want to see us then.

I have been reading Shakespeare in bed, and also Marius the Epicurean and Thais. Maurice Baring says they are 'out of date', and as they were both favourites of mine years ago, I was anxious to verify – and I find them as good as ever with nothing about them that doesn't seem perennial. Would you think of them as subject to fashion? except that the language of Pater is not simple enough to be always easy, but that is just a convention; like Dr. Johnson, one assimilates it at the beginning and then forgets. There is such a *solidity* of real work behind these books.

The world is lovely here dear B.B. – all colour, and snow ridges melting with blue shadows in the sky. But I wish I were with you.

Dear love to you both,

FREYA

16 December 1949

Dearest Jock,

I have read the proofs and changed very little but feel depressed as the book seems to me *too* condensed: are you sure it makes good reading? Anyway I am not sending the proofs till Stewart has seen them with a fresh eye.

I think more and more of 'Traveller's Prelude' with favour. Would you think it a good idea either for me in a preface or you on the jacket to explain that the book has been so little altered from its character of a private letter? I do say so at the end, but I feel perhaps the reader should *begin* knowing it?

I have been walking five miles, – but still get a lot of tiresome pain. I believe it won't go till I get *warmer* (though the house is beautifully warm now). Fearful struggles with bills and Xmas.

Love to you all, dear Jock,

FREYA

26 December 1949

Dearest Jock,

What a lovely stocking or valise of books. I am so looking forward to the (inevitable) end of this Christmas sunshine, so as to sit by the fire and read. This *Cornhill* is excellent, especially Isaiah and the Byron letters. The first one to his mother is terrific isn't it? The whole of *Childe Harold* and everything in it! Dear Jock, is the bookplate *your* present instead of mine? It seems all wrong, but it is a lovely present and just what I would have chosen myself; and Stewart loves it, and has come round to the mountain so that we shall use *both* for different sort of books and are longing to get to Venice to find a printer and some beautiful paper. Thank you dearest Jock, for this and so much else.

Stewart descended from a blue sky, all the Alps without a cloud behind him. May it be an omen! I met him halfway between Milan and Domodossola, as that is where they land in winter to be out of the fog, and we drove back through the Lombard mists and reached clear weather again in Asolo. It has been heavenly for Xmas, crisp and blue, white with frost in the morning and roses opening by midday and all the Christmas roses and winter jasmine coming out as fast as they can. We pulled ourselves together for Midnight Mass at Maser; I told Stewart that it would surely not begin till

Marina telephoned that they were ready to start, and sure enough, nothing happened till long after midnight as they had forgotten to send to fetch the Friar, and then he came without enough Communion wafers to go round. But only the plebs suffered, a meek little crowd right on the outer circumference of the little cold round church, in which we sat on two privileged benches just in front of the altar. After that we had a far too sumptuous meal at 1 a.m. (shrimps, turkey and plum pudding, champagne) and Stewart, between Marina and her sister, never got in one word: and then Xmas tree, and back at 3 a.m., and now here we are, cosy and idle, with no social engagements till tomorrow when we give a party of our own.

Much love darling Jock,

FREYA

SIR SYDNEY COCKERELL   Asolo
26 December 1949

Darling Sydney,

Your little book on William Morris arrived just as I was leaving to meet Stewart in Milan, so I put it into my bag and am half way through it, and enjoying it immensely. It is such a *sympathetic* life, and here in Asolo I feel a sort of affinity with it, as if W.M. would have liked and felt at home in this town of craftsmen. What a horizon it must have opened to you, to meet him when you were a young man. He must have been like an Atlantic coast, so bracing and boisterous and a giver of life. What strikes me in the book is how small a part is given to his family life, relations with wife and children. Is this because they really had rather a small share in all that richness of interests, or is it because they are taken for granted and not felt necessary to describe?

Stewart is very pleased with the house, bathrooms and all; and I am hoping he will be happy for a month of quiet and private life together before going to Rome in February. He is being kept busy with my proofs, going through them before returning them to Jock. Isn't it extraordinary how much one always misses of the things one knows quite well? I hope it is going to be a good book, dear Sydney, as it is dedicated to you. I can't see it at all clearly any longer myself, after working on it for so long.

This is only a hurried note, of love and thanks, and wishes for all good to you in 1950, and dear friendship always.

FREYA

152

BERNARD BERENSON   Asolo
                                           27 December 1949

Darling B.B.,

I think of spending my birthday with you on January 31st if that is a good
date for you? We would reach you on the 29th or 30th, and spend a few days,
and then go southward to Siena and Rome. I hope no horrible microbe inter-
feres this time (I am *still* not quite well, though much better). If you prefer
we can come later, on the way back: in fact we can make it any time you
prefer after January 28th: before that, Stewart has to keep himself free to
fly to London and back for an interview, which is to decide the future desti-
nation. I hope and hope for the Mediterranean, and so does he. St. Anthony
has been promised a big candle. Perhaps I should also try St. Jude: it seems
that he is so little sought after, because of the associations of his name, that
he has lots of time and looks after his devotees better than any other saint in
the calendar.

We have just got Kenneth Clark's book on landscape and reached the
point where he speaks of the love of landscape as a modern thing. I would
like to ask you about this; I feel very reluctant to think that the Greeks, with
their exquisite placing of everything they built, took no interest in landscape?
Perhaps people who live out of doors take no interest just because they are *in*
the landscape, and a part of it – like mountaineers or sailors with mountains
and sea.

Darling B.B., all blessings to you and Nicky for this New Year. I hope it
will let me reach you in summer at Vallombrosa.

                                                Your
                                              FREYA

SIR SYDNEY COCKERELL   Asolo
                                           24 January 1950

Darling Sydney,

A lovely letter I have of yours, lying unanswered. Nothing got touched
on my desk these last two weeks, while I wrestled with the negatives of
twenty years which have to go back to Jock before we leave for Florence,
Rome, and Malta next week. So you can imagine! And now I am just as busy
reading *our* correspondence. It is so warming, dearest Sydney, to go over all
these years of your good affection, such a treasure to hold. I have *lots* of
letters, so that many will have to be weeded out, and anyway, I find that
often one's dearest letters are the least suited to publication.

It is so cold these last two days. A powdering of snow and Bora coming
out of a blue sky,

153

> 'Bright reason will mock thee,
> As the sun in a wintry sky,'

all light and no warmth. But so dazzlingly beautiful, the folds of Grappa, the snow melting in its blue shadows into the sky and the knees of the rocks pushing through. And the pink light hits all the little houses on the plain, so that they look like what they are, a vast fleet of little human lives; they make me think of the little boats I saw in 1943 in Algiers, the whole flat sea full of them destined for Sicily. These are not thinking of attack, only hoping to escape all these beautiful modern inventions! But I suppose one can think of any human life moving out to conquer, at any rate, Time?

My autobiography Volume II is taking shape and I hope may be a good one and also interesting to me to write.

We leave for B.B.'s on Sunday, then travel slowly to Rome on February 3rd, and for a week to Malta where Stewart was once posted. On the 22nd, back for a week here in March and then for the second half of March to England. So you will soon see us in Kew.

Love to you darling Sydney,

FREYA

SIR SYDNEY COCKERELL   I Tatti,
Settignano
1 February 1950

Darling Sydney,

I have at last reached this home of peace and have a little corner of time to write to you. Your letter, with the wonderful tribute from Wavell to Rommel, came just before I left. I am so glad to have it, a generous noble document, in the tradition of all the heroes!

The fat bundle of letters has gone to Jock. I made a preliminary and provisional choice; I think it will make a very pleasant book. You will see that in dividing yours, I kept (a) to what you say about people you had known like Browning, Morris, etc., and (b) to anything that filled in the picture of me (not from conceit, but because after all that is the object of a book of letters).

Stewart and I parted in Padua, he for a Foreign Office interview in London (due back tonight with our fate possibly decided), and I for Florence. It was all altogether very hectic; four days before leaving we let the house to an American widow of a Russian diplomat who wanted an extra room for her chauffeur. At the same time a beautiful Venini glass mirror arrived for the

154

last of the bathrooms, with a workman to fix it up; and Stewart and I fell with our Vespa, giving me a useless ankle for a day. Having got clear of all this just in time, we woke in a snowstorm and drove to Padua with the mended Vespa loaded inside our car (as we propose to run about Rome on it) and snow piling up to the axles. All the trains were late and some cancelled.

B.B. is in very good trim, sending you affectionate greetings. Nicky radiating goodness and happiness. What a dear house to be in.

Every loving thought darling Sydney,

Your

FREYA

JOHN GREY MURRAY   Rome
11 February 1950

Dearest Jock,

Such a lark, we have Vespa'd down to Rome from Perugia. Of course it has been icy ever since we left Asolo in a snowstorm to come south (that awful Mediterranean cold that cuts through you like a knife): the Vespa had to be fitted into the car to get her to Padova. Then she had to be emptied of petrol and put on to the train. Then in Florence, rain, snow on the hills, huge cloudy skies, everyone said I was killing Stewart – so on to the train again, to Perugia. By this time we began to look on the Vespa with aversion as a holiday pet. We warmed to her after a fine day at Assisi, but then more rain came down and Stewart was all for waiting and doing the whole train business over again to Rome. But the little page boy of the hotel, who had become passionately interested in us and the Vespa, said the wind was in the right quarter (the North Pole it felt like), so there was no more dallying. We spent the afternoon going to Todi and slept in a primitive little set of rooms over the pawnshop – very cold, but Stewart was cheered by discovering a Roman forum and I would suffer a lot for a sight of the deserted *piazza* by night, those gaunt thirteenth-century palaces and churches staring at each other, with the wind swaying the electric lights, and puddles glittering below them, and the Song of History made audible as it were in the solitude and severity of it all.

Next day, yesterday, we came all the way to Rome – about eighty miles I suppose – along the beautiful ridges that slope down to Terni and then by a small despised forgotten non-tarmac road that reaches up and down over small ranges to the Tiber in the south. The sun came out, and a valley opened where every spur had either a small fortress-hamlet with walls and castle towers built into its houses, or some fortress-farm: it was just Romantic, and we might have been travellers any time in history between 1500 A.D. and the invention of railways – the Vespa is quite a good substitute for a horse and does for the same sort of country. We got here for tea and risked our lives across Rome where no one thinks of traffic rules but only gives a look to see whether the opposing vehicle is larger or smaller; of course the Vespa is fair game for anyone to run at!

Found a telegram from the Wrights which confirms Cyrenaica to anyone except Stewart, who is shocked at my hearing in this unofficial way *before* the official news. But anyway there it is, and such good news, though it may curtail England by a good deal. We hope to arrive on March 6th and will ring up at once. Would be much obliged if the dentist with the Highland name would keep me a long appointment for the 8th, as I have broken my front tooth and it's only holding on by its skin.

Love,
FREYA

JOHN GREY MURRAY   Benghazi
17 March 1950

Dearest Jock,

It is very pleasant and feels like a return to one's own world to be again on this side of the Mediterranean: the sun, the light, white minarets with green candle-snuffers on their top, blank walls with little ragged groups sitting round teacups or glasses on a tray – all the cheerful squalor, the gay dishevelled dirt and beauty mixed of the East, the dazzle of the sea so much more brilliant than any other; and here in Benghazi a tremendous feeling of the chaos and passing of time, brought by the damage of war. It took two years' hard work merely to clear the rubble from the streets, and I suppose about one house in four is still half ruined: they are being rebuilt, and it is a charmingly planned town, with marble porticoes and good square buildings, and the alternations of those in order and those in ruins give a feeling of time which usually takes centuries to acquire.

We had two days on the way in Tripoli (in the Volpi villa, a pleasant untidy set of rooms round a marble courtyard, in which it felt rather strange to be the guests of the British governor) and we had a morning in the old town – the houses of the French and English consuls who fought each other and stood on their roofs with telescopes watching for approaching ships and ready to buy off any countryman who might be on board as a slave. There is a pleasant square there on the edge of the sea, with an arch of Marcus

Aurelius half buried below the level of the pavement, and I'm sure every old arch in Tripoli was built on this model with the same beautiful half-circle curve. Benghazi has nothing so old, but it is a much better planned and harmonious little town, lying among lagoons. We found a dreary little semi-detached house assigned, but I was inspired last evening as we drove out past the town to ask who lived in some pleasant little houses in gardens, all isolated – and one of them is just vacant and we are getting it. It will make such a difference, as we are in open country, and have a garden with a well round it to play about in – and hope to be in as soon as we can find two servants (telegraphed to friends in Cairo). A fearful lot of things have to be thought for and provided: a cold winter as well as a hot summer, and everyone says it will be *weeks* before the stuff from London and *months* before that from Barbados arrives – but the hospital lends sheets, and Naafi lends blankets, and the Administrator's wife lends forks and spoons. Shops are gradually increasing: the chief difficulty is that the Arabs are unable to do any urban jobs – no upholstering, window fittings, furniture etc. – though I don't believe things will be a bit more difficult than in Aden in 1939 or even Baghdad in 1928 when I first went.

I have been with my hostess down the *suq*, looking at the sacks of henna leaves, frankincense, cloves, ginger, and unknown things with strange names used in food. The Italians built a beautiful meat and vegetable market, circular, on marble columns – such as we after two centuries in a land would never dream of building – and I went round it and saw a boy with a hooded falcon leaning against a column, waiting to sell it. The men wear what *must* have been the Roman toga, of rough white wool, voluminous and dignified, and little red skullcaps.

Must go now. The letters are safely here and I hope to start as soon as we are in the house and settled: we may go up and down the coast, about ten days, before this happens.

Love,
FREYA

P.S. We hope too for a little Italian cottage in the hills. You will *have* to come.

JOHN GREY MURRAY   Benghazi
                                            21 March 1950
Dearest Jock,

It is maddening not to be able to get to work – my days are wasting and we are deprived of all the comforts of life as all our luggage is either coming from Italy, Barbados or London, or lingering in a freight aeroplane. The house we have seized in theory has still to be vacated – and we have moved from the kind Residents to the British Club, ex-Banca d'Italia. We dined there last night, which happened to be one of the two in the week when there is no electric light, and the marble passages with lighted hurricane lamps on the floor at every door, and the dining hall with black and red marble columns, very shiny and slender, with white arches and mosaic patterns above and a mosaic pool and column-fountain in the middle, looked very beautiful in the light of candles stuck on saucers on every little table. It is so poignant to see all this poor Italian effort half bombed away and half given over to the waste of the Arab or the utilitarian hands of ourselves: behind all the bombast, arrogance, inefficiency, there was a genuine love for the civilised life. If they had only gone about it differently it might have made such a glorious success. If they had kept neutral in the war they would have got away with it and made it a national success if not a human one. One feels, when one sees these things, like eschewing human comparisons altogether and becoming a saint; and I believe the age of the great saints was directly produced by the general mess they saw around them.

Stewart is busy meeting all his Ministers etc.: the United Nations representative is expected. Already we British all feel passionately about the integrity of this little country and will resent any vagueness of committee-run nations. You may expect lots of contrasting points of view.

Love to you dear Jock,

FREYA

BERNARD BERENSON   Benghazi
23 March 1950

My dearest B.B.,

Here we are: we flew out from England on the 14th, after an incredible rush, and sailed over the shoulder of Mont Blanc, a white shoulder rising as it were out of a negligée of cloud – so beautiful and remote, an eternal world almost – and then we reached the blue stretches and landed in Tripoli at the Villa Volpi, where I did all I could for them, though the prospect of their getting it back is not very immediate. In spite of being very little ruined and much more like what it was before, Tripoli is not nearly so pleasing as Benghazi: there is an extraordinary feeling here, of the *matter* of history heaving and making. The charming little town, planned with real feeling, is still delightful though every third house is a shell. Your love for ruins will be satisfied; and they take on a beautiful peach-glow in the sunset. There is the pathos which one feels in the ruins of the ancient world, but so much *rawer*, like a freshly torn wound. As in the bombardments of the war, it is the small intimate details that touch one – bits of everyday life, and tiny loves and vanities, whose owners have vanished. In our nice new house for instance (we are not yet in but hope to be soon), there is a stair with an imitation carpet let in in mosaic, quite ugly, but evidently somebody's pride. When one sees this, and the little empty farms of the plateau now drifting back into the wilderness, one's heart goes out to the poor people with their fine labour and not ignoble pride: then when one learns what they did, deliberately trying to eliminate a whole nation, the monstrous cruelty and injustice – one feels that 'God is not mocked' in their ruin. If they had known the rudiments of justice, or even if they had had the sense to keep out of the war, this might have been a success instead of a failure – and I believe nearly every British official here is sorry that it was not so. What will happen now is very obscure: the really important, vital, question is whether this will go back to being a pastoral country or will carry on the experiment in agriculture. One should of course on the very first day have begun to prepare an estimate of the two ways of life with their relative advantages and revenues – for it is more than urgent and the whole future of the land depends on it: there *is* no revenue except from flocks or harvests; and if the latter is the means to a greater prosperity, it is necessary to settle a few experts here and there as soon as possible before the scrub and the nomad are back.

We are going tomorrow for a week to Barce, Cyrene and Derna. I will write and tell you about it, darling B.B. It is a lovely thought that you and Nicky are to come. We shall have a cool house near the sea, out of the town towards the sunset. But it is bitterly cold still, and I believe June would not be too late at all (as the plateau is very cool). This June? Dear, dear love from us both to you both.

Your

FREYA

JOHN MILLER Tobruk
29 March 1950

My dear John,

I must write to you from here, have been thinking of you so much.[93] We are here for two nights in the ex-hotel, now 'Ladybird' officers' club, with a

---

[93] John Miller had been through the Tobruk siege in 1942.

wide terrace over the harbour. Mines are exploding or being exploded on the perimeter, so it makes the atmosphere more realistic, and alas they are bringing in about two cases a day of wounded Beduin now the tribes are up here and are all keen to earn money by collecting desert wrecks. I can't tell you what an impression this makes, like the valley of death to drive along, by Ain Ghazala and all the familiar names, and yesterday to Bardia and Solum and Halfaya.

I wish you were here to tell us all about it. They have taken 180 wrecks out of the harbour, but *S. Giorgio* and a good many others still remain. Sad looking hulls are there, half out of the blue water. Most of the little hill is covered with ruins and there is very little accommodation. I wonder where you used to spend your time? The perimeter has nothing to show but a tank ditch and four little walls with shot-holes where the road goes in.

We thought we would make a tour straightaway before Stewart got too involved; now we go back and Benghazi, Cyrenaica is all the address you need. Why not come out to stay?

Much love, and thoughts from this place,

FREYA

SIR SYDNEY COCKERELL   Benghazi
                                                                1 April 1950

My dearest Sydney,

We have been here a fortnight, but there is as yet no settled feeling, as we have a house, but it isn't ready; and the furniture is bespoken, but not made; and the servants are found, but only arriving in a fortnight's time from Egypt. So Stewart wisely took the chance to see his country before settling down to advise about it, and we went all along the coast to the Egyptian border and got back yesterday. We have seen such wonderful things, a sort of palimpsest of histories, the most ancient of all and permanent, the desert rolling up from the south into pasture-lands of short thick grass nibbled by goats and sheep, the little pagoda tents of the tribes stuck among bushes here and there. As one reaches the headland of Cyrenaica that catches the north-west rain, the scrub increases, and blossoms all over with rosemary, arbutus, cistus pink and white, and gorse, and a carpet of anemones. The asphodel too is in flower, remote and elegant, like a flower in an Italian miniature. This is the basic world here, but there are so many others. The Greek Cyrene. We walked over its ruins, built over two breasts of hill with a shallow valley between them where the little shops trickled down to a flat space held by a retaining wall, where the temples and baths stood, and the cosiest semicircular theatre, where from every seat you look out over the shallow plain below and the Cretan sea. I got away from the escort, a dreary little archaeologist whose touch is like lead on all that living past, and went and sat on the steps of temple in the agora. It is a wide *piazza* built of rocks of stone, with the bases of its buildings standing, and a proconsul's marble pedestal and the foundations of the tomb of Battus, who brought the Cyrenaicans from Santorin and colonised them here. One could feel all the life of that little town, so very like a *piazza* in Umbria and about the same age. The good houses jutting out onto the square, the naval monument with dolphins, the temple steps. Down by the sea, half eaten away by its encroachment, is the port of Cyrene, Apollonia. A few Greeks are still there, and fishers from Crete for sponges, and a Christian church of the sixth century, built with more ancient columns and grass-grown, near the sea. How one feels the *age* of the Levant in these harbours; I think because they are so small, so obviously meant for use only by the tiniest, earliest craft. As I sat about in Cyrene I thought how *urban* all the Mediterranean is and how unlike us in the North. The first thing these people thought of, after frightful hardship, a failure on an island off the desert coast, and another failure on the mainland, was their city square and the founder's tomb and the temples, all harmonious on the fortified hill. I believe it is the climate which makes a *piazza* livable and clusters all the inhabitants about it.

From Cyrene we went on to Derna which is a charming little white-washed Turkish town of narrow streets and good doorways and a quiet little white square with tiled pool, a small covered market smelling of spices, where they sell woollen blankets and Beduin red and yellow shoes and stone kerns for grinding wheat or barley. I went there to buy a needle, one has to ask shop by shop, as everyone might have a little bit of anything. They are only like small boxes less than two yards square. A pleasant thing happened: an old man with a rather noble face and his white blanket over one shoulder sat in his shop, and, when he had offered me a small spear instead of a needle, asked how I knew Arabic. 'I studied,' said I. 'What is your name?' he asked. 'Faraya,' said I. 'Is it Faraya Stark?' said he. He knew all about me. It was such a friendly thing to happen, and we shook hands, mutually pleased.

Derna and Cyrene missed most of the war, but as soon as we got inland on the plateau, we came into the desert track of the armies, that vast battlefield. For over three hundred miles one is *never* out of sight of some derelict tank, lorry, armoured car or gun; they lie around in every state of demolition or disintegration. Farther in, the minefields lie untouched, over seven million mines still unexploded, and two Beduin casualties a day in Tobruk hospital. They were exploding all the morning as we sat in that naked war-spoilt H.Q. A few of the bigger houses are rebuilt, and a hundred ships big and small have been fished up in the harbour. But it still has an air of wreck about it, yet strangely gay owing to the light and health and emptiness of the desert around. The 'perimeter' is eighteen miles out, over the naked ridge and out of sight, and the whole place and all the desert around are full of ghosts.

We went right out to the Egyptian border and only returned yesterday after a week's tour. Stewart has collected a good panorama of ideas for his work here. I hope it may be successful; it is a tough job as they have to develop this country on a sinking tide and not a rising one. The Italians poured in money and people which neither Britain nor Cyrenaica can produce.

Goodbye, darling Sydney. Bless you and please write.

Your loving
FREYA

LADY RUTHVEN   Benghazi
                                                        1 April 1950
Darling Pam,

It seems very natural to be back among Arabs, though alas! that democratic fluency has gone and we both find that the necessary word is most often missing. But the air and the light and the cheerful guttural noises, and the suddenness of life, and the dust storms, are all here, and I hope you will come out soon.

We have been all along the desert way to Sollum and made a state visit to the Egyptian frontier officials. The main one was away and his assistant so frightened that he looked all the time like a lizard listening to a noise, and blinked at us from under an enormous military peak rather spoiled by a blue and grey scarf wrapped round his ears. All he did was to smile and say 'Ah!'; but I wasn't going to be done out of a sight of Halfaya pass, and he had to pack into his Studebaker, 'ahs' and all, and take us. And no doubt the sub-sub-deputy official who is spying on him will report friendly intercourse with a British Military Reconnaissance.

Oh Pam, I think of you so much here, and of Pat. We broke down and were towed to Tobruk in the moonlight and the whole desert seemed alive with the young, the gay, those who will never be old. It was strangely happy for the gigantic corridor of death, so many hundreds of desert-miles long. We drove by Ain Ghazala, a glittering solitude of ridges and sweep of sea breaking in long white foam on its empty beach. Never is there a stretch without some wreck of tank or lorry or armoured car, wheels gone, and chains lying loose on the sand, or sometimes only bonnet and shaft remaining, or empty gun pointing like a useless question to the sky. I think you would like to see all this, you must come soon. One understands so many new things, the hours of thought and loneliness for instance that must have comforted all these boys, the immense peace so august that I believe it made death more easy to meet. As we drove along and the afternoon melted all the low ridges, and the mirage built towers and white walls out of the scrub and dunes, and as the evening fell and a man or two showed walking towards the small tents pitched near a bit of grazing, and even the derelict metal took on a sullen sort of graciousness in the soft light, I suddenly had one of those happy times that come like a visitation, a feeling of enveloping *mercy* into which all this turmoil melted, so that one knew it cannot matter in the end. I am sure many must have felt this, and welcomed the end when it came. I believe I should do so if it came tomorrow, not from any dullness of life, but because the big adventure is beyond, and it would be nice to get rid of a lot of things, the constant irritation one causes to one's dear ones, for instance, by merely being oneself (and one can't not be oneself or try to change things that are quite good and nice. . . Oh well!).

Pam darling, will you tell me exactly where Pat was buried and I will go there, soon if it is easy to reach, and if not, will do it with you when you come. When will that be? I shall be away for September and October and would love to have you in Asolo in October or here any other time. I thought of going to Asolo by way of Greece and Zante; it is almost the same distance and a nice slow way.

Stewart has written what I think is a very good report on his first journey. Everything is to do, and I have a fear that we may have a lot of heartbreak, for what is this nation to be carried along *with*? We can't compete with the Italians, who poured all the money in they should have spent at home. I shall be much surprised if we don't hear how much better it all was under Italy in a very few years. Anyway, it is a fascinating work and I believe Stewart will be very happy over it, and is getting on finely with his Ministers. They are a nice people here, with pure Greek features as often as not.

Love dear Pam,

FREYA

Benghazi
                                                2 April 1950

My dear Sybil,

London was too short altogether but the sight of you was much too short:
I took it however as an 'extra', as there had been no plan for London at all,
and now I feel that perhaps it will not be so long before I see you, if only I
can make you feel how necessary it is to see Cyrene before one dies. Do you
ever go to places and think how terrible it would have been to have missed
them? There it is, a city of 1,400 years, standing in the gap of two round
hills with her baths, temples, theatre, held up by a great wall on the flat gap
between them, over a drop so steep it is almost sheer, on to the narrow plain
and Mediterranean shore – and a little harbour and resurrected church, built
in the days of Justinian with marble columns of temples that were ancient
even then. Two young naval men, Smith and Porcher, got the Admiralty in
1861 to help them with 100 statues which they carried down the slope and
loaded onto H.M.S. *Assurance* (such a suitable name) – and gave to the
British Museum. The whole place was underground then and the Italians
have dug it up beautifully. Poor Italians: their little white houses dotted
everywhere and falling to decay – we were caught by the night and saw the
flicker of Beduin fires built outside them against the doorposts. It is poignant
to *see* history as one does here – the visible swamping of the town by the good
old desert and its tribes. The great question here is whether this country and
its people are best with agriculture or pastoral as they have been for 1,200
years: and the fate of all those little white houses, and the 'centres' with
church, school, Fascist courts, etc. (covered with monstrous Fascist slogans),
depends on the answer. At present there is an Ozymandias feel about it all.

I thought often of your son[94] and his days as we drove by Tobruk and
Bardia to Sollum. The desert is like a great monument to all its dead: one
drives along its avenues of ruins, dead rusting metal ever in sight, with awe.
Please try and come, dear Sybil, either here or in Asolo: it would be a great
joy to see you with no *hurry* about it. One's life is getting too short not to do
all one wants to do with what there is – and that surely includes the sight of
friends.

Very much love,

                                                      FREYA

[94] Lord Rocksavage.

Benghazi
                                                                3 April 1950

Darling Nigel,

I haven't written before merely from lack of leisure, and too much moving
about, but I should have done so for I wanted to tell you that Marie is a dear
and that I am happy to have known her at last and hope she will give me a
little affection left over from what is there for you. She has the gift that I
know you need most, a *radiance* of vitality, a sort of spring of life inside her,
and she loves you. How strange it is how that subtle essence makes itself felt
on all around? I am sure you are to be happy together.

We are still so unsettled here with a house fixed but nothing in it yet, not
even the stair, and a frustrating slowness which doesn't matter to Stewart as
he is launched in his office and has lots of Ministers and things to see to, but
is maddening to me as I really *can't* start to write in the Memsahib atmosphere of the Officers' Club. I hope we may have you both out quite soon,
unless you come to Greece in September and take me up Mount Olympus?
Anyway, it is a long way ahead. What a godsend to be back in the Mediterranean world, never do I want to leave it.

                                                                Love,
                                                                FREYA

Benghazi
                                                                3 April 1950

Dearest Jock,

You *must* come here soon: Cyrene on its shelf with all the Cretan sea
before it and all romance around. There is nothing in a ruin if some of it
isn't buried, and here there is a whole landscape underground, appearing in
a few stones of causeway, a tomb, a foundation of farm or temple among the
limestone and rosemary, and cistus all in flower – and where the hills break
out and go steep down to the narrow sea-plain, the Italian excavations show
temples, forum, the agora and houses, mosaic floors, baths, pillars, amphi-
theatres, shops and tombs – all leaning against a high wall built from hill to
hill against the stupendous view. And there are 1,400 years of history, more
than in almost any site except Rome that we know. The little Fascist slogans
written up everywhere are poor in comparison! The most touching was an
English one however, in the bay of Sollum, a bombed desert pocket with no
gaiety except the shining blue bay and fig trees with very new leaves in the
sun: and among all the bombed houses one little one remained, half in ruins

and with the words 'Hotel of Happiness' written on its remaining half wall. I wish I could tell you how moving it is to go along that desert road.

Love dear Jock,

FREYA

JOHN GREY MURRAY

Benghazi
10 April 1950

Dearest Jock,

I can tell you the happy news that the Italian luggage has arrived (with all my writing material) so it is only *leisure* which is missing now. It is lucky Italian plumbing is so disastrous, otherwise there would be nothing in Benghazi to show us the more efficient people. It goes to my heart to walk up to the squalor, dirt, and general unimaginativeness of the places where the government of this place is now run from, and see the careful efforts, marble steps and stepped skirtings of marble, a lovely circular stair rail of beaten iron in the back of the British Information Office, half a ruined circle of fountain in a tiny dark court. I went across a lagoon to their cemetery yesterday, and there was a mixture – frightful Fascist pompous monument to the 'fedelissimi of the new Roman Hesperides', and at one side the rows of little dingy brown crosses with not even a date, only a *number* painted on them. The gates well locked, and evidently some care taken, the sort of loveless care not much use to anyone.

Did I tell you that a kind man sent me a lorry and five men to use for a day, and I have cleared every old tin out of the sight of my windows (while Stewart was at Kufra for four days). The view looks quite peaceful: a ruined pavilion, rather like a shabby Hindu platform, between two grassy plots and sandy roads, and the sea; a rusty old bleached ship, and the sunset. On the inland side are lagoons, now drying day by day with stretches of good hard sand for Vespa to race on. Stewart filled her with petrol and rode her with great splendour home from the customs wharf and I tried her up and down to the monument which commemorates the victorious dead – only there was no time to write their names in the marble slab.

Love dear Jock. Send news of Diana.

FREYA

BERNARD BERENSON

Benghazi
12 April 1950

Darling B.B.,

Such a joy – your letter of the 30th here two days ago: a little ship called *Gigliola* appeared too in the poor shattered harbour, with all my clothes –

166

brought from Venice in ten days. It is only the things sent by the Government from England that take so long – and this brings up a sad tale: *beds* will take five more months to arrive! We sleep now on horrid little iron operating tables that slide about the marble floor on slightest provocation. I hoped that we might be settled and comfortable by June, but it is not to be, and I fear you ought not to come out to us until we are all complete to make you comfortable. It will have to be later, and what you lose in time you will gain in the improvement of houses, hotel (at Cyrene), and roads. For you *must* see Ptolemais, now Tolmeita. What beauty, most of it still under the ground. A long street is cleared, just the bases of its houses and temples, with column or steps or white and black mosaic; and the square of the walls is a dim thing only guessed at like a dream, with a square western gate still standing and from it a sunken way of yellow daisies shows where the street once ran – all grass now, on a wide gentle bay, with lines of waves breaking on sand, like the years made visible, wearing us all away. Right out on the western shore the limestone shelf has been eaten away by the sea into smooth isolated piers or platforms, some quite square; and on one of them a tomb is still standing, with three plain walls and a squared door and niches inside, like the Palmyra tombs; and as we looked, a small falcon crept into a cranny of the masonry. You can imagine all the light, the sort of *transparency* of colour; and the columns of temples turned to churches, two great clusters, with the hills swelling gently behind them; and the later buildings still showing here and there, with a feeling of hurry still about them – for the walls were pushed up by Synesius to keep the Libyans out; and one can see older inscriptions upside down inserted in them. There are huge cisterns under a floor of cement, for water or grain. And now a tiny village on the shore, bitten by the wind and sun; and a little lighthouse to show that there are rocks, perched on a round of old masonry that must have been some fort or tower. Stewart wants to find a Minoan anchorage, and surely there must have been some, here between Crete and Alexandria? The guardian of the light came up and explained that he badly needed new trousers, and, as we were leaving, arrived with a tin full of eggs – he must have asked help from all his neighbours. We had to refuse them and he looked very sad; but, the trousers are being provided by the department of 'harbour lights', so he will be delighted to get his wish with no bribery after all. A nice tribesman *mudir* came along in a white toga and yellow (saffron yellow) boots: he came from the tribes near Sirte. It still seems enchantment to hear these names in ordinary use!

Stewart is hoping to combine agriculture with pasture under the form of olive trees: they grow wild here, and in fifteen years come to full bearing –

and as these next fifteen years they may have someone looking after them, they have a chance of being brought safely past the dangers of goats and neglect in their infancy. Then, when they have grown, even the tribesmen can gather them, and it is simple enough to make oil; and the grazing can go on around them. The Arabs are trying to settle in the hill farms and would not be so bad if only it would be agreed to whom they belong: of course no one will do much for an uncertain ownership. I cannot help rejoicing with you to think there may be one country on the Mediterranean left to the masters of flocks – those lovely slopes, with scattered patches of wheat, but mostly grass and browsing flocks among the ruins! The fact is that their trade balance was favourable until 1913 when Italy took over, and has been unfavourable ever since, though the population of the country diminished by half.

One's feelings are much torn: in the towns there is a poignancy about all the vanished Italian dream – so much care and expense and a wish to make their work beautiful for its own sake. I suppose the Swiss journalist here made the best comment: he said what a pity not to have done it all in Sicily or Calabria, and so avoid the troubles both there and here!

Love to you both, darling B.B.

Your devoted

FREYA

SIR SYDNEY COCKERELL

Benghazi

20 April 1950

My dearest Sydney,

We are only just back from a wonderful week visiting cases in the south. Jalo-Aujila is mentioned by name by Herodotus and there it still is, a little strip of palms, six miles or so, low down in a dip of the sands, 150 miles south of El Agheila. You reach it by a sort of causeway where the soft sand laps in a ridge under the car, but does not sink in as it does to left and right. The first green is tussocks: every living root has to push its branches up and up, making a little hill, until the heart inside comes to the end of its strength and the sand still climbs, and covers, and the hillock remains with only dead wood to cover it. And that is its life story. Just one long struggle, as one sometimes feels oneself! Then after the tussocks come tamarisks, and if there is water enough they cease being tussocks and shoot out a trunk and the outer circle of oasis trees appears. And then the people begin to fence their sand with fences of dead palm against which the outer desert bites and rustles and makes little tentlike mounds, very fine and white. And inside they irrigate and grow tomatoes, which make lots of money in winter when they reach the cold coast by lorries. That and dates and baskets with little red tassels are the products of Aujila and Jalo. The people must be Berber, they look different from the mainland (thinking of them as islands in the sea).

We lunched and slept (I did) in the afternoon at Jalo and then picked up our route again from Aujila to follow our own tracks by night. (We had circled our car on arrival so as to recognise the track!) So, as it is only an hour across smooth sand billows between the two oases, we came to Aujila in the sunset and I have rarely seen so peaceful a view – the fringe of the tree-tops and the gentle sands behind rolling away for ever; and the sun seemed not to give but to *take* its gold from the empty heart of the earth and use it to pour round the tops of the trees and brown huts and beehive domes of little mosques. There are about 600 people they say and over 2,000 in Jalo, and to reach or leave them one forgets the habitable world. The day goes by in a biscuit-coloured softness of sand, sometimes covered with the finest clearest jewel-like gravel of many colours where the car can race at will; sometimes brittle and light on the horizon, as if it were glass; sometimes darkened as a rim of mascara round an eyelid, and the horizon is near or far but with no detail between you and it; only sometimes a great feeling of being lifted up. Over it is a thin criss-cross pattern of old car tracks, or rather *under* it, as the wind has gone over them with its little patter of sands, and they are only ghosts; and here and there, even in this deep south where our Long Range Desert Group operated, some empty dead Ozymandias of an armoured car is left.

The Italians built even here. Aujila has a ruined fort with four round corner bastions, and Jalo a house for government and a gate with 'Credere, obbedire, combattere' still fresh upon it. The Italian ruins look very well and suited to this sand. We spent the night beside one, right out in desert about half way, built round an old Islamic core which must have been a shrine I think, remains of four central arches and a barrel vault cloister around. And now the Italian cantonments in ruins, and the star of Italy in front of them patterned out in stone and being eroded; and, most touching, a bowling alley of cement outside the walls in desert, with cement half buried under sand. They put up a petrol pump with the Fasces cast in metal, and there it creaks and groans in the night wind and a black rag still flutters on its door. I had forgotten the wonder of the nights: they begin like any other, with air still warm from the sands and dark clustered skies, but when one awakes at 2 a.m. or so, the sky has grown light and the stars are enormous and few, and hanging, with a transparent light all around them. One can watch them swinging round the pole and feel that one is looking to the whole circle, for even the horizon stars are clear. I woke up the second night and there was Perseus with six lamps as it were, suspended in a sky that might be cut in jade.

The workmen are pulling this house about so that it is misery to live in for the moment, but I hope the worst will be over by the week after next.

Your

FREYA

JOHN GREY MURRAY Benghazi
20 April 1950

Darling Jock,

All my work is here, ready, and I have found a fine solid sideboard to use as a desk – but can't start till the workmen stop hammering: they are taking a bite out of the middle of the house to put stairs in, and you can imagine the dust and noise, and a *khamsin* wind too blowing, hot and cold and full of sand.

How the 8th Army ever took Agheila front-on can hardly be believed: a tank tried the salty swamp and stuck, and they turned across the dunes south of the road; it took three weeks, and Rommel had *nothing* to hold it with – they found wooden dummy guns (all his stuff smashed at Alamein). South of the swamps for seventy-five miles the Italians had fortified the hills and laid a staked, mined fence of wire, and built a fort and a causeway. We drove there to the oasis of Marada across the worst surface and the most howling desert you ever imagined, stony and putty-coloured, and, for animals, only a dark wolf running along a far slope visible – though there were charming delicate little flowers and bushes of white broom. When we got half way there was nothing but a thorny jade-green tussock here and there, and then suddenly we came off the putty-coloured stone and down into a wide valley with tributary valleys, all white; the hills were flat and their upper crust, broken where the wind scooped it out, lay in slabs like a broken pie-crust on the sand-slope below, the shadows were green as if they were shadows in clear water; and a faint green on the upper rock gave an idea of grass. But I have never been in a place that gave so strong a sensation of *illusion*; it was very beautiful, but a deathly beauty; everything there was barren; the south wind ran a little white mist of sand along the valley floor, so that the bases of the hills were lost and they stood like phantoms in a sun-heat as bitter as ice; and everything was deprived of any human truth. The way was marked by old Italian signposts: some on their faces, but many standing, and their rusty faces blank; there were petrol tins here and there empty; and a car or two, standing in the whiteness, but when you reached it, empty, and ruined, and rusted. The only thing that continued its work was the barbed wire fence stalking up and down, mile after mile; and inside its boundaries the road, also white sand, marked with two rows of stones – sweeping round the solitary corners, leading as it seemed away from all human relation into a strangeness too different for us to know what it was – death in fact. The wide valley made a world of its own with all its tributaries opening fantastic shapes, white and faint, scarce pencilled on the horizon, and with no shadows (near noon) except those of the overhanging hilltops. It was a comfort to see the first tree, straggly in the whiteness; then grim gates of eroded rock, and ruined slopes; then a line of ragged battered tamarisk where a streak of moisture must run below; then more fierce tumbled rock and an eight-mile flat of salt marsh, desiccated congealed sand in bloated waves – and then the first green, covering low sand hillocks with faint thorns in a mess of dead brown; and the fences of dry palm leaf and the palms. A few poor huts of mud and palm and the black and white Senussi flag to show the Government – and then we were there. The oasis has 1,050 people drawing rations, and is fed by strange scummy pools that have continued bubbles welling up from their depth, and podgy swollen edges of mud. The place is run by a tough young *effendi* of Tripoli who was taken prisoner with the Italian army at Sidi Barrani, and entered the government service here. I went in to the harem where he has ten women and children depending on him, three going blind with the usual trachoma; a strangely fascinating wife with the startled eyes and pointed chin of an elf, and a look of magnificence, almost Elizabethan, they manage to give to their bright cotton garments by wearing them very voluminous, so that they walk about like vessels under full sail, with a look of pomp. There is a most extraordinary difference as soon as you cease to be official and drop into their own private lives – as if something dead had dropped away and the real person popped out again: the young *mudir* seemed to be quite another sort of person on the two sides of his harem wall.

Michael Stewart[95] has been for three days and we had him to picnic in this house and this morning I took him up to see the plain of Barce and its cornfields. Stewart has been trying to impress the necessity of getting the army to be a little less conspicuous in this country, if we don't want them to feel about us as the Egyptians do.

Would you please dear Jock telephone for me to the Army and Navy

[95] With the Foreign Office (and subsequently Ambassador to Greece). F.S. had worked with him when she was establishing her reading centres in Italy at the end of the war.

Stores and order a camp bed, of the light portable sort that stands quite low (about one foot) off the ground. I have my valise, and only want the bed and a mattress if they have a very slight and portable one, and would like it sent out at once, if you will kindly pay for it!

Stewart sends love. I long to hear news of the nursery!

Love,

FREYA

JOHN GREY MURRAY   Benghazi
26 April 1950

Dearest Jock,

The first sheet of Volume II is written! I have got a desk at last, made by taking off the front of a hideous Fascist sideboard, and a room with that and a chair and nothing else inside it, not much but a *little* out of the noise and dirt of all who say they are building but appear to be demolishing this house: and so I hope now to go on. It is a frustrating feeling not to be able to get to one's proper work – I had an idea that my proper work was to love and be loved, but it isn't: it is just to *write books*, so what is the good of not doing so? And anyway *you* will be pleased.

I am reading Byron with much enjoyment – but why all those asterisks? Quite maddening! The conversation with George IV for instance? Where one *doesn't* know what is left out, it is irritating, and where one *does* know it makes it just a little more masked than it would have been otherwise.

Today I Vespa'd into Benghazi, but not yet across the bridge of boats which makes our approach rather like Venice. I am going to be very rigid, cutting out parties here so as to write. I *hope* to do two chapters a month: that would make eight when you meet me at Zante or Asolo in September or October. Tell me soon which it is to be.

Love,

FREYA

MICHAEL WRIGHT   Benghazi
10 May 1950

Dear Michael,

You said you wanted letters, and I did write one to Esther, but I rather think her desk is like that lion's den, all sorts of things go in and nothing comes out again. Anyway, we have been here nearly two months now, and our house is still without a stair and full of workmen sitting about in happy little groups drinking tea.

It was very good to see Michael Stewart, even for such a glimpse, and he will have told you all the gossips and problems. The only vitally urgent one as far as I can see is also the most difficult one, and that is the army. There is absolutely no doubt that, unless it can make itself a little more unobtrusive, the same old troubles of Egypt will gradually gather here, though at present they are the cloud no bigger than a hand. But Stewart told me that General Lewis[96] was under the impression that this question is *dormant* and, my God, he is making a mistake if he thinks that. Every other day somebody wants a house, store, something or other in which the army is now settled; and every other day someone in or from Egypt points out the similarity between them and Cyrenaica. We are more or less all right with the generation that fought the Italians, but that is only good for another five or six years; and then there will be a young opposition who can scarcely remember any but British troops in sight in their country, and whose future opinions are being manufactured *now* (for it isn't as if the dear Arab produced *many* ideas, or at least he doesn't usually make one of them last for a long time). The army is as nice and popular as any army can be, and if they were up in the Jebel, getting on with the country Beduin, encouraging the growing of vegetables and fruit (by buying them) in the neglected farms, and doing all the things like hunting, etc., which the country people like, they would be a great help instead of a danger, which in the middle of every town, with all the hotels and best buildings in their hands, it is no doubt they are. They keep on telling us that people here should be grateful for all the economic benefits they bring, as if it were not by now one of the few really obvious facts brought to light in the economic world, that people grab the benefits and hate one for bringing them. It is no good bringing this *ethical* view to bear on human nature, especially Arab. And after all we need only to remember how we felt about the American occupation of England, right in the middle of the war, when they were actually fighting for us.

Dear Michael, what fun it would be to have you out here. I long to know how much you really care about the treaty? If the Emir cares more, he is surely in a much stronger position to impose his will? There is a time for standing on the platform and a time for sitting among the audience, and it seems to me that the Emir would easily understand if those are his and our places at the moment? But possibly the treaty is not so important? We are quite well out of it if it isn't, as it is very easy to twist it into an anti-Libyan-Unity slogan, and that is what the Egyptian voices are doing already, so that there is a lot to be said for any effort in its favour coming from Cyrenaica rather than from Britain.

[96] Major-General Sir Richard Lewis, Director-General Foreign Office Administration of African Territories 1949–52.

Poor Stewart is already up against an attempt of the Emir to secure the police to his nephew over and above all ranks and hierarchies. What a wonderful, rich, venerable history is that of corruption! But the people here are so nice, and still little spoiled, and such a lovely empty country. Every hill has the ruin of a Greek farm hidden among its thorns, and a little tent of nomads, filled with fleas, near by.

Bless you and Esther. If Cyrenaica is too far, please make it Asolo in October.

Love,
FREYA

SIR SYDNEY COCKERELL   Benghazi
12 May 1950

Darling Sydney,

All these accidents to my best friends! You well out of it, I hope, by now, and Lord Wavell too I hope convalescing. But to be ill in May is sad. Here we are not yet enjoying the feeling of spring or summer; the flowers are over, but the warmth not yet begun. A cold little wind comes indifferently from north, south, east or west, with or without dust. It gives an incredible cyanide blue to the morning sea, and then grows mistier and periwinkle-blue as the day goes on. I look at a strip of beach and blue horizon from the little room which a sideboard turned into a desk has made a study.

I am reading the *Quran* twice a week with a young teacher with a sad long face, rather under-nourished and beautiful, like a medieval picture. I think a lot of those interesting looks came from poor feeding. This man is very nice, he reads the beautiful verses with such feeling, after invoking the help of God and the absence of Satan, and one feels what a precious treasure is a Book, a thing to believe implicitly, an easy and perpetual comfort. It is years since I read through the *Quran*, and I am glad to return to it, magnificent language, like an organ.

I hope for a letter soon and to hear of your walking in Kew Gardens.

Love,
FREYA

BERNARD BERENSON   Benghazi
21 May 1950

Darling B.B.,

How I envy anyone who is in Paris with you – I would give a great deal to be near by when you walk among those beautiful things. France has been more or less left out of my life, even though I was born on the Rive Gauche, and there is no doubt that a craving for hats and dresses has interfered with my culture there! Now may you have a lovely spring and no cold winds: we have been shivering here in the real Mediterranean way – which is never really warm till June: but now it looks as if the still days were beginning and the sea about to lose its angry blue. We spent a good Sunday riding out about twelve miles from Barce to an estate laid out with great lavishness by an Italian called Jung: thousands of almonds and olives, and hillsides of corn, and plans for roads and sheds and water being carried on in the restricted way which is all the British Empire and the modest prospects of this poor little country allow.

If I were a millionaire (I am so glad I'm not) I think I would like to take Cyrenaica and run it; it would not be beyond one individual's capacity, and over a period of twenty years it might not even be a financial loss. But to keep roads, and restore and make a few good hotels, pay teachers for a technical school, and scholarships abroad, and start a few people in small industries, and buy tractors – one would see a country blossom in its own way, and perhaps prevent the coca-colaisation, and get much more satisfaction than most millionaires attain. I should not *really* enjoy it, because I dislike managing other people's affairs and like to feel a pilgrim and mere sojourner in this world – the Tents of Kedar, and after all if one creates even a paragraph or two, one need not feel it a duty to go around tidying up. But if I were burdened with money and had to spend it, that is what I should like to do to get rid of it. The ride was as perfect as a ride can be: earth tracks going gently up and down with no obstacle and a mile or so always in sight – so that one could go and go, cantering, and just waiting for the earth to turn at its horizon.

I plan to be in Asolo for October and Tatti in early November on my way south if you can have me then. And next year you must come here.

Love to you both – from Stewart too,

FREYA

CHARLES RANKIN   Benghazi
                                                         4 June 1950
Dearest Charles,

I was glad of your letter. You can imagine how sad it is – a big hole left in the world when someone like H.E. leaves it;[97] one suddenly notices how

[97] Field-Marshall Lord Wavell had died.

175

much it means to have them there, however rarely one sees them. Oh dear Charles, he might have had another twenty years and perhaps the happiest of his life and with time at last to sit back and enjoy his own stored riches. I am so sad too for Archie John particularly, who cares so much. It was a happy thought to think of him coming out here – on the anniversary of all this that happened here only ten years ago: and I think of it and find myself in tears at inconvenient intervals all the time.

UNO is here. What a shock it is, to see who runs us at close quarters.

> 'Divided we stand,
> United we fall;
> If we do quite slowly,
> There's something for all.'

My little reflection.

Love dear Charles,

FREYA

LADY CHOLMONDELEY
Benghazi
6 June 1950

My dearest Sybil,

You are my first reader except for Sydney and Jock Murray, and how dear of you to write and tell me you like the book. One pushes the poor little things out like a hen with a duckling – no real idea of how they will find themselves in the strange element of other people's minds – and it is such a comfort to get a letter like yours.

We have been seeing the United Nations at close quarters, visiting: what a shock! The chairman made a speech at a tea party on Independence Day, hoping next year to see the Emir head of United Lybia: *instant* protest from the French delegate. They are all camping among the ruins now, and then return to Tripoli. We in Benghazi meanwhile have been having the first election of the régime, and it was touching to see how seriously they went about it, with a bench of elders in their red caps and white togas, sitting there to watch over fair play. The carrying of the blue boxes containing the votes to the central counting place was like the Ark of the Covenant moving along. They are a good people – free, and decent, and dignified: I hope we can keep them so. Do come to see them before they are spoilt!

Love from both,

FREYA

Darling Sydney,

I have not written to you since the news of Archie Wavell, and there is nothing to say of that except the sadness of it. I had been thinking of him so constantly, here among his battles – perhaps the best year of his life in 1940? The desert will always be full of him to those who knew him. When already ill he wrote to me and said he hoped to come here, and I was hoping for it. It leaves a great hole in life; one of the great men gone, and there are not so many.

I was thinking of you this morning in a Greek sponge-fishing boat, a cool breeze and dark blue sea, but shining like a cut gem, a little twenty-five-ton boat, like that of Ulysses for sure, broad and scooped shallow amidships, with a mast for being tied to when sirens are about. It was a charming morning. About a hundred of these boats congregate from the islands during the six summer months, and dive for sponges in ten, twenty, or thirty-five fathoms of water. This one, *Hagios Nikolaus*, came from Calymnos in the Dodecanese. We climbed into it from a sister boat that brought us out from Benghazi, where the most of them were all tied up by the quay with their clothes drying on the booms and the Greek flags at the mast-heads (what a *pretty* flag, it melts into the sky) and sponges threaded on the shrouds as if on skewers. When we reached the *Nikolaus* a diver had just been pulled up and was resting to get his breath in his uniform all padded out with air, held up in the arms of the crew leaning over the side. When he got on board he turned out to be one of the most beautiful men I have ever seen, with a face like stone so hard set by his hard fine life. It was like one of those archaic Greek statues, and made finer by the sort of armour of the diver's suit, the riveted steel collar and wide rust-coloured garment below. What was so beautiful was the quickness with which the face woke from its hard beautiful repose to gentleness and amusement, so that it seemed as if the whole of civilisation were enclosed in it. I felt tears coming to my eyes, can you believe it? But it was the most moving thing to see such a triumph of human values in the poor bare life, such a *victory*. I got someone to ask the man his age, forty-five, and how long he had been diving, twenty-five years, and how long he could go on, another twenty-five years, and this with a fine proud smile, proud of all the things that are worth being proud about. He had been three times down into the sea, and that is as much as they can do in the day, and it is a harmful thing for them and can end in paralysis when something goes wrong with the circulation. In another small boat they were diving without a suit, holding a stone tied by a rope, with a little string they loop round three fingers to signal when they want to come up. They dive down and after a minute to two in the water are pulled up, the pulling being done by two men very quickly. The sponge they are making for is first located by someone looking through a glass-bottomed tin. We also looked through and saw the diver sinking down with his feet together and his head towards us, in a green, light atmosphere of water, as if the bottom of the sea were a great cathedral hall. There he squatted on the ground far below and then up he came, dim, up into the shafts of watery sunlight. We ended the morning with *ouzo*, baked octopus, and oily olives on the big parent sponge boat, and saw the morning's harvest on strings, all black and oozing what they call milk, and one wonders what first made anyone think of a sponge as something to wash with.

I am glad you are pleased with *Traveller's Prelude* and with the name which came to me one day suddenly by itself. I hope you will like the next one. I have done two-thirds for Jock to see.

Bless you, darling Sydney. Get quite well.

Your loving
FREYA

BERNARD BERENSON   Benghazi
                                                                13 June 1950
Darling B.B.,

You know nearly everything about the visible and a lot about the invisible world – have you heard of the painted tomb at Asgafa? They say it is first century A.D., and by a bad little provincial painter, but very lively, with three sirens standing straight up side by side with mannequin figures (out of *Vogue*) and frizzy hair, playing on instruments while Odysseus is tied to the mast. And there is a beautiful horse: I am sure the Parthenon horses came from here – their compactness and their strong necks so thick at the base are visible in every animal you see. All this is painted in four niches on a hillside near Abiar to the south, over rolling country that might be the Wiltshire Downs. We drove out on Sunday by a red earth track, and it was so pleasant to see the tribesmen with little sickles in their hands enjoying their own harvests at last: so *obviously* enjoying them. At Abiar it is all very bare, but there are eleven wells and it was like a return to Abraham, about 2,000 cattle, camels, goats, sheep must have been there, being watered or drowsing in groups with their heads bunched for shade together, among the rocks in the sun. And as we drove on and made for the Barce plain, we came upon one shallow basin after another, houseless except for an empty Italian farm fortified with round towers and shot-holes, but all rustling with harvests, the richest heavy-bearded barley you ever saw. What a land it must have been in its great days! On a gentle hill we found the foundations of a small Greek settlement – square enclosure, and a thick rectangle – evidently the strong central keep, and a number of circular foundations we think must have been storehouses for grain. So far south, these ruins must be pre-Roman, and held when the country was fairly safe. And we left them and came back through juniper woods and the sad empty little Italian houses with deserted vines growing over doorways here and here.

Yesterday this so-called democracy was launched at last with opening of its Parliament. All went beautifully, the police guard with black facings and black and white crescent-and-star fluttering in the sun: they came trotting down the street, and the Emir in a shining black car, blue suit, toga, dark glasses and red fez stepped out looking like a very dignified old woman encumbered with shawls. Stewart had tried hard to eliminate some of the lies from the speech from the throne, but the Prime Minister was adamant, and eleven long typed pages were inflicted. The throne itself would never have been ready but for a bevy of English wives who stitched the red velvet till midnight: we went to see the gold fringe being nailed on, and to prevent the Prime Minister from arranging the carpets like a café at the last minute. The whole cabinet, which consists of five, came wandering in to see that their friends were properly placed, and the Lord Mayor, who is enormous with a triple-sized toga, came and tried out his chair with a friend on each side to see that enough room was left in the middle. It was a wonderful sight to see them all trooping in next day, the fezzes and tarbushes and turbans, the coloured braided Turkish jodhpur trousers and here and there some yellow Beduin shoes – and all the white woollen togas so that the opening of the Parliament of ancient Cyrene cannot have looked very different. Most of the country delegates have Berber faces, rather square and straight and solid. The election day was very touching, they took it with such serious pleased conscientiousness – and 80 or 90% voted everywhere, even among the Beduin. It was probably one of the cleanest elections going: one man tried to impersonate his father, but as everyone knows everyone else he was instantly spotted; and as for the *reasons* for adopting a candidate, they were simple and sound – you gave your vote to who offered most tea and sugar to take home; and probably the result is as good as any other.

Our dear love to you both,

FREYA

179

Flying to Cairo
18 June 1950

Dearest Jock,

Arrived yesterday from a three-days' ride and found the happy news, and longing to hear the name; how does the poor mite not find one ready? and what does John feel about a brother? It will be fun some day to see *four* little Murrays playing on the Riva: I hope it may be soon.

The ride was over *wonderful* land, and coast: tombs and mounds and homely little bays where the ghosts of the swan-necked ships can still be felt drawn up on the white sand. And inland by tiny paths and limestone stairs under juniper forests and wild olives. The olives and the people are both descended from the old Greek colonists, I know. I am nearly dead as we started the first six-hour drive at 5 p.m. after a long motor-day; the second in the hot morning at 9 to 8.30 p.m. (only two-hour rest); and the third from 6 to 7.30 p.m. also with two-hour rest. Needless to say I had no hand in the organising and was livid over the timetable – and delighted to see Stewart suffering by the third day and unable to sit!

I shall find your reactions to the mss. when I get back and am very anxious to know. Dear love to you all,

FREYA

Benghazi
28 June 1950

Darling B.B.,

We have had the most delectable – though exhausting – ride from Apollonia to Tolmeita, along the coast until the cliffs come steep down into the water, and then we turned inland up the steepest imaginable wadis hidden in trees of juniper and carob. These beautiful Parthenon horses climb like cats over the limestone, worn smooth and full of round pockets eaten out by weather – but I had a bad moment when mine slipped with all four feet a yard or so backwards, and nearly panicked: however, I did stick on. We reached the top of the plateau and went on riding in the sunset, stopping at a tent for tea with mint and sugar, and on again over what looked like virgin wilderness, until one came upon the ruts of cartwheels in the stone – made by Greek farmers in their time. What a land! Riding by the solitary bays we found one lovely inlet with some old ruined heap on each of its promontories, and inside the curve, numbers of tombs cut in the rocks, inhabited by Beduin. The women in their wide bright skirts and great circular earrings, two or three in each ear, and bright check sheets that cover head and figure, were cooking at their fires, and it looked just like the pictures the travellers of the mid-nineteenth century brought back from Palestine or Syria. That is just what this country is like, as soon as one leaves the one tarmac road – and Stewart and I both think one should modernise it not to the motor age but to the age before and make good easy tracks for pack-animal traffic. We came on another site of old solid tombs, they looked Phoenician rather than Greek – sarcophagi with lids cut in a solid block. A little Italian centre had been built here on a hill, and the Arabs camped among the houses, all roofless and ruined by bombs, with bits of cornice and arcade of cement to add to the superior ruins of antiquity. And when we had crossed the wide estuary of the Wadi Kuf – huge stretches of salt pans blistering in the sand, and tamarisk dunes and swamp, and dead white skeletons of trees swept down – we came on a place of a few wells where cattle are still brought near the shore, and there, by a little promontory and a reef and two islets that make a tiny bay, is a low mound which I would love to dig, as it might be very early indeed – the sort of place where the *Argo* could have been drawn up on the sand. An acropolis with cyclopean bits of wall and later ruins is on the headland above; and we lunched in the shadow of a cliffside cave, and looked out on that incredible, unchanged age and gaiety of the Mediterranean. What a *satisfying* sea!

I am not in Benghazi at the moment, but at Burg al Arab with the Bramlys,[98] and going back next week; it is four hours by air from Cairo and everything is easy except the expense.

Darling B.B., I hope to see you in the autumn. May no Far Eastern cataclysm intervene: one does not know what to think and far less what to wish for.

Dearest love,

FREYA

CHARLES HARDING
As from Benghazi
28 June 1950

My dear Charles,

I am actually not in Benghazi, but was seized with a longing for fleshpots and flew to Cairo – it is only four hours and could be done oftener if it were also cheap. There I bought a trunkload of household things with only one

[98] Colonel Wilfred Jennings Bramly and his wife Phyllis. F.S. had first visited them at Burg el Arab in 1934.

little bit of fun – an old Vienna teapot and milk jug in the Muski – and now am finishing my escapade with old friends in the Western Desert. The house, built sixteen years ago of Ptolemaic blocks of stone, has a strange charm, as its rounded windows look out over rolling desert on every side, and indoors are beautifully polished parquet floors strewn with most lovely rugs, and old Italian cabinets and French pictures. The two who live in it are old now – seventy to eighty or nearly – and they stayed here while Alamein went on thirty miles away, and have done a wonderful work by just *living*: that surely is the best way of doing one's work in this world? They fenced a bit of desert and arranged the ground so that the rain should run into it when it comes, and an olive grove has grown up inside it; and it is all as peaceful as anything I know, with a nice feeling of tradition and independence about it. I am here for three days and then fly back to Benghazi – where I hope the workmen may be out of the house at last.

When I get to London next year we must have a real hunt or two for treasures. I feel it is impossible to face a five-year and perhaps ten-year job with only the squalid government furniture to look at – and even before I arrive myself, if you happen to see one of those nice round mirrors that bulge so that the whole room is reflected in them, and can have it sent out to me in Benghazi, I would gladly buy it. It would enliven us a lot. Not *too* expensive of course. But I know you would choose the right one. In any case I am planning to get six weeks or so in England next June-July, and to be very extravagant. If my book goes well, we might even buy a picture if you have a little treasure handy.

Ever yours affectionately,

FREYA

LADY RUTHVEN

Cairo
28 June 1950

Darling Pam,

Your lovely letter made me very happy, good news of you and my Skimper,[99] and Hermione, all giving a warm feeling when it comes. Darling Pam, don't let *anything* interfere with Asolo in October. I should be there, D.V. and *Inshallah*, by the 1st. Let me know dates as soon as you can, as I have just the one month, and it needs planning. As for Cyrenaica, we should be there with open arms from November to March, and April again in Asolo.

[99] Lady Ruthven's younger son (and F.S.'s godson).

We had a three days' ride along the coast, by little bays visited only by the Beduin and perhaps a pirate or a Commando since the days when the Minoan traders beached their boats on the white sands. Such a pure sea, made more of light than water. My dear, I shall never be able to let Stewart come exploring. He made a great scene and said I was to take no interest in anything, *everything* was organised and arranged. In spite of this I did put both feet down and make him telephone to ask about food and find out, to his surprise, that we were expected to bring it. Otherwise we would just have lived on a cucumber or two and the sight of flocks feeding far away. Nobody looked at a map with any eye for distances. However it really was all so beautiful, and the aches and pains go and the beauty remains. Coming into Tolmeita in the sunset can never be forgotten, with the cold waves lapping the submerged quays where the Greek promenade, by tombs and quarries, must have heard a lot of gossip in its time. Even there there was no firewood, no lantern, no water, and the beds not unpacked, and food only because mercifully I had refused to disinterest myself from that basic necessity and saw that a sheep with fat tail was dangling from the basket that contained my underwear (as saddlebags had also been omitted). What rankles of course is that, with three geographic medals, one should be even associated with such a shaming exhibition, and never even consulted. But we will sort it out and when you come travel by quiet stages and see that there is leisure to enjoy those hidden places and lovely wild villages. It is such a pleasure to come upon the people in their low tents, visible only by their smoky fires in the scrub, and barking dogs, and so happy in their freedom, and a good feeling to be in a land where no one need feel cramped for space. There are, I believe, about 200,000 to 250,000 inhabitants, and I suppose the Italians could have crowded in two million at the expense of the Beduin lives. It is not a very easy problem to answer, and a great luxury to keep a land empty in this age. But it is good to enjoy it while it is there.

Tell me soon when to expect you. Dear love, dearest Pam,

FREYA

BERNARD BERENSON   Benghazi
28 July 1950

Darling B.B.,

I was so happy to have your letter, and it came while I lay low with some miserable epidemic that is ravaging Benghazi. I am out of bed, but weak with that end-of-the-world feeling given by the sulphur-drugs.

I am glad to think of you back at Vallombrosa in spite of all the fairness of Paris. I hope to get to you early November and bring you the mss. of Volume II (Vol. I should reach you in September). Jock likes the second and there are only two more chapters to finish and I have tried to follow your advice and give more space to the world inside than to the sequences of events. I hope you will like it all dearest B.B.; it is one of the pleasures of the writing to think that you may be reading it.

We spent three days in a tent of the Sheikh of the Hasa – a low tent with lovely sinking lines, like a horse's flanks from the backbone, and made more beautiful than any Surrealist painting by the women's patchwork: their shawls, laces, tinsels, bits of old gowns, chintz from Europe, stripes from Cairo, were all sewn on anyhow with huge coarse stitches, and here and there a sort of Stonehenge of black material stitched on by way of ornament, and huge red cross-stitches wandering aimlessly, as if they had started and then changed their minds. With the bright carpets on the ground and this coloured roof and coloured border too pinned on with twigs of thorn, one felt inside the Tabernacle. The great art of the nomads is to have created a *ritual* out of their casual life: the little brazier hearth, the cheap enamel tea-pot, the lid of an army can carrying tea and sugar, the bazaar glasses: when the host sits down on the ground before it and starts on the long ceremony, the boiling; the pouring out (from as great a height as possible to show his skill); the tasting; the pouring back; a little sugar added; the whole thing all over again; another boiling and this time with a fistful of mint, or another herb they call *mardegusht* thrust in as a flavour – when at last the little glass is offered to the guest it has ceased to be its poor everyday self – it is a sort of triumph over everything material that stands in the human path. Looking at these people and hearing their soft voices so different from the harshness of Arabia, I think of them more and more as Greeks: *mostly* Berber – perhaps 70% – but of what remains, the preponderance is surely Greek and not Arab.

You would have loved to see them galloping their two horses, shooting off an old blunderbuss as they passed us, the young men dressed in the white togas, the horses with silver embroidered pommels, bits and breastplates, full of waywardness, tossing their long manes out of their bright eyes. It was like those French pictures of the Napoleon era – and of course that is just what we are finding here, the East is exactly that condition. When I get to I Tatti we must arrange all for next year – if only the world keeps quiet!

Dearest dear love to you both.

Your own

FREYA

Benghazi

                                                          10 August 1950

My darling Sydney,

How badly you, and everyone else indeed, has been neglected. For weeks now I have said every night as I go to bed, I *must* write to Sydney tomorrow, and then the world has been too much for me. And Benghazi, in the centre of three swamps, is unpleasant in summer, like Barbados intensified. Everything rusts or gets green mould on it. And today there is a south wind from the desert, blustering with dust, and even that manages to be damp. It is tantalising, because if we take a car and go one and a half hours up into the Jebel, the good dry desert air, still scented with thyme, makes us forget all trouble. And we have a secret hope that the Emir may think a summer capital up there desirable.

I was talking to a very good man here, the Minister of Interior, quite young, and said how sad it is to be faced with an apparently endless stretch of insecurity. 'I suppose,' he said, 'it is the natural state of things,' and I realised that anyone living in this country since the Italian war started in 1911 has never known what safety meant till 1945!

Dear love, dear Sydney. Please write to Athens.

                                                          Your loving
                                                          FREYA

Cairo

                                                          18 August 1950

Dearest Stewart,

I came away sadly yesterday – sad sad reasons. It is towards the end of life, so perhaps it doesn't matter. Anyway, Cairo appeared about 9.30 p.m. looking more beautiful than I had ever seen it, a cluster of coloured sequins in the darkness, its ruins and avenues, parks and gardens all made visible by the lights. I am going now to see to all the business and will add later.

                                                          Later

All tickets and hairdresser! Also the address of the Greek grocer is Pechlivanos, Kasr el Nil, and if there is war, I do think it would be a good idea to lay in a store of things like tinned ham, biscuits, pâté, eh? However, don't do it unless you think well of it! The news seems bad and MacArthur's plans about Japan depressing.[100]

[100] President Truman probably took much the same view. General Douglas MacArthur, at this time commanding the U.S. forces in Korea, was removed as a result of disagreement with the President over Far East policy.

I read *Vathek*, very remarkable. Extraordinary *colour* in the writing, and so much *felt*. That last description of Hell, with all walking solitary with their hands on their scorched empty hearts, is really terrible. What in his life could make him know that that is really so?

Most people here on leave. I long to reach that lovely Greek light.

19 August 1950

I have spent the morning in the museum, fascinated by the Greco-Roman and Ptolemaic, now that the background of Cyrene is familiar. It is mostly a shocking grimace after the Egyptian dignity, but suddenly there was a bronze head, nervous, sad, beautiful, a person one *knows*. The portraits are more interesting than anything else, those Tutankhamen women with their lips just closed, those Old Empire cut in stone. When all this has been going on for seven thousand years or so one *can't* think that it much matters what happens to us, only our own personal soul which each has to chisel out alone. That, and nothing else, I believe; that is, with W.P., a faith in the 'ultimate decency'.

Charming Mr. Henderson (who was in the Foreign Legion) took my passport and got me a 'special visa'. I dined there last night, a lovely flat, and pleasant wife and daughter, and easy talk going all round the table and most of the world. He described how he once force-landed in a nudist colony and was extricated and offered a whisky and soda by a butler with nothing on but a napkin over one arm.

I will write from Athens next and hope to find news of you. Hope you are happier all on your own! I felt I was just in the way.

Love anyway,

FREYA

CHARLES RANKIN   Cairo
19 August 1950
Dearest Charles,

So glad to hear of you at last. Here am I, sooner than I had planned, making for Athens and hope to be in Asolo by September 16th. The world looked so gloomy that I thought I must try to be there on the very day the lease is up. I seem to do two things before a war: (1) look at the Acropolis, (2) buy a hat in Paris – so I am keeping to my tour.

I am very exercised about Asolo and it seems silly to wait for war before deciding on a plan. My idea is (a) to get war-work in *Italy* which would

186

leave me free to spend part time in Asolo, and to travel sometimes to Benghazi where I imagine Stewart will continue (not as visionary as it sounds, as my work with those fifty-one little towns in 1945–7 was just of that sort). I assume, you see, that Asolo may be safe and the Mediterranean open. (b) In case of an overrun through or by Jugoslavia, I thought of getting Cici to find a few rooms in a peasant house in the mountains round Dronero: I can't think the Russians would want to venture in those little cul-de-sacs so very unlike the steppe; the people are safe not to go Communist; and there is local timber for warmth, cattle, milk, wool, leather, barley, potatoes, etc. . . . all the essentials. One might be marooned there but not destroyed. If the place were ready, lorries from Asolo could go across with most of our posses-sions in two days. (c) I could then with a quiet mind keep Asolo open and lead the good life till the crisis comes, and then decide whether to send the stuff, to transport the people as well, to go myself or not. Now, dear Charles, be an angel and tell me not in six months' time but *soon* whether you think all this is a good plan or no? And whether you agree that Italy is more useful to be in than Benghazi?

What a difficult world – but after all why shouldn't it be? I can't sympathise with all this wailing over spending on defence. Why not spend on defence? We have revved up production so that a hundredth part of our machinery can make more than what people need – why shouldn't they spend even 50% on so important a thing as being alive. What do we poor women buy at Elizabeth Arden and all except defence (against time, so much more inexorable than Russia)? The whole of life is defence, except love and beauty and the making of beautiful things; and that is not what the wailers about defence are worrying about.

With love, dear Charles,

FREYA

STEWART PEROWNE   Athens[101]

21 August 1950

Darling,

What country except Greece would show itself as mere radiance on the horizon? As we flew over the very blue sea, like an inverted sky, there was suddenly a whiteness; it had no clear line, it was just brightness, and that was the Peloponnesus. I am now on the terrace at Kephyssia, and the sun just

[101] F.S. was the guest of Moore Crosthwaite, now serving (as Counsellor) in Athens with the Foreign Office.

set; Georgette, the maid, came in to call me out to look at the view in the evening light. 'One must wait a few more days for the moon on the Acropolis,' she says. What happiness, to be with people to whom these are the realities – blessed, blessed Greeks. And their little houses are going up all over the place and a look of prosperity on the way up from Piraeus. I hope it is spread about.

I would like to send you half this delicious air, and the feeling of Europe gentle in the sun. Hope for a letter.

Love,
FREYA

Athens
23 August 1950

STEWART PEROWNE

Darling,

Such a pleasant day yesterday. The Nortons[102] have a cottage on a little pine-clothed rocky bay east of Piraeus and Moore uses it when they are away. We took lunch there, there are servants and every comfort. We bathed, lunched, slept, bathed again, and were joined by all the British representatives, Army, Navy, Dominions, etc., whom Moore assembles there instead of in a stuffy office. I do recommend it as an idea for committee meetings! I offered (being the only woman of the party by then) to leave them in their bathing drawers on the rocks, but they seemed to think that too informal, and left me to enjoy the sunset. Piraeus, Salamis, Aegina, Peloponnesus, all in sight. One of them, Colonel Wickham I think, was a D.S.O. of the *Boer* War. He swam much further beyond the shelter of the bay than any of the rest!

24 August 1950

Moore is a great dear, very gentle, considerate, and remote. He sent me out for a lovely drive yesterday through the King's woods over high shoulders of scrub with here and there a big oak, to a shrine to St. Mercury, where one looks over the water to Euboea, like a Lear picture, blues and reds and yellows melting away into the straw-coloured sunlight. It looked and felt like the last lap of the Pilgrim's Progress and I, who have been feeling very lonely, suddenly felt that there is no loneliness ever 'underneath, the everlasting arms'. Strange, how these comforts come.

---

[102] 'The British Ambassador and his wife.

188

I spent last sunset on the Acropolis, looking along the inside of the Parthenon colonnade towards the west. It was as if one were in the heart of a rose, a pink-yellow rose; and then I went on to the Parthenon and looked back and saw the Propylaea fade to dove grey against Hymettus, like dying roseleaves under a strengthening moon. I missed you and thought of you.

I shall be here till the 10th. Am going to Delos on Tuesday to Friday, and then Moore has some leave and will take me to Yannina, and back through Thessaly; and, if we can get it in, a sea-trip to Aegina and Idhra, all places missed before.

This morning I spent wandering over the theatre of Dionysius, so pleasant, with the names on the seats still inscribed, and then to the Herodian theatre, where they were rehearsing a ballet. Extraordinary what a different *feel* in the Greek and Roman theatres.

Love darling. Let me find news at B.B.'s on the 14th.

FREYA

STEWART PEROWNE
Athens
27 August 1950

Darling,

We have just been bathing off the rocks, the sea dark blue and Lady Norton arriving in a white caique with the Red Ensign from a tour of the islands. You would like her, she has turned to a sort of leather, with no worry about looks, but the nicest young blue eyes and evidently doesn't care a damn for anyone. She has now landed and strewed the cottage with Rhodian embroideries, painted peacocks, Wedgwood and Italian plates, and every sort of bric-à-brac collected from the islands. In a few days another eccentric, Mrs. Noel-Baker, is arriving. Moore tells me she spent all last winter marooned in Euboea. Two people got out to her with an escort, but the escort was murdered on the way home. However, she kept the bandits off purely by prestige and turned up in Athens in a large picture hat in the spring when the road became safe. I am longing to meet her.

Yesterday we had a cheerful party down here with Paddy Leigh Fermor and Joan and two young Pallisers – Paddy looking in this wine dark sea *so* like a Hellenistic lesser sea-god of a rather low period, and I do like him: he is the genuine buccaneer. He is writing a book on Greece for Jock.

I can't keep up with all there is to see. Daphne, and back towards the Acropolis in sunset, Hymettus pink and all the little hills and boxlike houses

189

illuminated by heavenly radiance. I am sure the Daphne heads are portraits, they are so individual and strong, but not the splendour of Ravenna.

28 August 1950

Last night was full moon. We spent the day at Cavouri and saw the sun go down and moon come up simultaneous and equally big, across innumerable bays, promontories and islands, and the lights of Piraeus like a tangle of little ribands far away. And, after dinner, came back to see the Acropolis, which is open for three nights at full moon. What a vision! As if it had been steeped in milk, those noble propylaea climbing into a shrine of moonlight. We crept in under the barrier to the little Victory temple and sat there, and the city like a bath of lights below. The moonlight does wonderful things to the caryatids of the Erectheum: they looked out at life and beyond it with a blank grandeur they never have by day, till one felt across the time and space how near the hands were that chiselled them in stone.

I must send this. Am going all alone to Delos tomorrow, and it means two nights at sea with all those choppy little waves. But perhaps Apollo will visit me and touch me with a feather of gold if I sleep on his island. After that Moore will take me to Yannina, rather protesting because I want to visit Missolonghi, Acheron, and Dodona on the way. Today we went to Phyle, a fifth-century B.C. fortress on a height of Parnes where the middle road to Thebes comes down. Thrasybulus watched from the walls of the older fortress and saw Athens with its thirty tyrants far away below as we saw it, sitting on the old walls with the noise of the wind and the pines. The thirty tyrants have been reduced to the mild little man Venizelos, who seemed quite pleased when Moore, obliged to congratulate and yet a truthful man, exerted himself to say, 'Eh bien, Excellence, ça va assez bien?' Some pleasant Embassy people came – all are being so nice and cordial.

Bless you. I do hope to hear more details soon.

Your loving
FREYA

STEWART PEROWNE Athens
31 August 1950

Darling,

I am distressed about the 'flu, so sorry you got it when I was away and no one to look after you, and I hope it didn't run you up to those temperatures that make one feel miserable. I shall hope to hear, and so grateful for your telegram meanwhile. I ought to be writing this from Delos, but I went to Piraeus only to find that the boat had left three hours earlier (these little Greek boats keep to Ulysses' traditions of private enterprise). So we start for Yannina today. We have been having great fun looking it out on maps, and do you know that in one day we hope to include the places of three famous battles, Lepanto, Missolonghi, and Actium? We potter about round the Amvrakian gulf after this evening in Delphi, moonlight I hope on those olive groves of Itea. The waters of Acheron are being drained, so I am hoping to see them before the picture in Homer's mind vanishes forever; and Moore has been calculating roads and distances in a rather dubious way, as it is a singularly roadless bit of country. The whole of Greece is meant for walking really. Luckily he has a Land Rover, and we are taking it from Yannina over to Meteora and Larisa. I was touched because, when I was to sail for Delos, he telephoned to Piraeus all on his own to ask if the sea was rough.

Love

FREYA

STEWART PEROWNE   Agrinion
2 September 1950

Darling,

I have just a few minutes while the car gets itself together, and two packed days to tell you of – Delphi, Lepanto, Missolonghi, the ferry across Achelous to a fortress of the Macedonians. What a *Macédoine* of history, and we began with a visit to Lethe, perhaps the genuine one? A little stream already a bit polluted (and after all Lethe has a lot to pollute it) coming out of a rock at Livadia and winding in a gully by the town, with arched bridges, and little cafés under plane trees, gardens untidy with sunflowers and women washing. I dipped one toe in, as there are a few things I would like to forget, but not many. High above is a ruin, towers and battlement walls, and a cave with steps where the faithful go. What they call it now I don't know, but apparently it was the oracle of Trophonius who told everyone such depressing truths that their faces were melancholy ever after and he became a byword. And we got to Delphi in the last of the sunset by Arakhova, which is one of the most beautifully placed villages in Greece. They are recovering, but it is miserable to see the burnt out ruins in every one of these quiet places, and crosses *filled* with names of the murdered. There is a fine resolute air about all, men and women, and great beauty here and there, and intelligence everywhere.

The moonlight in Delphi! It crept up behind the great rock that rises as if it were an Ascension from the deep olive bowl below. The old pillars of Apollo seemed to grow and become a part of the mountain from which they were cut, and we sat on the theatre steps and looked down on the orchestra flooded in light. It seemed to make a full circle with the bowl of the valley. There is no place I know so numinous as Delphi; I sat wondering what I would ask if the oracle still answered, and thought I would ask what I should feel at the time of my death. And the moon came out of that great blackness and began to peel away the shadows one by one, and I thought the oracle had answered gently, to wait and endure till the darkness is over.

We left and bought food at Amphissa and then drove up and down behind the steep sea-hills by a shocking road, along the River Mornos, fine and big country with patches of corn and high scarce villages, and down at last to Naupactos (Lepanto) which still has a castle and walls all round the town, coming downhill like Asolo, and a little circular walled port full of caiques from Zante loading hay. One wonders *why* the Turks were at Lepanto, not even room for a galley to move freely in the port. We left it at about two, and bathed by the wayside with the mountains of Peloponnesus opposite, and drank coffee in the square of Missolonghi. I am so glad to have seen it: a bleached little town with a strange quiet sad feeling, the houses peeling and the lagoon in front. What surprised me was to see the mountains with lovely healthy country so close and I suppose it is very much drained since Byron's day. It is all mountains and lagoon in this corner of Greece. We left the main road and went west across a lake by a causeway, looking for an old fortress called Oeniadae (last touched by Alexander V of Macedon), and what a time to find it, lost among quiet little villages in roads so deep in dust that we could neither breathe nor see. Here we came on the Achelous, the largest river in Greece, and were ferried across and baked through other even dustier ways and at last reached the nearest village where a man said he would guide us, looked at our car, and rushed away to change from his neat best trousers into a set of rags. The people are so friendly and one can only sometimes tip them without offending; usually it is cigarettes and handshake. And as one gets into remoter places such beautiful human beings appear here and there – the straight Greek features, and the quick eyes and clever nervous hands, all among the shepherds in their poor half-burnt villages, for it is all destruction, Italian, German, and then bandit.

Well, we finally reached our ruin just at sunset, and there were bits of great walls, third century, polygonal and two yards thick, declining down the scrub to a marshy plain with streaks of red sunset on its western watery end, and shepherds in mud huts with their flocks. It gave a feeling of the end of the world, and Acheron quite near, and the ruined town with five miles of wall and a bit of gate and arches and palace and theatre, but nothing else remaining, was like the last Greek effort swamped in the barbarian world. We drove back in darkness through the dust, and crossed what in the light of the headlights looked like ferrying Styx with Charon, and finally about 10.30 reached Agrinion, a dull little town, and went next morning to Arta. Arta itself is down near the swamps, with three old churches in fancy thirteenth-century brickwork. We were taken over them all by a man we met in the street who spent an hour and never thought of being paid.

After lunch with all the market people in a pub on the square we left. A lovely Epirote, sitting just behind me, attracted Moore, until she spat on the floor and wiped her mouth on the tablecloth, but after all one can't have *everything*. Her husband never said one word to her, and apparently it isn't done to speak to your wife in public. They wear two long plaits down their back, with only the ends showing under a black kerchief; but up here you still see the old high-waisted dress and little Turkish embroidered jacket, and the shepherds in black jodhpurs with a jaunty little cap on one side, and their coat worn over one shoulder, which gives it an air.

We deviated again at Arta. We have been almost all round the huge Amvrakian gulf, and at its very tip in the north-west is the promontory of Actium and the town Augustus built to commemorate the victory. Its walls are still there, with beautiful Roman brickwork and gates every 100 yards or so in sets of three and one, with steps going up on each side of each group and a ruined battlement, where I suppose one could walk. There is a theatre, ruined and overgrown, and a palace; and from the top one sees both sea and gulf and the wild mountains and views made all of blues and jade-green pasture and swamp, and cloud from the steamy lowlands rising to all the wild north.

When we left it, I still wanted to reach the shores of Acheron, but the man at Arta had assured us that the Sacred Lake was close on our road, to be reached through the grounds of a children's summer school. This seemed improbable both for geography and psychology, but Moore was delighted with anything that saved us from exploring the northern swamps in the late afternoon; so we found the children's school, and there was the Sacred Lake, and it certainly looked as if Charon could be expected at any moment. It was dark dark green, with a blind sort of light, only on and not in the water, and a little wind that lived only on the lake and made its little dead waves and a whisper of reeds all round it, growing out of deep water. The hill was high and steep all around, and behind the hill another farther and higher skyline, and the sunset sky and a cold remoteness.

We reached Yannina in cold and rain, the people all warmly dressed in frieze and the houses with eaves, and a northern look. A little Turkish town with painted woodwork and the old fort standing out into the lake and two mosques, one at each end, with pencil minarets, up one of which we climbed to see the view. We spent an afternoon going over a very rough track to the valley to the north where the ruins of Dodona are spread all over a low hill. A huge theatre stands there, its stones tumbled about like spillikins by earthquakes, and the whole place has scarcely been touched. It is so remote it wasn't even discovered till last century when an Englishman told a man in Yannina where to look and there he found it, the huge theatre in the lonely pleasant valley, with villages, now half burned by the bandits, under trees.

It is so touching to see this people building itself up again, always being knocked down, and still cheerful, interested and alive. If one had to describe the look of all these peasants, from the tiniest little girl upwards, I would choose the word 'resoluteness'. They all have it, and perhaps it is what our people have neglected for the last fifty years or so? Anyway, it is a fine thing to see on the faces you pass, and makes you feel that the world can recover, whatever may happen.

Next day we left and did an arduous nine hours' drive over Pindus by a road where even the Land Rover threatened to stick in the shady turns where the mud lies. There is plenty of going and coming of soldiers however, all very well dressed in American kit and looking as if they meant business. It was a moving sight to see them with their band marching through Yannina, with their steel helmets and bayonets, yet looking so very like the young men of their friezes, 2,500 years ago. They are all out in the hills looking for eighteen Albanian agitators who have crept in, and the Pindus is the only northern road from west to east. We climbed up by steep tilted corn-patches to the pine trees and Metzova, the highest village, and then down by beech trees and pines and slopes (I think) of myrtle to Peneius, which the guide book calls 'a river in Thessaly'. That little sentence seems to me to hold the essence of Romance, and what a valley, open and smiling, with the rocks of Meteora at its opening in the plain. They are hideous, with sub-human likenesses, like things imagined by Dali. I wondered why there are no Greek legends about them and we noticed that the Greeks did not like the monstrous, contorted, *diseased* imaginings like the barbarians. Even their pictures of Hell have a decent humanity about them. Incidentally, when we reached Larisa and read about it, we discovered it to be the place where Perseus killed his grandfather, and that when carrying the Gorgon's head across Libya the blood that fell from it turned into snakes which are still there. And one drop turned into Pegasus who flew straight up into the air to Helicon.

It poured with rain in Larisa. The poor little town was shattered by earthquakes in 1941 and the Italians then instantly bombed it, and it is still very much like Benghazi though more cheerful. A little hotel trying to pick itself up out of the débris and the café and restaurant carrying on cheerfully in the *piazza*. We came back in pouring rainstorms, over six passes to Athens. What a country it is. If you ironed it out flat it would be quite huge. As it is, these five days took us over 1,400 kilometres as varied and lovely as any on earth.

Darling, a packet of mail with two letters from you – so distressed at all you tell me, your 'flu, the P.M., etc. I am only thankful that you will be coming away in a day or two after this reaches you. I think it will be all right if you go slow and steady. There is nothing in this world so expensive as sitting on platforms. The trouble of your life is that you happen to enjoy it, and there is a prejudice in England against people who enjoy it, and fundamentally a right prejudice. There was bound to be difficulty with the P.M., but you have to remember that he, too, likes to sit on the platform and that, unlike you, he has less other capacities to rely on. You can look upon anything that hurts *your* vanity as a godsend, for it can release things in you so infinitely better, but he hasn't got them, so that this is all he has. I hate to think of it all happening as soon as I left.

I go to Delos tomorrow, will write, and after that wait for your coming.

FREYA

SIR SYDNEY COCKERELL
Delos
9 September 1950

Darling Sydney,

This is a far place from which to write to you, far from us all today but so near to the heart of everything. One feels a sort of exultation in its cleanness: sun and air, the soundless wind with no trees but only marble columns to stop it; the sea, sapphire blue with white waves on one side and golden ridges on the other, and tumbling over rocks; a handful of tiny scattered houses, a few sheep, cows, fowls, and turkeys browsing on stubble-fields enclosed in stony walls; and a caique and two fishing boats by a shingly spit where the sacred processions landed. All around are the other Cyclades in a circle, and one can see why the Greeks made Delos holy, with their instinct for the drama in landscape. It is like the cup in the middle of the altar, lifting its small tumbled hill of stones, where a very old holy place with roof of great slabs taken from the hillside shows something that the earliest Greeks already found existing.

I am sure that a hard time is before us, and it is a comfort to come here among the island people and see them free and happy, with their lovely strong walk and careless courtesy, the beauty so frequent and the intelligence universal, and to see that this has carried them through everything and brought them out safe and vital through thousands of years and wars. They have a strength of a tradition to which they can hold, and of course an island does make it easier, and that perhaps is our English blessing too.

I stopped in Mykonos, and there is a little whitewashed town tumbling downhill like a waterfall, half oriental in its details of chimney and trellis-work over doors, and with classical columns standing at unexpected corners. Here it is all ruins, dug out by the French, and the whole roofless town is clear with its flagged narrow streets and marble door-frames and windows leading to mosaic courts with pillars. They have found a house with stairs, and it is growing more modern with every new discovery.

So glad you have seen the plan of the book and approve. I will alter the introduction in agreement with what you say – in fact, am revising all the introductions as soon as I get home. I have taken a complete rest here, if such a journey can be called rest. But it was glorious and I am glad to have done it. Delphi, the grey columns in the moonlight, will be a memory for ever, and so will much else.

Love, dearest Sydney,

Your

FREYA

STEWART PEROWNE Mykonos

10 September 1950

Darling,

It is surprising what a lot I can talk about with twenty words of Greek. I discussed all the meals with my landlady, got safely off Delos with three changes of time for the boat, and promised to return next year with you for a long stay of a week. But what beastly manners the French have! I came with a letter from their own Ambassador, telling them to be particularly nice to me. Their School is all there is on the island that talks anything but Greek. And I sent my letter at once. Monsieur went off in a few hours without a word for Athens (having five young men to send round). I met one of them, and asked, and he rebuffed me as if I were asking for gin out of hours.

11 September 1950

Just reached Athens and horrified to get yours of the 1st and news of relapse. Am telegraphing to ask if you won't come to Asolo direct; you do need to do something *different*, not people and lectures, to get a rest – just unwind in the garden. Do think of it. I do hope for better news. Love darling,

FREYA

LADY RUTHVEN
Athens
11 September 1950

Darling Pam,

Your letter has just reached me, very sad news no Pam and godson this autumn. But please keep to April or May, only not at Benghazi but Asolo. I mean to do all I possibly can to see my tulips next year, never yet seen since planted in 1946!

I am now back from Delos, which is far more difficult to reach from here than London and took me from 8 a.m. one day to 4 a.m. the next, beginning in a gay little boat shipping buckets of sea, and ending in a Greek steamer with all the cabins full and seats taken but a quiet warm night and everyone matey. The faces are such fun to watch, lots of classic profiles in the island, the round chin just inclined to be heavy and going Hellenistic instead of classic as it gets older, and the earlier Minoan type with the straight thrust-out nose and firm mouth. They are a wonderful people, so close-bound each in his island, so sure of themselves and free. As for Delos, it is tiny, one can go over it in a morning. The ruins lie at one end glistening white in the sun, and there are scarce any inhabitants. But it has such a feeling of cleanness, gaiety, and peace. I would love to spend a month there. Why don't we one year? The boys would love it and learn all about sailing. Even I could swim to the next island in water as blue as gentian and the inn came to £1 a day.

Love,
FREYA

JOHN GREY MURRAY   Asolo

                                                      22 September 1950

Dearest Jock,

Just arrived with Stewart last night and must use this paper to say how
beautiful the *Prelude* is. It really is superb: pictures, engravings, print, paper
and all. I only hope the contract is up to it!

Will write when a little of all the mountain here is cleared.

Love and congratulations,

                                                                FREYA

JOHN GREY MURRAY   Asolo

                                                        2 October 1950

Dearest Jock,

Lovely arrival of telegram with breakfast in bed – so exciting and I hope
for reviews soon. Are you tasting wine somewhere? I have taken a room at
Metropolitan for November 24th–25th; till you come am going to Diana at
Chantilly.

I am working like a slave. Lavender Wilson is here for a week and
angelically typing and here is Chapter 1 meanwhile. I hope to get them done
in time, but John Miller is here writing *his* book (good I think); Lavender
just arrived; Cici and baby arriving tomorrow and contemplating separation
from Franco, the carpenter planning redoing all our windows, the architect
planning double front door and porch, painter doing the shutters, Venini
coming for weekend. What chance has Literature?

Love dear Jock and thanks for your dear and constant affection. One must
say this when a book comes out. Would you like this book to be dedicated
to you?

                                                                FREYA

SIR SYDNEY COCKERELL   Asolo

                                                       10 October 1950

My dearest Sydney,

It is good to hear from you and to know that *Traveller's Prelude* goes on
giving you pleasure. I am waiting for the reviews, and hoping that Osbert
Sitwell has not put us too much in the shade! But Christopher Sykes has

written me such a heartfelt and glowing letter and tells me he has written a review and this is more than any other regard – the praise of one's fellow-craftsmen.

I am busy with Volume II and hope to get most of it settled with Jock in Paris, and then to spend the winter over III, so you should read them all, anyway in ms., in 1951. It is hard to fit in all there is to do in these few weeks, and Asolo so lovely, one would like to spend all the time in the garden and walking about the little hills. We have had the house full, and have been both to Venice and Ravenna. We motored, lunched at Arqua and saw the little study where Petrarch wrote, with a quiet view of the hills. I like seeing the places where things were produced, so much of them *must* have gone into the works that were created. One feels it very much in that little house and garden. Then we passed by Ferrara and looked at Schifanoia and reached Ravenna and spent the next day there, the morning with mosaics and the afternoon in the *pineta*, full of blue shadows with the tops of the flat pines floating above them as if it were a thin sea of air. We followed the broad canal to its winding through rice flats to the sandy shore, a desolate landscape with only here and there a sad house in trees, and little fishing huts like the lake houses of neolithic men, on poles in the stream with shallow nets held open at the four corners and resting empty and suspended on wire cords over the middle of the stream. These things went all along the open canal almost to its mouth and were more lonely than any solitude of nature, with the deepening twilight and last light catching patches of swamps here and there, and, as we neared the coast, sand-dunes covered with evening primroses opening like stars.

Ravenna has a Communistic municipality, but the people all looked like anyone else, prosperous, gay, friendly, and polite. I think that these mid-Italian towns revive their ancient republican independent feeling and call it Communism. One must go very cautiously with these generic names!

Your affectionate

FREYA

STEWART PEROWNE Asolo

15 October 1950

Darling,

I waited to write yesterday till some little word might appear, but only a card has come, with no life-giving words upon it, so I shall keep this till I return from Venice and find a budget I hope.

I spent two domestic days doing all the dull things, linen cupboard, stores, visits from the old Asolani including poor Monsignore with a swollen tooth. He was so pathetic, so old and alone and always worried by parishioners. His door is open and anyone walks in and I offered to write a notice for him to hang up and say he was ill. He was wrapping an old black wool round his face, and I longed to do it for him and felt he would so like some kind arms round his poor old neck, but there he is, near eighty, and I suppose it will soon be over, and he safe with someone who is better at loving than we are.

17 October 1950

I found Harry Luke here (this is Venice), looking like a wisp, all his little tummy and cheeks melted away. I am sure sitting still in Asolo will be good for him, he has a sad little pining look, like a baby. Then Nigel and Marie arrived, very nice to see them, with twenty-six trunks and packages. Nigel is going on to find a house and get it furnished while Marie stays in Greece – a wonderful arrangement I thought. He is not at all pleased to be going to Baghdad.

Lovely reviews: Christopher Sykes in *Observer*, Raymond Mortimer in *Sunday Times*, portrait now in *S.T.*, couldn't all be kinder. Only hope it sells.

I miss you, and now there are lots of places in Venice where I think of you.

Love,
FREYA

JOHN GREY MURRAY
Asolo
19 October 1950

Dearest Jock,

Such a sudden world this is. A telegram from Esther Wright says *imperative* to see me London; it is sure to be something to do with Stewart, Benghazi, etc., so I must make it (and only hope I can get him to refund me the fare!). I thought I would fly by the night aeroplane on November 1st, which only costs £10 return; if no, go back with you, which I fear is more expensive. Am packing now.

Love,
FREYA

Asolo
                                                              22 October 1950

Darling,

Last letter from Asolo and very glad to get yours yesterday and to hear
that you found all welcoming. I long to hear about Benghazi. Am very
vexed at having to go to London, but it will be helpful to take you the news
from inside I hope. Darling of course I won't find Benghazi 'bleak' so long
as you are not bleak! The climate is made inside the house.

Something that touched me was said by my hairdresser who, you know,
has ruined her life for our one Communist, a revolting man who will never
marry her and whom she adores. We were talking about all her troubles and
I said, 'Well, you mustn't mind too much, one is only beginning here, and
there is a much greater life beyond.' 'Ah Signora,' she said, 'I shall have so
much to suffer when I get there.' I can't believe that one can ever be
punished for loving so much that one consciously accepts the penalty of Hell
at the end of it and that is what the poor woman does. I suddenly found
myself with tears and tried to undermine Monsignore by telling her that I
couldn't believe in a Padre Eterno worse than my own father, who would
certainly forgive.

No other news except much love. I miss you.

                                                              Your
                                                              FREYA

Benghazi
                                                              11 November 1950

Darling B.B. and Nicky,

Thoughts and thanks have been going towards you, and with them there
is a general thankfulness for the happiness of finding you well. Do keep so,
darling B.B., so that I may find you flourishing in March. It was a short
glimpse, but it is extraordinary how little time counts: one's whole life seems
to be divided into long quiet times of preparation and then something or
other flowers and gathers it all. I always feel I Tatti as a gathering together
of this sort.

We flew to Malta and then on in beautiful clear weather. I have never
seen such gay clouds: they were tossing their heads and looked like those
angels with lots of drapery floating around them, dancing on the floor of the
sea – and that was white and hard and stippled with little ridges, as if cut in
metal. The Greeks said that Ixion fell in love with Juno and was given a

cloud to embrace in her likeness and from it the centaurs were born – and one could see how the Greeks saw the centaurs with tossing manes in the sea-clouds.

We found Stewart very well, and the house with two pleasant tough Arabs instead of the Sudanese. Two Sheikhs came to tea, and all are hoping for rain: the land is all yellow and empty and burnt. What a terrific difference between the two coasts of this sea.

Love from us all,

FREYA

JOHN GREY MURRAY   Benghazi
                                                          25 November 1950
Dearest Jock,

It seems a long time without news, and I let every day pass hoping to find a letter in the mail. Am also still very tied up with servants: there was a tribesman with turned-up mustachios who took all the tea and sugar and has walked off and not been seen again – and now we have two who don't know more than rudiments and those on good days only, but seem to have nice natures. We rose yesterday to a dinner to the Resident and his wife with the quarter of a sucking pig which was sent out to the Barbary Club to be cooked and rushed here across the harbour in time for dinner. I insisted on good Burgundy, and the pig was beautifully cooked, so we are all resting on our laurels today.

I haven't *looked* at the mss. since Paris, but hope to get started next week. The house seems to be watertight and the garden is nearly planted. We have five little olive trees; some day, when we are long forgotten here, I hope they may make a nice little walled patch of shade.

I spent a pleasant hour with the Emir's wife, looking at her treasured albums – photographs of the Emir in shorts playing golf at Gezirah, and punts on the Thames near Oxford. What strange little miniatures float in and out of our lives!

Have you read Duff Cooper's novel?[103] I was much moved by it. The whole of our (my) generation is in it, that went to die so innocently in 1914. I can so well remember the fear that the war might be over before I got into it.

Love dear Jock,

FREYA

[103] *Operation Heartbreak.*

Benghazi
                                                    25 November 1950

My dearest Sydney,

Do you get out to see your friends in Kew Gardens, and would you ask
them a question for us? We are very anxious to know more about the ancient
main export of Cyrenaica, a medicinal plant called *sylphium*, which our
Herodotus says casually in a footnote, is *asaphoetida*. Is it? Does Kew know
anything about it, and could one, if it is *asaphoetida*, lay one's hand on a
picture of that plant?

We have just spent three pleasant days in Cyrene. There is a government
rest-house, where one sits round a good fire of cypress and sees the sea below,
beyond the ledge of the first escarpment which is about 900, and Cyrene
1,800 feet. One feels as if one leant out of a great balcony, and the sea fills at
sunset with streaks and patterns of lemon-coloured light. The highland that
catches the rain already has millions of tiny green spikes out of its red earth,
like the thin hair on a baby's head, and the sheep are so greedy for these
tiny grasses, their heads are down to the ground all day long. In the shelter
of thorns and in stone pockets hard to reach, cyclamen and small starlike
scented narcissus are in flower, and the sea is cobalt and full of sun as if it
were summer, though really the wind has a little icy shiver that makes it
very treacherous. We took Harry Luke, who is staying with us, to Tolmeita
yesterday and thought to come back by the old Turkish road that climbs the
plateau under juniper trees and looks back from its grassy stony zigzags to
the sea between two hills. When we got half way up we found a huge hole
and thought an unsuspected mine must have exploded. We had a little hoe
for digging up plants, and smoothed a way up the side, only to find a tree
trunk laid across a little farther on. We pulled this aside with some labour
and then reached two deep trenches blown up across the top of the pass and
spent the last hours before sunset filling in the first, where the car stuck. So
there we were, luckily with the remains of a sucking pig for supper and I left
Stewart and Harry and went up to find help and walked for an hour across
the plateau fading wild like a moor with yellow sunset into the night.

I came to a house in the last light, but the people are afraid and don't
leave the shelter of their walls if one calls. The little Italian houses have their
windows bricked up and their doors stuffed with thorns, and you can only
come upon a little glimmering fire and lantern on the ground if you walk
round to the back. This I did and found only a woman and two children at
home, the men all away 'at the ploughing'. So I went on again, and it was
full night with only the cry of a bird now and then and when I came to the
next houses I realised that the dogs would tear me up before I could get

round to the back. They are fierce at night and used to attack, so I went on till I came to one little house with a light in front and made for it. The dogs rushed out snarling to within a yard of me, but a woman came out and called them off. And there inside were two strong men on a mat on the floor eating their mess of supper out of a wooden basin together with the son of the house, aged five, while all the women and daughters sat around. I told our story and they promised to help, and I waited while they finished eating and then still waited, 'for bakshish' they said. I thought this an effort at blackmail taught by the Italians, so said severely that my husband would provide the bakshish in good time. But it was for and not from me that they wanted it. A great rummaging had been going on among the women, and at last three hard-boiled eggs were pressed into my hand (and very welcome they were).

We then set out, I and three men with picks and shovels, and they strode along at a terrific pace, back for an hour to the car and dug it out while I sat with Harry by a fire. We thought it rather hard that one of our very few roads, which was built by the Turks and survived forty years of wars, should be blown up by the British army merely for exercise, and there is going to be a fuss about it and they will jolly well have to mend it. 'Britain can break it' Stewart thinks of as a motto for the Sappers.

Love,
FREYA

JOHN GREY MURRAY Benghazi
29 November 1950

Dearest Jock,

Such a long time without news of you: was it that week in Paris – too strenuous? – or have you come back unable to write without a *coupe de champagne* every two hours? I meanwhile have the most ridiculous piece of news to give you: I am to be made an Hon. Doctor of Laws by Glasgow University. Did you ever hear anything more exhilarating? So many laws I have broken. It is just what happens to those young men in the *Arabian Nights* and delightful to find in real life – and will take place in June next year. You become it without a lecture, but only a hat and gown to buy which of course is pure pleasure.

As well as this excitement is the enclosed proposal to make a film of Luristan. I have written to say that I should love to see my books filmed but that *you* decide all these matters.

I am sending Robert Byron's *Byzantium*. What a first rate book: I think the analysis of the Greeks in his first chapter is masterly. What a pity he died, and stopped writing anyway in the welter of war.

Love dear Jock,

FREYA

BERNARD BERENSON Benghazi
6 December 1950

Darling B.B.,

So many days gone by without writing. I came and found a nice cook, full of goodwill but no cookery: and a sort of minor Byron of a parlour-boy, with twirling mustachios and a gay way with life – but not domestic. Since then a second parlour-boy has come and gone, brown ebony from the Fezzan who told me he got drunk 'only on holiday' and said his luck was bad. 'Well,' said I reasonably, 'you might make it better by working a little?' 'Perhaps,' he said, and added 'but perhaps I am lazy.' We now have a nice earnest young Berber, and I am teaching him from the beginning and hope to be settled in time. It is frustrating to have to devote so much time and energy to mere *living*, the mechanical parts of it I mean. I have done seven pages of Volume III in all this month, and that is all. I hope that you have got the *Prelude* by now?

Our King[104] is not yet really made, but everyone behaves as if he were and the buses have new flags with a red stripe not nearly as smart as the former black and white but I dare not say so as Stewart helped to invent it. We went last night to leave a letter at his palace out in the country, and there was an inscription of congratulation over the door in electric lights. I hope it may end happily for him: he is gentle and benevolent, and yesterday in the afternoon, as I was coming home from my walk, I met his outrider, and grand red car behind, and police jeep behind that – and he and his Emira were having a quiet little country drive together side by side. It is rather unusual and pleasant to see that in a Muslim land.

When you were here did you go to see the (wrongly called) River of Lethe? It flows under the limestone floor through 'caverns measureless to man' and a zigzag of steps go down through slanting shafts of sun into a huge shadowy cavern where fifty Americans were trapped during the war. They lived for weeks and finally surrendered, and their gear, bits of iron, wheels, etc., lie strewn about in the water, shallow and muddy, where blind crayfish move about rather terribly – they are so pale, turquoise-colour, and fleshless with rectangular joints, and move very slowly feeling the ground,

---

[104] The Emir was to be King of Libya.

without eyes, and with a spinsterish frustrated horridness about them. I suppose one might be like that if one lived in Lethe in the dark.

Darling B.B. I hope for lovely days with you in March. Keep well and get no colds through the winter. Here a cold blast is coming in from the desert south, but narcissus and crocus and cyclamen are out among the rocks. Stewart sends love – so do I, always, every day, to dear Nicky too – and Christmas thoughts.

Your

FREYA

Benghazi

9 December 1950

JOHN GREY MURRAY

Dearest Jock,

I am in a bog of servants and royalty mixed. I thought a party for the Emira to meet the British ladies and her own Ministers' wives was demanded by Conscience. What a mistake to listen! Fifty little notes were written by hand (mine); waiters found, milk ordered, a whole morning spent looking for chocolate; cakes, eggs, etc. etc.; the evening before it all was to happen, a casual remark from the Emir to the Resident who happened to be calling, told us that she was in bed with chill on liver – and everyone had to be put off. The cakes distributed among orphans – and now she says she is coming on Monday and all is to do over again. So your first chapter is only at page eight.

We are going for Xmas to Derna.

Love dear Jock,

FREYA

Benghazi

10 December 1950

LADY CHOLMONDELEY

My dearest Sybil,

Your book delighted me on my journey: it seemed to me to put the Institutionalists just where they belong – and surely it is time that the difference between charity and philanthropy were understood. I think a lot of the trouble is due to the prudery that glossed over the fact that the word charity and love are the same – and the things the same too – and so that cold horror of philanthropy crept in?

We have been hunting foxes this morning on the Barce plain. It is sixty miles away and we go and sleep there, get out at seven, and come back to lunch here, and the 16th Lancers who run the pack gave me a well-trained English horse. It is twenty years since I hunted (and then very rarely) and I am frightened all the time, and *very* insecure – and one misses the smells of the English grass and bracken under dew. Even the foxes seemed to be practically scentless – we saw them, and they just melted away. But it was good to see the hounds swishing along with wagging white tail-tips, and the horses full of fun, and the variety of the land, and also a rather nice *English* feeling of being all together doing something we like, and not just looking after people who are saying things about us.

There are crowns, flags, speeches, Constitutions flying about here and I have the Emira to tea tomorrow to meet fifty English ladies and no one knows whether to curtsey or not. No one quite knows, I believe, how much or how little this Three in One is to hang together either: the Cyrenaicans, being compact, comfortable and with no minorities are not anxious to join themselves too closely to anyone.

A happy Christmas dear Sybil to you both from us both – and very much affection.

FREYA

BERNARD BERENSON   Benghazi
                                                Christmas Day 1950

Darling B.B.,

Your letter like a little dewdrop, brought to my room where I am spending a hermit Christmas – for the stirrup broke and I fell on my head out hunting (*after* the hunt too, while cantering home). Very annoying as it will be six weeks before I can get at my book again.

I am glad of what you say about the *Prelude*: I feared you might think it *all* too like a chronicle. But as you see, there were too many people intimately involved in my life, so that it was all walking on eggs to write about – and so strangely dramatic that I felt there was no dealing with it except by distilling down as it were to the most essential narrative I could. The next volume is in Jock's hands, and I hope you will like it – for there I have dealt with the narrative part by letters of the time and prefaced them with a *contemplative* introduction to every chapter, so as to make a sort of orchestra of bass and treble.

Must not write more darling B.B. except to send you and dear Nicky constant love.

Your
FREYA

Benghazi
21 January 1951

Dearest Sydney,

Only a little note with my love as I am still using my eyes very sparingly. The animal we were hunting was a fox. They are large, grey, and *very* swift so that they outdistance the hounds when running in sight. It was rather touching to be joined by one of the pye dogs who led our hounds and took the greatest part in the enjoyment of it all. A Beduin also hastened to saddle his shaggy little beast with a silver pommelled saddle, to enjoy himself with us.

Love dear Sydney,

FREYA

BERNARD BERENSON Benghazi
29 January 1951

Darling B.B.,

I am getting on so slowly with my poor head that I think of leaving earlier for Asolo than first planned. Would you have me for a week on the way up from Rome about March 4th or 5th? The wind is blowing icily, from the Sahara and the Alps alternately, and the world is not nearly so warm as it looks in the bright sun. But there is a beginning of green, lovely, bright, and soft, and the first flowers, and all the asphodel. What an *elegant* flower.

Dear dear love to you and Nicky,

FREYA

STEWART PEROWNE Rome
9 March 1951

Dearest Stewart,

Such a busy time after the leisure of Benina. A hasty but pleasant hour in Tripoli and a bad arrival at Malta. It was also rough, and hours late, and we reached Naples in fog and Rome in a downpour, and it is still cloudy. But such beautiful municipal planning as makes me think pathetically of you struggling in Benghazi. The little beds on the boulevards all bursting into daffodils and hyacinths, and tidy green grass outside the station round the walls of Severus.

It is gentle to be with Lolette,[105] in the old familiar *mélange* of poverty

---

[105] sc. Biancheri. The family had been neighbours at Mortola.

and splendour: tea out of the china that was made by the Imperial factory in Petersburg, and the plumbing all anyhow, but with great and kind efforts a bath emerges. And Della Torretta,[106] the most charming old Sicilian ex-ambassador, comes and sits in the evening over the bedroom stove, so much more cosy than the very forbidding Louis XV drawing room.

Bless you, dear Stewart. I long to hear how the domestic situation goes; well, I hope, for they will have only entertaining and *no cleaning*.

Love,

FREYA

STEWART PEROWNE

I Tatti,
Settignano
14 March 1951

Darling Stewart,

I am going to an oculist today, but the head is much better and only returns once every three or four days to torment me. We have had two lovely quiet days, and the sun came out and B.B. and I took the car high up beyond Vincigliata, with Fiesole in sight on its ridge, and walked down among red oak trees and pines and cypress and sharp deep edges against the sky, and little streams trickling down under the brown leaves; and B.B. told me about his youth, and how he met his wife (who must have been a terror, a *devourer*) and then how Nicky came. It is like a great panorama to talk to him, with all the expanse of his eighty-seven years before him.

Tomorrow Marina arrives, so there will be a sort of hurricane of activity. I really long to reach Asolo, and look with anxiety at every daffodil here that goes over, wondering if I shall be too late for them there.

Bless you, I hope for a letter soon.

Your

FREYA

STEWART PEROWNE

Asolo
19 March 1951

My darling,

Things are so sad and superficial between us that I have long been feeling that they cannot go on as they were and have only waited to write or speak

[106] Lolette Biancheri's stepfather, the Marchese Della Torretta.

because I could not bear you to think that any trivial cause, or want of affection, made me do it; and also because I hoped that you yourself might feel this thing so near your heart as to make you speak before I left.

I don't know whose the fault, anyway it doesn't matter. If it were just that the thing has failed, it would be simple. We are both independent, and we could separate and go back to where we were. I do care for you, but I have tried to take myself out of this account and to think of the whole thing without any bias as far as I can; one of these days I believe you will discover that you do care.

Let it be friendship meanwhile, and not just acquaintance. Half a dozen people around us tell me their hearts more intimately than you do. Better just to come and go as friends and that I will always be. There is nothing but true affection in my heart.

I have kept this for a day before sending, feeling perhaps that I might not send it at all, but there *must* be a truth between us, and it is the truth. Let it not make any difference to what we are to each other, such dear friends, and with true and safe affection, let it only take away what there was of pretence. I long for you to come here and you know it is your true home.

Love,

FREYA

BERNARD BERENSON
Asolo
19 March 1951

B.B. darling,

The happy days, how swiftly they go. Thank you always, so much more deeply than I can say. I Tatti mean happiness to me, and not the happiness that so many have, only recognised when it is over.

I have written to Stewart and sent it, with a pang, making it as gentle as I could and leaving every door wide open except that of going on as we were. Now that it is done, I feel how necessary it was: a lie that one goes on living is like a working poison.

I have just been reading the letters of Synesius together with Hodgkin – fascinating it all is: the descriptions in Synesius make the history so vivid – his apologies for not being able to send oil to his friends in Egypt because the ships were afraid to put in to Cyrenaican ports, etc. . .

Very dear and grateful love,

FREYA

Darling,

I have sent you a sad letter, which I had to do, and now I am glad it has
gone and I will think of it no more, but await your coming with happiness,
glad of whatever we can gather from ourselves and our years. Bless you,
darling, however it may be.

I was so glad to have a letter at last, and to hear of the Jebel, of course
lovely to see with Steven[107] like a torch beside you. His *Synesius* is here and
a delight. All sorts of things come to life in the letters: the people in the farms
being murdered and only the people in the towns surviving; the brutal
fisherman from Benghazi who came to power and introduced thumbscrews,
etc.; the fact of silphium, far from being extinct, being grown in his brother's
garden. You will revel in the book. That and Hodgkin are keeping me right
out of this century yet almost as much *au fait* as if I were reading the newspapers today.

It *is* a rest here with Emma and Maria and the house shining in every
corner! Today it is fine for the first time. The beauty is ineffable, almost
unbelievable, the blossom drifts in pale clouds over the little hills which are
green and *luminous*, and mists filled with sunlight play about the plain like
those little wreaths of angels the painter saw. This morning I spent in the
garden verifying the new tulips and iris, all pushing up happily. The
magnolia buds are fattening and the little fruit trees I planted three years ago
along the grassy path are like little candlesticks with lights against the landscape of Bassano and its hills. Reginato came and we measured out the new
terrace and talked over the design of the glass door which he is to do to
scale. Alas, I am going to be poor and in debt again, but no doubt Volume II
will come to the rescue. So glad you like it.

Just this minute a letter from Jock about *Spilt Milk*.[108] He isn't at all too
discouraging. Of course, I believe you thought of getting by with much less
hard work than is necessary. The lighter the work, the more polish it requires, like the shine on shoes, and possibly when you look at it now you will
see places that can be pulled together. I long to hear what Jock said to you
about it. He is very cautious, so I think it is not at all a discouraging verdict,
though evidently, like most authors, you must sweat over it a bit. That is the
real hardness of writing, the *hatred* one feels for one's work before the end.

                                                          Love,
                                                        FREYA

[107] sc. Runciman.
[108] An unfinished story.

21 March 1951

Darling,

The foundations of the Babylonian terraces are being dug in the garden. It is ruinous, but very exciting, and I have been spending my time going round to see what is still alive (quite a lot, apart from the daffodils which Checchi says he watered to death). It is going to be so exciting to see one thing after another come out. This year the clematis sown three years ago has flowered, huge white canopies hang at the corner of the house and I will try to trail them over the old archway to make a lovely entrance to the town.

The proofs have come. Thank you for this promptitude. You will always have to read my proofs, you are the only person whose alterations of punctuation I can ever accept and the only one whose corrections of text I would be disposed to take on trust. I have incorporated all you suggest except two trifling ones, and have sent the whole book to Jock (at cost of a hideous headache yesterday). Today I am pulling out Volume III, but doubtful if I can yet do anything in the nature of work.

Love,

FREYA

STEWART PEROWNE   Asolo
24 March 1951

Darling,

I wish you had been the procession last night. The tail was just beginning at the church door when the head came back, and nearly all men. They had no banners and gaiety of course, only a dark crucifix with spear, hammer, etc., but all the houses were lit up with little oil wicks or candles. Ours were on the spikes of the railing and made a huge crucifix of candles so that we had by far the most ostentatious illumination; but the nicest was the little back street where snail shells had been filled with oil and a tiny wick, and put into the crannies of the wall. It was very touching to see, all down our street, the people's figures bent over in the night at their windows, lighting those humble little lights that must have gone on for thousands of years, certainly more years than the Christian.

The Santini gardener came and promises to plant poplar trees to screen the nuns opposite. What a blessing I came back in time; after next month would be too late and we would have to look at that blank wall for the rest of our life.

Love,

FREYA

Asolo
31 March 1951

Darling,

So glad to get a letter at last; they do take a time, *more* than from Barbados which doesn't seem reasonable. What a day yesterday. We went to lunch at last to some persistent neighbours (Fascist, but so silly that it doesn't matter). We stepped into an immense palace filled with ancestors and brocades, and there, moving about among vermouth and chairs, were the ancestors themselves, all bent, shrunk and out of drawings, a collection of antiques you *never* saw: the Baron in green cloth waistcoat and side whiskers with eyes that looked as if they were loose like a rather old doll's; his ancient sister with what they call a *toupet* of neat false hair just like the green stuff in which the daffodils were stuck on the dining table (only grey of course); the old Mama, bent to a right-angle and toothless, but full of fun and with a *toupet* less tidy but being mouse colour more dashing; a middle-aged relative nondescript; and the hostess herself playing and singing *Kiss Me Kate* in English at the piano. It was wonderful, you would have loved it, Proust or Balzac dried up and preserved and almost inconceivable in the modern world.

After lunch we were taken first to a room of stuffed birds and then to an eighteenth-century children's room with a small beautifully rococo merry-go-round for four, two horses and two chairs; a little theatre, Palladian and about three feet high; a glass case with Tantalus inside (you fill it with water to his neck and then he moves his tongue and eyes because he can't reach it); a lion's head that moved its eyes and mouth from side to side and roared; and the most haunting pictures of human profiles entirely made up one of fruits, one of fishes, one of animals, and one of human beings, so ingenious that you could not tell at a distance and only felt a growing discomfort as you drew near. Good tough old eighteenth century, no one worrying over Freud! After this we went to the museum, a huge long room filled with heads of animals and antlers, an elephant one end with large flapping ears, and a giraffe at the other, and all the occasional tables made either of rhinoceros hide or with hippopotamus's feet. The lamps, which had been suspended by stuffed pythons, fell down and were lost when the R.A.F. bombed the house during the war. But all is now rebuilt, and there is a portrait of the husband with a whip with long thong in his hand, hat over his eyes, standing with his body thrown back and feet well apart, ready to tame a lion. All this in the quiet flat countryside.

Those horrid nuns won't put poplars; only *alberi preziosi* will they accept. I am going to try Monsignore but fear there is little hope.

Your
FREYA

Darling,

I am still immersed in barbarians and now in the reign of Theodoric the Goth. The gradualness of the whole thing is so remarkable. I imagine no one quite knew what was happening while it went on, while Theodoric for instance was building his new palace in Ravenna and giving Italy thirty years of perfect peace. I do feel that one ought to read those years of history to understand our world today, far more useful than newspapers.

I have been thinking hard of *Spilt Milk* and do approve of your intention of working on it. Writing just isn't thrown out spontaneously. I'm always being told that people do it like that, but never fail to find hard work when I look into the matter. I think there are two things to do: (1) to put yourself in your reader's place. I think I now do it automatically, stepping outside myself and looking at the thing written or to be written with the eyes of a stranger. You will then nearly always find your *transitions* too quick or too slow; you have to arrange them so that your reader can keep an easy pace just behind you. (2) I should read through a detective story or two, and then a book by Peacock or David Garnett and then decide which sort of method you want. If you want the thriller, it must have more excitement in the plot; but if the latter, it must be polished up and every little picture finished, a lot of work, but very rewarding. I do hope this is useful advice; anyway, the best I can do.

It is good of you, too, to offer £100 for the porch. It would cover half and I wouldn't mind borrowing for the rest as I could pay in the autumn. But don't do it unless it is quite easy. The house is, after all, well on now and all the remaining things can wait (except the bookshelves which I *am* doing).

There is an excellent review of Grahame Greene in the *Literary Supplement* of April 6th. It assures Mr. Greene that 'Christians have no corner in sin' and is altogether sane. I think he is a dangerous man, he says apparently that even as a child he discovered that Humanity was not black and white, but black and grey. Nice people discover it to be white and grey as they go on.

We must go again to Ravenna. It seems that in 1854, a stone's throw from the great mausoleum, some workmen digging came upon a skeleton in armour, with gold helmet, breastplate, and sword, all jewelled. Before the news reached the authorities, these things had vanished, probably melted down, all except one small piece of the breastplate which is in the museum. Hodgkin thinks this was most likely the body of Theodoric, pushed out of its great red sarcophagus when the Catholics came and the Arians went.

The loveliest of tulips has opened in the garden, pale lilac with a half-cup at the base of pure gold, from Crete. As for the landscape, it is just unearthly, or rather like a quintessence of Earth translated into something, luminous like an illuminated missal, every little hill shining with flowers.

Dear love,

FREYA

STEWART PEROWNE Asolo
12 April 1951

Darling,

Margaret and Rosamund[109] are packing busily, trying to get all their shopping, sabots, berets, baskets, and hideous little bric-à-brac from Venice, into already bulging suitcases. They go back looking transformed as the hairdresser has been in and given them a 'Latin Wave'. I have enjoyed having them and they are wonderfully good about letting one work in the morning. They are both like you, but in a rather Jekyll and Hyde way; Margaret yesterday began to tell me how hard it is to have a conscience. I felt I couldn't deal with a niece's conscience as well as an uncle's and advised her, rather vivaciously, to arrange her life so that her poor old conscience might not have to be worried and given a rest. I have been making noble efforts to be equally nice to both of them and I think they are both happy with their stay.

14 April 1951

They have gone, with picnic foods for the day and last instructions to the bus to deposit them at Padua station. I sent the parents a little note and a tin of olive oil. We had a grand finale by going to see *Tosca* in Bassano. The three principals were good voices (though Tosca was a poor actress), but it *is* a poor opera, don't you think? There are only two goodish arias and the orchestra is nothing but church bells for Sacred and drums for Profane. On the other hand, it is a wonderful good drama, and of course so much more touching today than any time in a century before. The nieces loved it, though the song in the prison, which always makes me weep, left them quite unmoved. We went early to Bassano so that they were able to look around while I went to look at the plans of desk and bookshelves, both very satisfactory though the important point of the price hasn't yet been reached. But

---

[109] Stewart Perowne's nieces.

they both promise to be lovely pieces of furniture and the book problem should be solved for some years.

I went about looking for a present for your birthday but couldn't think what you would want except a new bath oil smelling of pine-woods. Tell me if there is anything you are hankering for more than a bath under pines!

Love,

FREYA

STEWART PEROWNE Asolo

19 April 1951

Darling,

Such a relief, *three of* your letters came together this morning, exactly fifteen days after the last. I have now been thinking hard over the problem of your job, and it seems to me that you are right to enquire about the I.P.C.[110] as a thing to fall back upon; but the fundamental thing is that people keep you if they want you and get rid of you if they don't, and after all every government job in war was liable to a month's notice. The only thing to aim at is to be useful enough to be wanted. Now I think you have the chance in this interval, which is fluid so to say, of doing three things: (1) making your advice a matter of course to Emir and Ministers, and indispensable; (2) giving them a feeling of *safety*, by being always ready to advise and never grasping the credit, so they will come to rely on you without a feeling of danger to themselves or their vanity; (3) giving the *British* confidence in your readiness to work by choosing the important things to do and seeing them right through from beginning to end. I feel that you have been sometimes injudicious in not putting first things first (I may be quite wrong); one must delegate work, but only when one is sure that it will be carried on. In fact, one is never free of the responsibility till the job is finished. You must make people realise that you do mind, deeply, if the little country is a success or no. If I were you, I would make a list of what is needed in order of importance, i.e. agriculture, and what has to be done, in order; transport; etc., etc. The fact that it isn't all your business doesn't matter so long as you are quite disinterested and not out for kudos for yourself. I honestly believe that if you work upon these lines, and keep nose to grindstone this summer, that you need not worry about a contract. They will want to keep you for yourself.

Those four cases of books are at last through the Customs, though I had

110 Iraq Petroleum Company.

to take a car and go to Venice on purpose yesterday and was taken to the Douane to talk to a little man straight out of Stendhal. As we had nearly an hour to wait for him I was surrounded by a most friendly group of Customs officers when he arrived. They had apologised in a nice Italian way for their existence, saying 'Everyone always thinks of us as rogues' and had been charmed to be reminded that anyway St. Matthew had been one of themselves. They went wandering about among their wicked papers murmuring 'Gia, gia, San Matteo' with beaming looks; and when the Inspector came he was already vanquished. It was the four Roberts volumes that got him down. 'You must admit, Signora,' he said, 'that they are not of a normal size to carry about for study.' One couldn't very well contradict, but I explained that it is very sad to sit in foreign lands with nothing of one's own beside one and that you always like to travel with a bronze figure of a dancing girl far heavier than the books. The end is that they are to reach Cornuda station on Monday.

Martin Coleman took me for an exquisite drive. Do you remember that little village we lunched at, Lugo, with the Vespa when we went up behind Marostica? Close by is Palladio's first villa, with what a view, the Astico river winding among its white stones, exactly what Veronese painted at Maser, and in this villa, too, there are landscapes so exactly like (except badly touched up) that it *must* be the same hand. The villa is far more fortress-like, but so beautiful. A wonderful great room, and terraces, semi-circular, and terrace walks with statues. A whole civilised life.

Love,
FREYA

Asolo
27 April 1951

STEWART PEROWNE

Darling,

Dear Zara,[111] I got her off to Venice yesterday and felt I must take her and devote one day and give her a car. She is such a dear and so unused not to being looked after. Sandy sent three telegrams in five days merely to say that he misses her. I got her in to the Bucintoro. It does seem hard for the Governor of Windsor Castle's wife to have to find the cheapest place in Venice! But we drove there in a gondola (it was her first sight of Venice) and then we pottered about looking at all those bogus little shops which she

[111] Countess of Gowrie.

much preferred to Art. And then I had an early dinner with her at the Colomba and I left, having entrusted her to the Venini girls.

The Day of Liberation was celebrated, and today that nice St. Liberale who gives his name to the Bank. Emma has been reminiscing about the day six years ago when a German armoured car came lumbering up the hill and this house had a tommy gun at every window. The partisans were here ready to enfilade, but the surrender came just in time, and while the armoured car crew were taken off to the Teatro Duse, Emma was invited to go and help loot the car. All she got was a despatch case of very superior notepaper, which she still uses!

Love,

FREYA

LADY YOUNG
Asolo
29 April 1951

Dearest Rose,

I have written to Jock to add a word about Hubert's music – I would like to add much more, not only about him but about so many friends: but it is like a picture, you have to be constantly subordinating to the main theme and never let the detail swamp you. I wonder why it is that people realise the difficulties of painting so much more than those of writing? I don't think there is too much about you in the book: you see, it all has to be focused on what affected me (as it is an autobiography) so I give the impressions as they came to *me*; and I have only given you more prominence because you affected me more *intimately*. I think people often forget this and write bad autobiographies because they think that an important event must be given more space than an unimportant one – whereas the thing that counts is what the particular event did to the person who is being written about. It is all very difficult.

Dear love,

FREYA

CHARLES RANKIN
Asolo
29 April 1951

My dearest Charles,

I had begun to think it about time for one of those rare letters, and I was so glad to see it arriving. I've been here a month, and I begin to think I never want to leave Asolo again. You must take a spring holiday sometime and see what it looks like, and if I am away and it isn't let, you shall have it on loan for the honeymoon. I am so interested and hope I may meet her anyway, whether you topple over or only hover.

At the moment I feel that a garden is far preferable to any husband, and I don't even feel like Eve, looking round for someone to share an apple with. Tulips are out and roses beginning, and I am designing my patent writing desk and never looking at a paper. On June 13th I shall be in London for five days and hope for a glimpse of you; but I hope too to be a little less hurried later and to have half July and all August in England – though mostly out of London. I go to Scotland to wear a red gown and become LL.D. – such a good *easy* way of doing it: you will have to tell me what it really means. I only wish I could try the gown on beforehand: I feel sure that tucks will have to be taken in at the last minute.

Everyone here asks after you.

Love,
FREYA

STEWART PEROWNE

Asolo
10 May 1951

Darling,

We are all gloomy with the continuing rain, and the house covered with dust from masons. But the porch takes shape, and a lovely design of beaten ironwork for the door has just been spread out on the floor by Reginato.

I have been thinking hard over your precious leave, and feel that you would want it as soon as possible; so unless I hear soon to the contrary, I shall consider the first available day, September 16, as the happy day of your arrival! If, however, you prefer to go to Stamboul, I will try to join you there; but think that a home is a precious thing and needs a lot of building and care like every human affection, and that, in the world as it is, you may not have the chance of enjoying it for long. So make your choice and let me know.

A note has just come from Cici to say her separation is decided on, a sad little note poor child, though it is sadder for Franco as he is the one who cares. I wrote to him and to his mother to say how sorry I am, not that that will help much. It is hard to feel that whatever you do you can't make your-self loved; and I only hope now that Cici will find someone and care for *somebody* or she will end with just herself.

My fourth chapter is done and only one left, and I now come on all your early letters. What a long time ago it is, London in 1938 and '39. It all comes back as one reads and really, if one keeps letters, one mustn't be afraid of one's past. I have kept yours here, but all the rest go to Jock and I rather think I may never read them again.

I have just been told that I am being given the Sykes Memorial Medal of the Central Asian Society on June 13. It is very flattering. I wish you could be there for some of these occasions. Do you realise this is my fifth award? I wish I could *wear* them!

Love, dear Stewart,

FREYA

STEWART PEROWNE   Asolo
                                                              21 May 1951
Darling,

We had an avalanche of people and filled up the Sole; the Robinsons straight from Germany telling us that the Germans are again terrifically strong and just as aggressive as ever and now send food parcels to England; the Gileses, a charming young couple, *Times'* correspondent for Italy. I now have John Miller coming for two days and then a quiet time, I hope, till I leave on June 7th.

The moon reached the full this morning at 5.45 a.m. and I looked anxiously out, and there was a cloudless morning so one may hope for a change at last. How can one imagine that one doesn't react to a moral climate if the physical one has such a tremendous influence?

Love,
FREYA

STEWART PEROWNE   Asolo
                                                              24 May 1951
Darling,

I feel as if I had been ages away after two days in Venice. We went to S. Giorgio Maggiore and Redentore, but Palladian churches leave me cold. The Gesuati I loved because of the magnificent Tiepolo ceiling, but the best of all was the Ospedale Civile the day before, where rows and rows of white iron bedsteads filled with people are ranged in huge, high medieval vaulted rooms with windows out of reach above, all looking extremely like Goya.

We lunched in great splendour at Hotel Gritti, which has fresh flowers and an Old Master in every bedroom, and the dear Freccias gave their motor launch, so that it was all very luxurious and so lovely with a blue sky at last.

Even so, nothing is quite as good as the garden here. I am sure you are right about the country. Its fibres go so deep, there must be some lack of *continuity* in people who only live in towns. It is curious how one needs the country more and more as one grows older. And a day in the garden, not doing anything more strenuous than embroidery, being that is to say quite receptive and almost passive, is like a week's rest cure or more so.

The Freccias showed me pictures of the 'Almond Feast' in Agrigentum when, on February 24, the Greek temples are filled with almond blossom and the girls wear their little brocade jackets and the men black corduroy breeches and white stockings. What a nice world where these things still exist.

Love,
FREYA

STEWART PEROWNE
Asolo
25 May 1951

Darling,

I have had a pathetic visit from Cici's father-in-law, who evidently thought I must be conciliated. Such a nice man, long-winded but kind, and very anxious that Franco should not lose factory as well as wife. I couldn't agree more, and said so, and he went off very friendly and much more optimistic than the state of Cici's mind warrants. I am all, however, for her making it legal while she is about it. I think it quite possible they may come together again if Franco continues in his steady devoted way. I think the feeling of something *reliable* counts very much with most women.

The Emir's visit sounds awful, and why weren't you there? What I feel is that it is no good blaming *them* if things go wrong, we can only blame ourselves who undertook the shaping of them. And if they don't make a success, they will turn and rend us. I have personally never believed Libya would work since proportional representation was accepted; it decided it for a Tripoli-*effendi* state, and from that moment the Emir could only work in Cyrenaica. This will not be accepted, as it is unpopular. But you will see that so it will turn out.

The municipal elections are on tomorrow. Cadona has bought himself new teeth and smiles all the time and canvasses himself so that it is useless to think of him as a carpenter till this is over. Such awful things happen in people's lives. Our nice fat respectable municipal secretary has one adored only son doing well at the university and his parents' pride; and now is being prosecuted for improper behaviour and some municipal enemy published it in the paper and the boy and his mother are hiding themselves in the country. I met the poor old man and went across the street to talk to him and he was drunk, a thing he never was before. I came home feeling as if everything in the world were spoilt.

Love,

FREYA

NIGEL CLIVE

Asolo

25 May 1951

My dearest Nigel,

How strange to think of you and Maria in Baghdad. I often think of places I have been in and feel how peculiar it is that they go on in their small old way when oneself is so far away. Even your address, Al Waziriyah, brought so much back – the old Defence man (what was his name?) and innumerable tea parties in those roads where one's car always broke down and there was nothing to take one home. Has it gone on growing I wonder; and what has happened to our club-house; and is Jasim with you or elsewhere? I would love to have my little carpet and drop in on you.

Love to you both,

FREYA

STEWART PEROWNE

Asolo

27 May 1951

Darling,

The election here is over. I haven't heard who is in, but Martin says it was very funny in the *piazza* yesterday, like a ballet – dozens of small boys with ladders pasting up manifestoes for the Demo-Christians. Then someone came along with opposing manifestoes, and the little boys pasted them up side by side so that 'Vote Baglioni' and 'Vote Communist' seemed to go hand in hand. Then the electricity men came along and hung up little lights and sat at the café singing the 'Internazionale', till someone asked them for the Demo-Christian hymn, with which they obliged, and finally for

'Giovinezza' which they were also able to produce. Not a political place, Asolo!

Yesterday I had the Mother Superior and two hospital nuns to tea to see the garden. I thought it would please them as they get so little in the way of outings and they went around swishing their black capes among the roses and saying 'Paradiso', and Checchi got them a huge bunch of flowers. I wish I could tell the roses to go slow, they are all trying to rush out together like people interrupting – like a conversation at Maser.

Thank you for the two wonderful parcels of coffee (so precious in case of a war, both to drink and in place of money!); they have gone straight into the strong box and I will only use them for the house when you come.

Love,

FREYA

Asolo

STEWART PEROWNE

28 May 1951

Darling,

Why did I ever undertake the Dark Ages for a lecture? It's an almost impossible task and is getting me down. I only manage 700 words a day and do want it done before I leave. Can you tell me by return how many words there ought to be, for not more or less than fifty minutes?

It was telepathy again about Cyrenaica and Tripoli, as your letter came this morning. But why don't they see these things in time? The whole art of governing is seeing in time, and it was mathematic that the thing couldn't work with the Emir and proportional representation. One or the other, but not both. Why, oh why, do they do these things?

Love,

FREYA

Asolo

STEWART PEROWNE

30 May 1951

Darling,

Two days have gone without writing to you, and it is all the fault of the lecture which is also giving me the most troublesome headaches what with the vastness of the subject, the business of writing in Italian, and the feeling of the Winged Chariot. How I hate writing in a hurry, it brings that tension which always ends by making me ill. But anyway, I have done three-quarters of it and am now polishing off the Lombards. Did you know that they were originally neighbours of the Anglo-Saxons in Germany? And that they parted their hair in the same way and wore loose linen clothes 'qualia Angli-Saxones habere solent' (first mention of the name in history)?

The election has gone to the peasants. All the Asolo citizens are flabbergasted; such a thing has never happened before. There is only one educated among them, the Professor of the Filippin school, who will, I suppose, be *sindaco*. It will be interesting to see what they make of it. I don't, myself, think that it is the general list of them that counts. All depends on whether there is one man among them who will give time and work and get something done.

One lovely new lily has appeared, very dark maroon, so beautiful. The others, alas, I shall miss I am afraid. Already suitcases are appearing. I feel I have only been here a week; and the poor *tessoria* is only just beginning to lift its head, very languid. It is touching to see how they all, Caroly, Checchi, Emma, Maria, spoil me as soon as I remain alone – a sort of gentle cherishing goes on. One wonders what one does to deserve the devotion of one's servants. It is such a one-sided affair.

Back to the Dark Ages. The Popes are getting *awful*.

Love,
FREYA

STEWART PEROWNE   Asolo
                                                  1 June 1951
Darling,

That terrible lecture is done. It is probably very poor and stodgy, but I believe very few lecturers for the publicity department of the Embassy read *twelve volumes* before they give a lecture. I have enjoyed that part of it enormously and am glad that I chose a subject that I knew nothing about to lecture on. Today I took three lovely hours off in the garden and drew a *fiasco di vino*, every straw almost! I can see why people find it the only wholly satisfying occupation; it completely obliterates the self while one is engaged on it.

Whatever happens, you must get next April–June in Asolo. It is such a succession of beauty. The flowers are more like a mannequin show than anything else – they take each other's place so smoothly and show themselves off so well.

I am reading *Antony and Cleopatra* in readiness for the 16th. What magnificence, what amplitude, what magic. Like a great wind of Eternity sweeping through the lines as if Time were a dead leaf on the way. Oh, why shouldn't one live romantically and nobly and grandly when one has only one life to spend? Whatever Shakespeare thought about when he wrote those lines doesn't matter – he must have *lived* them to write like that. I'm so glad that, for once, this play is to be there when I go. I wish you could share it.

Your
FREYA

STEWART PEROWNE

Paris
9 June 1951

Darling,

I am quite an *habituée* of my little hotel and was greeted like a friend, rushed off an hour after arrival to try the velvet gown, which is magnificent, and have bought white gloves after all, not kid, but *antelope*, like whipped cream so soft and lovely – and washable so that one can wear them for day, too. But I thought that if there is an evening reception with the King and Queen, I shall have to have long gloves. Six guineas, your present. Thank you ever so much; it was nice of you to want me to wear something from you.

I had a very good journey out, leaving Asolo sadly as always. In Milan I found a sleeper all to myself. It was dark through Switzerland and misty but the green electric flashes from the train lit up the landscape in a sudden and surrealist manner. At Paris a little Frenchman and I got out together with the same porter and he told me he was going to Glasgow. 'So am I,' I said, 'I'm going to be made a Doctor there.' He was so impressed he left bowing backwards!

Paris is more and more expensive, but so gay. I was taken to see Christian Dior's dress show, and this afternoon we went and looked at Toulouse Lautrec's show. He is not great, not in the range of Manet or Renoir, but with a very human quality, wistful and sad over the sad world he looks at. It seems to me that the difference is that the nineteenth-century artist is still on the side of the Good when he is painting the underworld. The Graham Greenes and Mauriacs have really crossed over, however much they disguise it from others and themselves.

It was the French Derby and there was a huge lunch-party at Chantilly, two tables of fourteen, Duff at one and Diana at the other, all in ravishing clothes. The most extraordinary thing was that four people at my table had been to my own house in Asolo and I didn't recognise one of them! Shaming, but there it is.

Tomorrow to London and will write from there. Hope to find a letter. It is rather nice of me to be thinking of you in Paris, isn't it!

Love,

FREYA

STEWART PEROWNE Paris – train
12 June 1951

Darling,

I am sitting in my train with the plays of Racine. (I get one classic on every visit to replace what the Fascists took.) Those smooth verses, so courtly, like a great river, with not a ripple allowed in the surface – the consummate art, never allowed to show, and what one still sees here and there in clothes. I thought Dior a little cheap, but yesterday dropped in to see Lilia Ralli, who is now one of the pillars of Dessé's, and sat for half an hour looking at the show. *Dreams* of clothes. I told her that they have far more poetry than any-thing I have seen in Paris, and she told me to come either in March, September, or December and bring my own material and they would do the making at cost price. Isn't that exciting? I think the sensible thing is to come to Paris only once in two years, or even three, and then get several at a time (say *three*) and spend the interval copying them at home. One gets so many ideas just by looking. The Dessés are all very gentle, aprons and ruches of lace, cascades of frills everywhere. My Mme Grès is ravished with the *tessoria* silks and is ordering scarves for the autumn. I do hope to be able to get some-thing going to stop our little private slump!

London

14 June 1951

Such a lovely lot of letters waiting and yesterday your telegram handed tactfully by Jock just as I was going in, feeling ridiculously nervous. There was the usual little gathering, always so very touching, all the old people who have done things in their day and are now handing on. Sir John Shea gave me the medal, a lovely silver one with a rather Persian design, and

Sir Howard Kelly sat beside me, and they were all so genuinely friendly and pleased to do this kindness. We had tea and then heard Kingdon Ward telling us about an earthquake in Burma: all the outlines of the hills in their lovely valley became *fuzzy* and the earth roared, and the hills shook down their stones and forests. Can you imagine anything more terrifying?

Darling, I must hurry. London is a whirl and my little book already full. I dined with the Jocks last night. The Festival[112] is rows of lights and the trees are floodlit emerald green and bronze, charming. Osbert[113] and John Piper have designed little gardens I must go to see, with fountains and puffs of smoke and everything but flowers.

Did I tell you that I gave a little before-lunch party at the Ritz for Marina, about ten people? Marina is enchanted with England and especially the *people*. It is nice to see these good patient stodgy qualities recognised.

I do enjoy being in Albany. Who would ever live anywhere else in London if they could choose? You step out into Piccadilly, yet there is not a sound and a wonderful collegiate, cloistered feeling about the hard bare stairs and the closed-in harem seclusion.

Darling, I send you this with my dear love and miss you often.

FREYA

STEWART PEROWNE

London
15 June 1951

Darling,

I have just been having a long talk with Roger Allen[114] and must tell you before I get it fuzzy in my mind. He was very frank and friendly and may come out to Asolo in September. We agreed, of course, at once about the problem – necessity of finding a good man in the palace and all the things you know. But the two important points were (1) the future *line* to follow, and (2) *your* future. I asked him about (1). I said one must *know*, as it is a question of giving a push of the rudder right or left and our only wish and job is to carry out the F.O. wishes; and he told me the position has changed a good deal in the last year and Tripoli is now just as important as Cyrenaica or perhaps more so. This, you see, means a considerable change of outlook and it makes a very nice balance necessary between the *effendi* and the Beduin state.

[112] London was decorated for the Festival of Britain.
[113] sc. Lancaster.
[114] In the Foreign Office. Later Ambassador to Greece.

227

As to your position, Roger told me that you had seemed 'a little unsettled' and asked me what I thought about it all. I had a rapid decision to make whether to be completely frank or conventional, and decided to be frank. I told him I thought you would be better in your work in the future than in the past because it had been difficult to switch over the Acting Governor to the Adviser. It was especially difficult for anyone who enjoys sitting on platforms, but that you have been switching over and that it seemed to me to promise quite well. I think Roger was pleased with such a balanced view and went away very cordially.

Last night I went to *Antony and Cleopatra*. What an evening. Laurence Olivier a fine Antony, easy, a soldier, simple and kept all through less prominent than Vivien Leigh, who rose from splendour to splendour. I never want to see another Cleopatra. I am sure Laurence gave the part as the gentlest compliment to his wife and she added no fancies of her own but just let the great words and the great love of three centuries ago speak through her. She was not even beautiful, getting thinner and thinner, with scarcely any make-up as the great end came near. I wept all the way back down Piccadilly.

I lunched with Lulie and her Mama, a nice little Arab lunch on a tray with a little Arab maid from Zamalek. Today am going to see Sydney in Kew.

Dear love,

FREYA

STEWART PEROWNE   Train to Glasgow
                                                  18 June 1951
Darling,

Three lovely letters, pressed into my hands as I was leaving Albany this morning. Of course I love to get all the chit-chat, it is almost like being with you and it is all the little things one likes to know; and I am pleased when you send me a little of your fan mail. Why shouldn't one be pleased when people like one – so long as one doesn't make it one's objective? It is the flowers in the hedges that make the road pleasant, though they are not the road.

So many things in your letters, and this such a wobbly train. The English counties rolling by, green and pale yellow with showers and sun. Dear, kind, gentle land. Yesterday I walked with Sydney in Kew Gardens, such beauty and peace, and all the people scattered about and the air sweet with azaleas.

Sydney sent his love. He was in very good form, eighty-four years old. In the evening Osbert and Alan[115] took me to the Festival Gardens done by Osbert and John Piper. You never saw anything so gay, obelisks which are fountains lit from inside, the trees emerald green and bright yellow, lit from below, the dance hall a Moorish tent billowing out into little tents for sitting out, the kiosks an Osbertian dream with walls of wickerwork and mirrors, and puffs of smoke coming out of pineapple obelisks, and two friezes of figures against the skyline done in wickerwork, just the human frame, like the mannequins in dress shops. The whole so gay and mad.

I wish so much you were here for these Ceremonies. Do you think I could wear my gown as a theatre wrap? I would buy one if I could do that!

Dear love,

FREYA

STEWART PEROWNE

Glasgow
19 June 1951

Darling,

Just off. So glad of your telegram. I have a telegram, too, from Asolo Municipality. Rather touching! Very nervous and wish it was you and not me being robed. I would enjoy it so much more. The Clerk of Senate yesterday told me that the doctorate gives me the right to decide on points of both canon and civil law. I said they seemed very rash, that I was just thinking of writing a handbook on smuggling.

It is such a comfort to be with the Kers;[116] they think of taxis and *everything*.

21 June 1951

The cap is on. All went well. There are still lunch, dinner, and two celebrations today and I am nearly dead.

22 June 1951

It is just 11 a.m. I have slept like a god and got up with the wonderful feeling that the day is my own (and not feeling a bit like a doctor inside), have sent off five telegrams of thanks including one more heartfelt than the rest to you, and have had three letters from you in the mail. So good of them to come so rightly timed. And now I shall tell you all about it.

115 sc. Lennox-Boyd.
116 Charles Ker was brother of W.P.

I got up on the 19th in a train about half a mile long and found the station dotted about with sweet girl undergraduates all in red gowns and dear Charles Ker. We called in and took an enormous sheaf of tickets and introductions from the Senate House and tried on the gown and cap and asked about the wearing of decorations and all that, and next day gathered in the great hall of the university to watch the delegates of two hundred other universities and Learned Bodies hand in their addresses. I seemed to be the only person not wearing anything academic! The delegates were all one more strange, coloured, and gorgeous than the last, the French going in for gold and ermine, the Lutherans for ruffs, the Rhine for great medieval robes with velvet collars. It was fascinating to see how medieval the *faces* became with these robes. There were three women delegates, an English one in blue and silver, a French and a Belgian. Will Spens[117] represented Cambridge in black and blue (but only came next day). The Scottish Academy wore a maroon-coloured velvet cape with gold tassels on the sleeve and (as he had a gold beard) looked like Sir Walter Raleigh. The old Chancellor with white bushy eyebrows and a cape of black and gold sat in his chair and the delegates came one by one, handed in their scroll, and bowed before him. Some little orientals brought their greetings in the Office Folder and I thought suddenly of the policemen on the Western Desert road. There were Indian universities, Madras, Malaya, in red silk. I suppose there is nothing left so colourful as the academic world today.

Well, after this ceremony I came upon my fellow doctor, Dorothy Russell, who turned out to be very friendly and easy and the professor here with whom she is staying added me to his lunch party. From there we went on to the solemn procession and service in Glasgow Cathedral and that was beautiful. The sun shone, and the gowns glittered and wound in a semicircle with the dark Gothic walls behind them and the only slight anticlimax was the Moderator of the Church of Scotland who appeared to be sleeping all through his fellow clergyman's address (but he *may* have been thinking with his eyes shut?).

The Kers live half an hour by car outside Glasgow (and refuse to let me pay for any of the daily taxis I have been using) so I just had time to get back and dress in my white Paris frock (and diamonds) and get to the dinner where I had a Canadian doctor also getting his degree on one side and one of the Glasgow professors on the other, a charming lawyer obviously immensely relieved to find me Normal and not Academic. In fact about a dozen people have come up these days and told me how pleased they were to find me 'feminine'.

[117] Sir Will Spens was then Master of Corpus Christi College, Cambridge.

Next day I joined the sixty-seven other graduates all robing with far more concentration and fussiness than men are credited with, and we were formed into a long double procession by the harassed Clerk of the Senate, Divinity first and Laws after. The doctor ahead of me was a nice old boy, adviser to the College of Surgeons, and the one behind was the most charming ex-professor of medieval history in Oxford, radiating gentleness and goodness and humour. We made great friends and I told him how much we would enjoy a year or two of quiet research and he said, 'Let me know if ever you think of it and I might arrange some sort of grant' – and I'm sure he really meant it. He was smaller than I am, and the next man was Sir John Reith of the B.B.C. who is six foot four. I was so glad not to be next him, the man who put his hood on had almost to *jump* up to reach. Churchill, it seems, always calls him 'Wuthering Heights' and he made me think of the hero of *Barchester Towers*. He looks so bitterly righteous and incapable of being happy. He was one of the speakers and made a very heartfelt sentimental speech but so egotistical down below that it jarred (I wonder why sentimentality and egotism go together so?). The best speech was by the head of Princeton who also got a degree. But his was all later. We are still going in slow procession onto the platform past a mirror into which every single man turns to look as he passes, with slow music, and a packed hall and galleries in front. We sit in tiers and then the Chancellor's procession comes in and he sits on his throne. And then one after the other goes down, kneels, is touched on the head by a huge purple velvet sort of mushroom cap very worn at the edges, gets up, shakes hands, and has the hood fitted on from behind and retires. I had tied my hair tightly and neatly in black tulle and carried it through, I am told, with composure, and got a great clapping. But the audience was so nice and wise and gave the greatest ovations to the foreigners and especially the coloured ones. I wish the Barbadians could have seen!

After this long morning we had a great lunch and then there was another reception in the afternoon which I skipped from sheer exhaustion. I went out again in the evening in the black gown with the red and purple LL.D. over it and a little black veil on my head just covering the eyes, which I thought rather dashing, and the black enamel and ruby pendant which looked very fine, with my little white cross of St. John beside it. The whole of the City Corporation with the Lord Provost at its head was there to receive us and we shook hands and bowed and went on into the huge ballroom. Everything here was done very solid and good about 1880; solidity is the word. This was a very pleasant evening. All sorts of people came up and I really ought to be very rich, because everyone seems to have read my books. A nice little professor from Denmark who is an orientalist came along and told me how he had lost his wife after twenty-five years and how lonely it was. And suddenly everything seemed so much less important than that one human fact. I looked about at all the faces and so many are pinched and made mean by worrying about their honours, promotions, degrees; when one saw them in rows it was just like those pictures we have by de Monvel of the Inquisition trying Joan of Arc, the world writing hard things on the features. But now and then there were lovely faces, made noble by their years, to whom all this was play and the reality elsewhere. I suddenly thought of my lilies just coming out in the garden and felt relieved to know, quite surely, that my reality is in a right and peaceful place.

Yesterday was the last ceremony. The King and Queen had to cancel and Attlee took their place and we gathered again in the great hall to hear the Royal Address and then two speeches, Macmillan and Attlee. They both stressed the necessity of the humanities to balance our overdose of science. This is becoming an accepted cliché almost, so we may hope to see it penetrate into life in our time. I had Will Spens to sit beside me at an informal lunch and, as we had two hours before the next reception, he took me to look at the picture gallery, which is a very good one (a most enchanting Watteau, a lovely Van Gogh, and many others, including the two Whistlers – of his mother and of Carlyle).

There was another great University reception, the Scots Guards (rather dim in contrast to the Robes of Learning) playing on the grass of the quad till a shower drove them in. Then back with just time to bath and dress and return for the dinner given by the Senate. The wives were being entertained separately, but we academic ladies were with the men, four of us, including the Vice-Chancellor of London University who made a speech really *shaming*, arch, argumentative, and inaudible, in a squeaky voice. I had said to my Glasgow professor (who was again my neighbour) that every woman who deals in education should have a past. So now, when it really was too appalling and I said to him, 'I could make a better speech than that', he said, 'Well, of course, you have a past.' 'Several,' said I! There must be something terribly wrong with female education when it is taken for granted that an academic woman is to be avoided. There was a charming principal of Utrecht University opposite me, a German from Cologne next, a Canadian and a New Zealander, and they all drooped and then looked even sadder when the Principal of Yale University spoke and explained how the young universities make up by energy for their lack of time and how they mass-produced universities in America after the 1914 War. It was fascinating to watch the tacit rejection on all the European faces.

Today and tomorrow is devoted to trips on the Clyde and to Loch Lomond, but I have given up and feel I must now see my own friends, and devote this morning to you.

Some day when I can afford it I think I must get a cap and gown. You can't imagine how noble it looks with jewellery and décolleté – far better than ordinary evening dress!

Love,

FREYA

STEWART PEROWNE

Lunga House Hotel,
Ardfern, Argyllshire
27 June 1951

Darling,

We are not on an island at all, but surrounded by them, a beautiful land-scape like a northern version of Greece, with not a house in sight or anything more than a few fields of cultivation. All the rest is jade-green slopes of turf and bracken and oak-woods in the clefts. It is so exciting to see the long summer light for the first time. Mary Smith and I sat yesterday on the shore and watched the life: a seal swimming with its head up in the middle of the loch, a sandpiper dancing its head and tail, very agitated because of a nest nearby; oystercatchers, terns, gulls. Mary knows them all and one can see how the old Irish saints came to be on such familiar terms with the animal world, as the human one is so very scarce. Today her son, who has bought a little island here, is taking us out to fish in Loch Awe (that is to say they will fish and Mary and I walk about). It is wonderfully restful. If Pam were here we would walk barefoot on the turf, it is so soft and fine. I am reading *The Lord of the Isles* and it is quite different here in its proper surroundings.

Back south on the 10th, Royal Garden Party on 19th. *Wish* you were here. I am frightened to go alone and hope to find someone, perhaps Sybil.

Love,

FREYA

STEWART PEROWNE

Argyllshire
29 June 1951

Darling,

It would be such a pleasure to me if you were here. You would have enjoyed yesterday so much. Mary's doctor son bought an empty island two

233

miles long, all wood and grass, and keeps it as a holiday place for friends who help to build the little house. They have done it all themselves and it is already weathertight and warm. Yesterday they took us all with our lunch to look at the islands which fringe the sea where the seals lie about on the rocks. The seals are just like a barbaric version of the civilised legend of the sirens; they lie about in the same way, only clumsy and not quite knowing what to do when their moment comes. So they turn their heads and soft brown eyes to look at the strangers, and then flip and waddle down to the slippery seaweed and slide into the water. In the sun they go quite light and blond.

We watched six of them there on a little promontory, three beautiful young sleek grey mothers with their children; and when papa had looked at us, he turned his head round and told the harem to get away, and they all slithered down and disappeared, a sleek head bobbing up now and then to see what we were doing.

We next visited an islet where the terns and gulls lay their eggs. It was full of little pale-blue spotted eggs laid on patches of grass or in crannies, and bigger gulls' eggs, some just hatching with a little pink mess and beak inside, and dozens of tiny fluffy speckled chicks already knowing that one must sit quite tight and hope for the best in this world. One had to look out for every footstep for fear of squashing some baby, and the poor terns kept up a great wheeling and crying, and a shrill sort of trilling in the air, waiting for us to go. One feels so much here as if it were the edge of the world. The Irish hermits of St. Columba must have had the feeling, for it is what they have sent down through the ages, a loneliness, and a familiarity with birds and beasts in a world which belongs to them more than it does to man. As soon as one gets inland among the lochs, one comes to landscape and life taken in the most obvious way from Walter Scott.

1 July 1951

We leave tomorrow and spent yesterday in one of the white and red steamers sailing round Mull to Staffa and Iona. Steven's island in the distance, north west, but faint as it was a wettish misty day.[118] Staffa is a small rock, flat and green on top and the columns it is made of very strange indeed: they look just like the mosaics of Warka.[119] Some tremendous pressure must have made them fit so close one to another, and at the entrance to Fingal's Cave they make a sort of buttressing, bulging out in an architectural and noble way with the steps of the basalt below, all dusty black and the sea very

[118] Eigg.
[119] Sumerian (in Iraq).

green, and a feeling of nature enjoying herself in private. We then landed in a drizzle on Iona, a gentle island sloping to sand and green short grass with sheep grazing round the three Celtic crosses, and the cathedral beautiful in shape and in the harmony of its walls made of rough irregular stones, pink and green and silver, and bound by grey arches and buttresses, with a great feeling of time. Dr. MacLeod, who has started the 'Iona Community' was on board and took us ahead of the other visitors and told me that St. Columba must have gone there because it was the centre for the Druid religion, and thinks he converted the chief Druids and through their help established himself on the mainland so quickly. When we left Iona we went on round Mull, alas, hidden in mists; but we did see the island of Ulva of which, you remember, the Laird eloped with Lord Ullin's daughter. And if the sea were rough, it would be a very easy place for drowning. Yesterday all was calm. We came back with the inlets and islands shining in the last light and tomorrow we leave. It has been such a new window, this western northern edge of land and sea, the long light, day till almost midnight, and the loneliness, and the people so much firmer and kinder than most.

I believe that if your job came to an end it would be a good idea to look for another, not from any British institution, but direct from some Arab government. I think the day of the direct British Civil Service in the East is over for the moment and that the most useful as well as the most rewarding work is direct adventure on one's own. If one is clear of one's own Service, there is a lot to be said for offering oneself independently and on one's own merits to any country you like. I shall be interested to hear what you think of it all.

I have just finished my proofs and sent to Jock. They read very poorly to me and I only hope they are better than I think.

I think of you, and hope and wish all good.

Dear love to you,

FREYA

STEWART PEROWNE   Edinburgh
                                                               7 July 1951
Darling,

Yesterday's drive to Edinburgh was mostly hidden in mist but the bits that showed were huge, steep, naked Border hills, grass-covered, and good for sheep, very lonely. A surprising lack of *incident* about those smooth high slopes, like the first idea of a hill, endlessly repeated. A charming miner sat beside me and thought me Italian so was very demonstrative and gave me coffee when we stopped. He asked if I had a nice house, two storeys and hot water, and I said yes, and a bath. So has he, and says it's the greatest pleasure when you come from the mine (so much for the old story of coals in the bath). He said they were struggling to obtain a fortnight's holiday instead of a week in the year. Can you imagine anyone keeping underground with only a *week's* holiday in the sun? That alone settles me in favour of the miners. How shaming that they should have to struggle for a thing like that! And a sweet good woman said to me, 'Of course, most manual labour has only been getting a week.' As if most labour is shut up in blackness underground.

I am now waiting for the Newcastle train to spend the weekend with the Geoffrey Youngs and came early to the station to avoid 100,000 Orangemen who are making a procession, though no one seems to know why. What a beautiful town this is! It isn't afraid of monotony so the grand terraces go up and down its hills, all the same, built in a good smooth stone, and one feels as if it were some fine old city in a picture.

Love darling, do write lots more poetry.

FREYA

STEWART PEROWNE   Northumberland

7 July 1951

STEWART PEROWNE

Darling,

I was reading again what you say about born soldiers. I think Wavell *was*. When Archie John chucked the Staff College, his father said to me, 'He isn't like me, he doesn't enjoy the military problem for its own sake.' I think it is something like the matador and bull, an art. I believe I should have had it if I had been a man, the delight of seeing a pattern work itself out and the excitement of the material with which it is done, the lives of men. I don't believe you can be a real general without that feeling, and you can't have the feeling without the gift of imagination.

9 July 1951

This is so beautiful, high up above the valleys and yesterday we drove even higher, between the North and South Tyne along the Roman wall. The land is big and strong, immense grassy fields divided by low stone walls, with stumps of trees, but all lifted and open under the vault of the sky, all dotted with cattle and sheep, with little tarns shining in hollows, and all tilted towards the north and breaking in low cliffs of dark stone dressed to the lip with grass. The wall runs along the cliff tops and looks down on the ghosts of the Picts below, or over the grassy summits. Every mile had its tower and we wandered over one of the forts that held 500 horsemen or 1,000 men. The plan is all there, the rounded enclosure, four gates, towers, H.Q., and chapel for the standards, and sanitation (like Ostia), and the houses outside where the families lived and a town grew up no doubt. The names one sees are all barbarian and I imagine that very few *Romani di Roma* lived along the wall, tough Gallic mercenaries mostly.

It was so beautiful, such a mixture of landscape and time, and the Youngs such good people to see it with. They drove back by Redesdale and Otterburn, and you can't imagine how legendary it looked: the Border country and the valley of the Raiders, at 9 p.m., under the shining sky, the sun throwing great shafts from a lattice-work of cloud, and the low smooth ranges like an arpeggio, one behind the other in gentle gradations to the west. I read the two ballads, 'Otterburn' the Scots', 'Chevy Chase' the English view. The place where the Douglas died under the bracken bush is marked by an upright stone on a pedestal in a little wood. The English came riding up through swamp in a very foolhardy way and got it in the neck. There is a nice little touch in the Otterburn ballad which says that those who had servants got them to attend to their horses and the rest had to do it themselves.

I showed your poem to Geoffrey, who told me it was 'very pleasing'. He is bringing out a mountain book this month. He has done a great work, inspiring a sea and a mountain school which each take about 1,000 pupils for a month's course every year; that is, they have a hundred or so a month at a time for ten months in the year and put them through very tough courses. The boys come from industries and all are volunteers; the time is taken out of their working time and many employers contribute. It must be one of the best things done in our time, and I have promised to go and see the school next time. It must bring so much happiness to so many lives. There is a charming atmosphere here, very little money and no care for anything except the really necessary things, beauty and kindness, many books, pleasant and shabby objects, and the two people getting old together, loving their own society, and with such clear and young and happy eyes. Jocelyn the son has just arrived with his bride, a blonde and steady Dane and he dark and romantic with blue eyes. He is schoolmaster to the little Greek prince.

11 July 1951

Back in London, and lots of your letters. I would just stand on the position that you are out of the Colonial Service and the F.O. are morally obliged to keep you going for the five years for which you were led to believe that you were serving them? Then if all falls through, I would apply to Nuri direct and get the F.O. to back a job which you will already have found for yourself.

With dear love. Bless you.

FREYA

STEWART PEROWNE

Sissinghurst Castle,
Kent
16 July 1951

Darling,

This is the enchanted garden, the Sleeping Beauty might be anywhere about.[120] It is all divided by old brick walls or hedges of clipped yew, the roses have rambled about everywhere, little old roses out of French embroideries, blue roses, green roses, musk and damask. There is a garden in which I am writing, all white flowers and pale silver leaves, huge silver thistles like armour tall as men on horseback. In the middle is the old tower with two turrets and weathercocks, a flag, and clock, like the painting behind a capital letter in a missal. And there is such a gentle life in it all, Vita wandering about in her orange trousers, with a cigarette in a long holder and her wolfhound behind her; and Harold with grey hair that would like to curl and his charming face of a little boy pretending to be grown up. Benedict is here, the elder son, who edits the *Burlington Magazine* and has given me his room, which looks out over a gentle slope with a church spire in the distance and haycocks in the sun. Harold told me that I could measure their affection by the fact that they never have anyone to stay, they keep their outer life in London and come here to the enchanted place; and I do feel it is far more of a reward than to be made a doctor, to come here as a friend and intimate into something so perfect and self-sufficing.

Love,
FREYA

STEWART PEROWNE

London
16 July 1951

Darling,

I am so sorry, this blow was bound to fall.[121] I am longing to know that you take it rightly and then, like most blows, it will turn to blessing in the

---

[120] The Nicolsons had created the fine garden at Sissinghurst.
[121] The end of the job in Cyrenaica.

end. Luckily we can wait a little before finding something else, and think it over in Asolo. I wish I knew what to say that might help and comfort.

Roger Allen is coming to the party today and I will try to hear something, but Jock advises not to go purposely to see anyone and I am sure that he is right. If you do have any other job out there offered you, I imagine you will take it. And I suppose it may hasten or delay your coming north. If the former, I will either meet you at Mortola or expect you here.

Bless you darling. Don't be too sad: let us look upon this as a new beginning and make a quite new and different programme for the second part of life.

Your loving
FREYA

P.S. I had only a few minutes in a crush with Roger Allen, but said to him, 'What is this I hear about booting out Stewart?' 'I know,' said he, 'but Stewart didn't seem to mind at all.' (Now why, darling, quite such an unnatural impression?) I think he would like to help all he can.

STEWART PEROWNE
Hatfield House
22 July 1951

Darling,

I would so like you to be here instead of entangled in those miserable intrigues. There is only one other guest, an American, and otherwise I have the Salisburys to myself and am just now going down to the muniment room to read Lord Burleigh's diary. We drove through the park yesterday; there are oaks a thousand years old, one is mentioned as the landmark in Domesday Book. My room is the one prepared for Prince Albert with an 'A' over the mantlepiece in a sort of altar decoration, and Victorian portraits all around. There is usually a touch of affectation about the Victorian pose, but here it is made extraordinarily different with the terrific Elizabethan background; it becomes just a part of England. I love being here. It *is* England, the tradition, the simplicity, the dogs and grandchildren coming from their house in the park, the interest in things all over the world, the feeling that one is a part of all that belongs to this land. We went to the great hall to see two new portraits of the Burleighs just arrived. They were in the Woburn sale and the Salisburys couldn't afford to buy them, and the Queen has bought and presented them.

Last night we were talking about Wavell and Lord Salisbury told me how

Churchill protested against Wavell's withdrawing the Black Watch from the fight in Somaliland. Wavell wired back, 'I don't count the courage of my men by the butcher's bill.'

Dearest love,

FREYA

STEWART PEROWNE Hatfield House
24 July 1951

Darling,

It is extraordinary how the day goes by in a country house weekend. I got up to breakfast at nine *en tête-à-tête* with Lord Salisbury, who has all the Cecil magic in his conversation. It is like a thoroughbred horse, always pushing on anxious to find where you want to go and to go there; conscious, too, of the stream of history that lives in this place. One feels the passionate love in every detail. After breakfast I asked if some time or other I could be taken down to look again at Lord Burleigh's diary (no one is ever left alone with those priceless documents), so we went down under vaulted passages and opened locks made in the shape of hands holding bars which lock both ways, and finally sat down with the precious book of thick rugged paper and spent the rest of the morning over it. The atmosphere of that old world sank in slowly until it seemed today. The notes were written at various times, sometimes with beautiful careful letters, sometimes hurried. After a week's reading they would be easy to decipher, but as it was we had to pick bits here and there, the Queen's progress from or to Windsor, letters from Scotland, my Lord of Norfolk visiting the Queen of Scots, the massacre in Paris (St. Bartholomew), Lord Oxford (Burleigh's son-in-law) 'made by lewd persons a stranger to his wife', a grant to Sir Walter Raleigh and the like to Sir Francis Drake, an increase of Scottish news as the Armada approaches and orders to the lords of various counties to arm two, three or four thousand men, the whole life emerged slowly. Lord Salisbury told me he had never read so much in the book before and I hope he will have it transcribed. It has never been published or even photographed.

When we came out we went to the flower garden and worked at tidying the roses. The old Tudor barn is there where Elizabeth and Mary lodged and were kept prisoners, with a wonderful ceiling of rafters with a cross-pattern. Of course many countries are older than England, but very few go on *living* with their old things in this unbroken way.

For lunch, the Australian head of Shell came and the South African who is now head of Smuts's party, and we were all taken all over the house full of pictures and treasures. The fascination of the pictures is that most are contemporary, the French look horrid people; Leicester looks a thoroughly unreliable tough but certainly with a *way* with him; and the Van Dykes are wonderful.

Love darling,

Your

FREYA

STEWART PEROWNE

London

26 July 1951

Darling,

Back to find two letters of yours, rather sad; I do wish I were with you, and yet I don't suppose it would help. Haven't we known what governments are from the very first? I believe in the long run it may all be for the best if we take it wisely. What about beginning all over again and spending three years on a degree in archaeology? We can afford it. I asked Steven what he thought, and he is for it; he says it would give just the 'mental discipline' you need.

I am rolling along to Henley to lunch with Peter Fleming and Celia and go on to Cliveden. So dear of Nancy, she has got Pam, and asked me what men friends I want and I have asked for Christopher Sykes and Fitzroy Maclean. One's friends are wonderfully good. I sometimes wonder at what age this kindness stops, it would be too much to expect it to go on for ever.

Cliveden

28 July 1951

This is the room with the view you love, a still summer day, a little haze lying on the river, the trees as if cast in metal so warm and still. The most peaceful view in England.

Nancy not peaceful! I think she is desperately unhappy inside. She has gone for the public things and now begins to find them dust and ashes I suppose, and here is Pam on the edge of a penniless marriage with the only person she has ever felt like loving since Pat died. Everyone is at me to dissuade her, but I can't find it in my heart to do so. All I suggest is to live in sin for a couple of years before deciding, which is advice that none of these old ladies would approve. Christopher is in Paris but Fitzroy is here and very pleasant, and also Professor Rowse the Elizabethan, an arid little combative man.

Nancy says she wants to become a saint so that everyone may feel her influence when she comes into a room. I told her I have only known two people who gave this impression of making a room different, one was Gandhi and the other the Mufti and neither were saints!

Waldorf looking better, wheeling himself in a chair around his woods. How beautiful they are. The long garden a dream, all colours shut in by the box and cypress.

Love dear,

FREYA

STEWART PEROWNE
Cliveden
30 July 1951

Darling,

Pam and I leave in time for lunch in Windsor today, and I must send you a line or two from this place you love, all basking in a perfect summer day. The tree shadows are blue, as if they were veils drawn over the dark spaces; there is an incredible smoothness and peace, as if the feeling of a safe and inexhaustible income still clung to the landscape. The river below is without a wrinkle.

Fitzroy has written an excellent speech on the Middle East, and tried it on us last night, and then gave us the story of how he shepherded Tito to Rome, a wonderful saga, with Tito seeing the sights of St. Peter with two tommy guns escorting him up the aisle (supposed to be strict incognito).

I have been keeping a little aloof, revising Volume III, and thinking of you and wondering what is to come to us. If there is no job in North Africa, I think more and more kindly of a new career and a degree because it would give you something to carry on into old age and take away the blank wall of retirement. But I must wait for your news.

Windsor

Darling, this is Norman Tower and your letter of the 25th waiting. I simply can't believe they can want to let anyone as useful as you are go just now. Owen Morshead, the King's Librarian, dined here last night and told me he is on the Colonial Office selecting board. They used never to take a third degree except for very exceptional reasons, and usually an honours first or second. Now they are content with 'passes' and hardly any are gents at all; and even so they can only fill two-thirds of their lists. I don't think this is bad, it merely shows that the gentry is gone back into trade and farming and we get Elizabethan again.

Pam's two boys have just arrived, Grey beautifully free and kissing me straight away, little Skimp a shy little schoolboy full of constraints, both beautiful. This afternoon I hope to meet Derek Cooper, whom all the coil is about. You know that Zara can't bear the thought of Pam's marrying a penniless man. My dear, he pays super tax. I'm afraid I strongly urged Pam, if she cares, not to play about with him and risk the awful judgement of levity with such things.

Poor Nancy, she is terribly unhappy now. I suppose she married Waldorf for a few wrong reasons and treated him off-hand for years, and now, suddenly, she told me, he hates her; and I know exactly how that happens, he has given and given and given, and suddenly it is an end. And now I daresay she would give anything to have a chance to get his love back. He was so nice and asked after you, and so did she. She is a very true creature, a good friend.

It is rather pathetic here to see these old people[122] carrying on their job, surrounded by crowds and crowds, a little murmur of voices like waves rising all day long from sightseers below, peering into the garden, glancing in when you open the door, and crowds of strangers, Australian, all sorts, to be received and entertained. It is a poor life for old age, though Zara has got herself drugged to like it, but poor Sandy would be so happy walking about his courts with a dog and a gun. The Castle has a wonderful spick and span bogus air, one feels as if Hans Andersen might have invented it, with the scarlet soldiers at its gate and the scarlet geraniums in the sunk garden before it. I don't know how it manages it, but it looks bourgeois in spite of all. Perhaps the miles of gravel, the arrangement of trees in the park, perhaps the fact that the pet dogs in bronze are put in the places where fine baroque nymphs and gods would have looked well. The best moment is at night, with the lights of Windsor below and the silhouetted towers. But Cliveden is *far* grander.

I have just refused an invitation to lunch and visit Syon House with the Queen of Rumania. I must be getting blasé, it seemed quite unalluring. Fitzroy tells me he is now really happy only when writing, and I think I was right in *Perseus* to say that loving and creating are the only two happinesses that last. I hope for your poem and think of it with pleasure.

Love,

FREYA

---

[122] The Gowries. He was Lieutenant-Governor and Deputy Constable of Windsor Castle.

Darling,

Grey is playing Chopin. It seems wonderfully accomplished for eleven. I suppose that is something you and I must think of as a possibility gone by, not like drawing, to which I mean to give all my days at Mortola till you come. I have just posted the ms. of Volume III to Jock, finally revised for the printer; what a relief, and what a job to do it in this social whirl. I wonder how yours is getting on and whether it is a pleasure to you.

How lovely that there is Asolo. It is such a refuge to think of when life goes wrong. I am longing to hear what you think of my idea for your retirement with archaeology, for one really could do it in Asolo with four months or so at a university to gather the material to work on. And it would be the proper preparation for Euphrates.

Harold Nicolson came to lunch yesterday and says he thinks of visiting us in Benghazi. I didn't say we might not be there as I have mentioned this only to people who I thought might take an interest and help. He has nearly finished the King's life[123] and seems to have enjoyed it. Isn't it funny that the present should seem to us so much more important than the past or future? This Palace of Windsor has been going since William the Conqueror first shovelled up the mound which makes the Gowrie garden; in fact, there was an earlier palace close by. Nearly every king has lived, jousted, or been imprisoned here since, such a packet of human history. King Richard II kissing his queen many times as he said goodbye in the gateway, never again to see her; the King of Scotland writing poems to the girl he married as he watched her from a turret; the chapel where Henry VIII and Albert are remembered together; and what one feels is this flickering moment of today, crowds of loyal democratic and very plain people walking about the ugly self-satisfied walls of George IV. Pam has resigned from being Lady of the Household and I am glad as I think it is the most cramping life, but the old people will be pained I fear.

Love darling. Bless you. I do so long for your arrival.

FREYA

Darling,

I have been spending such a wonderful hour with Sir Owen Morshead in the Library here. It could easily have been a few weeks. I think I have

[123] The biography of King George V.

learned more of English history this summer than in *years* before. First, he showed me the King's miniatures, the finest collection in the world: Holbeins, more beautiful even than his big pictures, and Isaac Olivers; Charles I, Oliver Cromwell and his mother (good faces in spite of what you feel about the poor man), Ben Jonson, Raleigh, Donne, on backgrounds of lapis lazuli. And then letters, touching royal family letters: the little boy, Edward VI, writing to his 'whipping boy' in Paris to tell him not to compromise him by going on Papist pilgrimages; Queen Mary II's six-monthly account book, with pathetic little notes asking William (who must have been a horrid morose man) to forgive her for the 'faults' (the account never tallies) and saying she doesn't know what the right sum should be 'but I know that it is gone'. Then a beautiful illuminated book left to George III by the Cardinal brother of the Young Pretender who was made by his adherents to call himself King of England. When Napoleon came to Rome, looting everything, the old Cardinal, who was a very harmless man, fled to a monastery near Padua and George III sent Mr. Coutts to him with £2,000. It was Xmas time and the Cardinal did his best over the dinner: the turkey was a success but the plum pudding was, said the Cardinal to Mr. Coutts, 'what you would call a Pretender'. George III gave him £5,000 a year for the rest of his life!

There is another nice bit about George III. He used to buy books and ordered his librarian never to try to make a profit out of the sellers of books. There was a copy of Shakespeare that had belonged to Charles I which he coveted and lost as being too expensive twice, but bought the third time for 'the enormous sum of £5.0.0' (note on the title page). It has Charles I's signature and, written by him in his captivity, 'Dum spiro spero'. They have all the little notes sent out by him from Carisbrooke Castle to ask for a rescue, and to ask again and again that his mistress be sent in to him.

There is a charming little trio of letters from the Young Pretender as a small boy (Carluccio) to his father, who answers with warmth and affection. One can see the Italian family gentleness coming in. And then we saw the embroidered shirt in which King Charles I was beheaded. And came to Napoleon's letter when he took refuge 'comme Thucydide' with 'le plus puissant, le plus noble, et le plus généreux de mes ennemis'; and from that to Churchill's instructions to Alexander to 'eliminate' the German and Italian armies in Africa and Alexander's reply telegram to say it had been done. What a morning!

Love,

FREYA

245

Houghton Hall,[124]
King's Lynn
4 August 1951

Darling,

The train was more like the weekly train to Transjordan than anything I have met in England. It got slower and slower after Cambridge, browsing along the wide open spaces and stopping at stations much too small for it so that only the people in the middle had a chance of getting out. Sybil came to meet me and it was a perfect summer day.

My last day at Windsor was spent on the river with the two boys and Pam's Derek, Pam not being available. We took an electric canoe and went through the lock and had tea under the bank and a great tree just above Cliveden. Those woods looked so lovely from the river. After tea, the boys slipped one on each side into the water and were instantly nearly drowned. Skimper was splashing about but had the presence of mind to make for shore. Derek had gone in after him, when I saw Grey sinking, gurgling, and sinking. I gave an agonised cry and Derek rescued Grey and handed him to me to hold from the boat side while Skimp was rescued and we got them both safely in – with a salutary fear of rivers I hope may last them a while. It might quite easily have been a disaster. Derek is a gentle, very loving creature. I can see why Pam is drawn to him. He is a very good companion and seems to have found me so too, for he told Pam I was the nicest woman he had met except herself, and that I carried about me an atmosphere of peace!

Dear love,

FREYA

Houghton Hall
5 August 1951

Darling,

Queen Mary came at 4.20 and left at 7.15. She was very erect in grey glacé kid shoes, the kind of 1910 with little waisted heels; and a Liberty silk of pink flowers on pale blue under a pale blue coat with little cape, and pale blue marabou; a high tulle collar of the sort held up with whalebone; a pearl necklace, diamond brooch and earrings of a little diamond and huge pearl; a very pink make-up, and blond-grey hair nicely waved; and a pale

---

[124] Belonging to the Marquess of Cholmondeley.

blue toque with a bunch of pink and yellow primulas and a white narcissus among them; and a grey silk parasol with a Fabergé handle of crystal and diamonds. She came along very anxious not to get her feet wet, with Lady Wyndham (whom I had met years ago at Petworth) very dowdy behind her with untidy hair. Perhaps a Lady-in-Waiting ought to be a little dowdy? Sybil made me sit on one side while she sat on the other and she said, 'I know all about you. I've read your books.' She has a wonderfully short, decisive way of speaking, but kind, with a readiness to be interested in anything that comes. Everyone offered her little bits of the conversation that might please her. I was very shy, as you can imagine, but I did talk a little and showed her my ring which amused her, and told her Lord Wavell's answer to Churchill from Somaliland at which she looked at me with a *flash* of the eyes. It must have been terrific when she was young. I think it is this spontaneousness and kindness together which charms everyone. She remarked on Lady Wavell's shutting of her eyes and imitated her.

Sybil was so kind and had me tell her about the submarines in Aden, and the siege of Baghdad. Then, when Sybil talked of Sweden, she tried to remember a name and couldn't. 'Very aggravating. I forget things since two years. I used to have a magnificent memory.' She was lamenting because there had been a little rose garden just below her window at Sandringham and 'the Queen has had it taken away, I don't know why.' After tea, which we had sitting at a round table, we all took a photograph of her. I do hope it comes out. It seems that she likes being taken and sat beautifully for it. At 7.15 we all curtseyed and kissed her hand, and she drove off and slowed down for a little knot of people in the park who waved their handkerchiefs and cheered. As she went she wrote her name and the date in the visitor's book and wrote 'aged 84' after it. Wonderful woman. She gives me the feeling that she *enjoys* every bit of her job, and likes her people, and to know about them, and to give them pleasure. She makes up her mind instantly on anything that comes before her and if she thinks it nonsense, says so in that crisp little voice that no one would contradict.

Sybil has thirty Wrens to visit and to tea today, but they both love showing the house and can afford to keep it. You never saw anything pleasanter than the library, a mellow serenity, a sort of warmth hangs about it. There is not the tremendous sense of history of Hatfield, but a pleasant livableness of civilisation. How lucky to be able to see this in the world today.

Love,
FREYA

London

16 August 1951

My dear Gordon,

You asked me to write down a suggestion for the influencing of Persian opinion through broadcasts. What I had in mind was a plan I had made during the war when there was a great deal of German intrigue in Persia to struggle against. I came to the conclusion that one of the most effective ways of getting at the old-fashioned religious opinion would be from Iraq, through the religious Shi'a leaders in the Holy Cities of Nejf and Kerbela. Their ramifications are extremely wide and powerful, they go into Afghanistan and India and all over Persia. It might be difficult to induce them to do anything openly, and it would need a very careful, skilful and diplomatic approach, but if you could induce them to speak, or even to give an opinion to your people to put on the air, I think you could work it to good effect.

I suggest that Salih Jabr, who is a Shi'a himself and minister in Baghdad, would willingly help. He is a friend of mine and you can use me as an introduction if you like. He is a better man to ask than the younger and more 'progressive' Shi'as who loathe their Holy Cities and would underestimate their influence.

Your affectionately,

FREYA PEROWNE

JOHN GREY MURRAY   L'Arma,

La Mortola

2 September 1951

Dearest Jock,

How beautiful *Euphrates* looks. The books get better and better, as far as their outward appearance goes – it is a lovely production, and it pleases me too to see your name inside.[126] How wonderful it is to have *finished* a book, and sit back and see it doing all the rest of its work on its own.

Cici's Paolo has been giving us a dreadful anxiety by eating figs in private and getting a high fever which has not left him for four days. He is now being given one of the new drugs and seems a little better this morning – but what agony when small children are ill: it seems as if a puff would blow them away.

Stewart is arriving with all the chattels from Benghazi, and his car, in about a week and I hope we shall be in Asolo by the 15th and able to make

125 At the B.B.C.

126 *Beyond Euphrates*, the second volume of F.S.'s autobiography, is dedicated 'To Jock Murray, the gentlest companion'.

plans for the winter. Almost sure to be in England I should say in November or early December – and perhaps I can induce him to go to Smyrna after.

Dear love,

Your
FREYA

SIR SYDNEY COCKERELL
L'Arma
3 September 1951

Darling Sydney,

It was a very short little visit I paid you, and already it seems a long time ago. I have been here over a week and done no work except two little articles for the *Observer*, and the days go by as if they were liquid and flowed. Cici has rebuilt the open loggia where I used to sleep and has made it into a beautiful room with windows all the length of three sides and a bathroom on the fourth. One looks out to the sunrise over Bordighera, the sea horizon, the point of Mortola. There is all the Mediterranean gaiety, and the hillsides are full of little terraces where men attend to roses, carnations, or vines. I go down about eleven or after and then everyone gathers from the villas around and bathes. There is a whole colony of writers: Henry Green has just arrived, William Sansom is here, and Alan Ross, whose book *The Bay of Pleasure* about Naples is coming out, and the Hills are here, who keep a bookshop in Curzon Street. They are all very pleasant and I find it nice to be welcomed as a colleague and taken as one of themselves and notice that I have never been in a coterie of writers before. Travellers have been far more my companions. It is pleasant, too, to come on the younger generation who thoroughly dislike the decadence of the twenties, Evelyn Waugh and that depressing generation. They tell me that the 'between-war' point of view is quite dead.

What a good summer it has been, a real revisiting of England at last, so many old friends and new places. I hardly know which was best among so much. A good world, dearest Sydney, and the better for your presence.

Very dear love to you,

FREYA

NIGEL CLIVE
Asolo
23 September 1951

Dearest Nigel,

I had been thinking of you for the last few days, and your letter came. I was so glad of it. We have lots of news, the chief thing being that the post of British Adviser in Benghazi was suddenly eliminated and Stewart left without a job. He has three months' leave and pay and then a pension, and is here and planning Xmas in England and then may know if another job appears. If not, I am hoping he might think of starting life all over again by studying for the degrees that are needed in archaeology, and that might take him out to the East in a pleasant way. Anyway, we shall know more in a month or two. I am now planning to have a look at Asia Minor and learn a little Turkish next year. You don't happen to know of an inexpensive boarding house in Smyrna?

We are only just back in Asolo. It is heaven, the blue sky and gold world you remember, day after day, and all peace in the garden and over the little hills. But it is let from October 15th for the winter. I am furnishing the top room where I used to write before the war and have taken a little bedroom and tiny shower-bathroom out of the *tessoria* so as to keep a little bolthole even when the house is let. You must remember it; there would be just room for you and Marie.

I had a lovely English summer, all over everywhere: and then three weeks at Mortola with Cici who has just got separated (but alas no divorce in this country). A negress who came to be interviewed as a maid in Barbados, when I asked her why she had never stayed long, said, 'I comes and I goes,' and that is what marriage seems to be. Not yours, darling Nigel, bless you both. Do let us see you soon. Give *ever* so many messages to all the friends. They are the nicest of all the Arabs in Iraq.

Love,

FREYA

SIR SYDNEY COCKERELL   Asolo
                                                                12 October 1951
Darling Sydney,

I hope the book pleases you. It comes out today. It is almost like Xmas, all the labours over and one sits back waiting for reviews. I had a very dear note from Vita Nicolson saying that she and Harold like it. I hope to be over, if only for a few days, some time this winter and then must tell you about plans for what comes next. It is rather pleasant to have a little time meanwhile with no writing to do. Asolo beautiful, just turning to autumn, and cold but bright, with yellow persimmons on the trees under a blue blue sky.

I am reading Dante, the *Purgatorio* and *Paradiso*. What a happiness to come again and again to what the human mind can achieve at its height. It is an honour to all of us of the same species.

Love, dearest Sydney,

FREYA

Asolo

14 October 1951

Dearest Sybil,

Stewart has been offered a job in Paris on November 1st.[127] So he leaves for a few days in London to see about it, and I go to lecture in Milan and Genoa, and all being well we meet in Paris and look for a small, quiet, inexpensive hotel on the Rive Gauche. It is fun to think of, as neither of us has ever *lived* in Paris (except when I was born there). It seems to me that it may be more probable to see you there than in Asolo? I hope so.

I hope you will like the book. It must feel like getting a débutante daughter safely married.

Much much love, dear Sybil, to you both,

FREYA

STEWART PEROWNE I Tatti,

Settignano

29 October 1951

Darling,

It is lovely to think of Paris on the 5th, less than a week. I shall drive straight to Bristol Hotel if I don't see you.

I haven't told you all the wonderful conversations with Lena Waterfield over her youth. Her father, who ran his estates like water through his hands, took her to Paris at the age of *three*, curing her of sea-sickness with champagne and pepper! He met her future stepmother and presented her with a cheque for £10,000 on the first day of the acquaintance and, of course, Lena was left penniless. And reminiscences of Vernon Lee whose father never would lie down. I now remember my mother told me about him. He lived in Florence and had a sort of sarcophagus padded in which he could sleep tilted and almost upright. He thought his wife was a teapot and tried to pour her out! And Vernon Lee's little nephew was born with one eye, like a cyclops. What a place, the Continent in those days! How tame we have become.

Cici has tried to enliven life for me by making another drama scene, and I really feel it is too much. Do you remember how I rushed to Milan and sat there in August to help with her baby? She said to me, in the way of all my aunts before her, 'Some people might remember that you made me walk about' (quite good, too, as a matter of fact), 'but I am willing to remember

[127] Liaison with Arabs and United Nations.

251

only your kindness.' Now this is just German, or Freud, or something extremely unpleasant, and I told Cici that she would have no more maternal interest or advice from me; she is young, rich, free, and has had plenty of time and chance to settle her own life, and, I am really rather hurt by it all. She is now full of *prevenance*, but there is something very wrong, some little megalomania, and I'm blessed if I mean to go on being treated with such *cheek*.

B.B. and Nicky are both radiant, B.B. skipping down the hills like a sprite, and both send their love and expect us in March.

Love darling,

FREYA

JOHN GREY MURRAY   Milan
                                                          4 November 1951
Dearest Jock,

All packed and ready in Milan with half a day left over. The fact that my mail has lost me leaves a beautiful feel of freedom. When it catches up I daresay it will contain some reviews? So far only Harold's has come, but I hear that the others are good and some call it the best book. What a relief that is and I wonder what makes it so? What *does* make a book good? Anyway, what a comfort to think now of writing not about oneself!

I wonder if you can help me to procure a copy of W. M. Leake's *Journal of a Tour in Asia Minor*, published by Mr. Murray *in 1824*? He was such a good man and gives references and quotations to all one wants to hear about before him. It was the Golden Age of travellers.

I wonder if I shall have time to do things like study Turkish and a bit of library reading in Paris? I would like to get ready for a preliminary wander by September or October next, from Smyrna or Adalia inland. And what a comfort it will be to have all this ready and planned if Stewart gets no further job to hold him next year?

B.B. was in splendid form and a charming New England old couple, Judge Hand and wife, were there, and we spent a night on the way down with Lena Waterfield in her castle. What a place, a quality of magic about it. And then down for two days to Siena to show Cici, who had never seen it, and S. Gimignano where when I last was there the American deserter stole my car. The wine was just as good, but the town a little more everyday. It and Assisi and Bordighera all have that same indefinable patina given by innumerable innocent, elderly British Victorian travellers eager for romance

252

in the background; not vivid, like the people who want it inside themselves, but a little bogus, with edges undefined.

We came back here with a night in Parma, exuberant with fertility and food; saw twenty-eight saloons of pictures (a few good – two wonderful Spanish portraits, author unknown), and the wreck of the Farnese theatre with just a wooden painted horse or coat of arms stuck to splintered walls.

Do write. Love dear Jock,

FREYA

JOHN GREY MURRAY   Paris
                                                    15 November 1951

Dearest Jock,

A lovely letter, and I am glad to hear how the Publisher's mystery works, and delighted to have at last crossed that whirlpool of the $17\frac{1}{2}\%$ out into the gilded lagoon of 20%! It looks as if the bathroom may be paid for after all.

My drawing comes along nicely and charcoal nudes decorate the walls of the Bristol bedroom. I go every day to Julian's Atelier, quite near where I was born, tie my head in a handkerchief and wear a burberry and look as like the Left Bank as I can, find an easel, shove it in amongst the young shock-headed girls and boys, and sit down to take whatever view I like of the model. Twice a week the Professeur comes around and with a stroke here and there revolutionises the efforts. Otherwise Mlle. Joubert, with a blue overall and lots of chins and kind old sensible eyes, waddles around and gives a hint as to how you foreshorten, or shade, or take away. It is wonderful how the time passes; and it is like adding a new *sense*: I begin to feel the delight of a pure line, the beauty of the bone at wrist or ankle, a whole new world of delicate pleasure. Perhaps dear Jock I shall never write any more and only make pictures? Anyway I believe I may be able to illustrate.

I do nothing about the United Nations except sit at lunch with a delegate or two now and then and take the Iraqi wives to dress shows. Stewart is at it all day. I would take a hand if wanted, but I'm not really and do you know, I am glad to be left out of it: it is a temporary affair, and too much like what the three witches in *Macbeth* were cooking. After fifty one wants to emerge into the more substantial world. Diana and Duff now live in it: she tells me she goes to bed at six, Duff comes and reads and they dine in her room, with time for walks, garden, friends: the only way for ageing. Paris is crowded: the dresses *dreams* – Dessé's had a grey evening gown scarfed with black

253

chiffon and held in a sort of Milky Way of diamond stars. How I hope I may go somewhere in the next world where clothes are worn (and with a nice figure to wear 'em).

All concrete plans are still hazy, though I did go and buy a book on the Roman frontiers of the Euphrates.

Love,

FREYA

SIR SYDNEY COCKERELL   Paris

16 November 1951

Darling Sydney,

I was sad to hear of you confined to bed, but Sybil tells me you are up again and well, and you know that a heart is only in need of *care* both morally and physically, and will be kind if you treat it kindly. Do be careful, dearest Sydney.

I see nothing intimate of UNO except lunch with Mr. and Mrs. Casey who were friends in Cairo during the war.[128] Nuri Pasha was there, glittering with impishness and mischief, and the Turkish ambassador and the Lebanese, a nice philosopher with a halo of wild grizzled hair; but, otherwise, I see only our Iraqi's party with whom we spent a delightful Sunday at Fontainebleau, driving through the woods before the last leaves fell, visiting Millais' house where the young Barbizonians now exhibit their modern works, and eating at Les Pleiades, a delicious meal of lobster pastry. The fact is that everyone is hectically busy, away all day on committees, and the leisurely feel of the old days in Geneva has gone. We go to a cocktail party at the Embassy tomorrow, but there too there is a desperate feeling of trying to cope with the floods of people – UNO, European Defence, Atlantic Pact, American Aid, a huge octopus organisation. I wonder if the delicate little flower of peace will live among them all?

As I have all this time on my hands, I decided to devote these three months to learning the elements of drawing. I long to show you my efforts. It is a great delight, like discovering how to walk, or swim, a new capacity. If people concentrated on developing all these things in themselves, each one working at anything he is capable of to make himself as complete as possible, wouldn't it be better than all this worrying about other people all the time?

Dearest love, dear Sydney,

FREYA

[128] R. G. (later Lord) Casey. F.S. had met them when he was Minister of State in Cairo in the war.

Paris

16 November 1951

Darling B.B.,

I am going to disappoint you if you are expecting to hear news of the United Nations, for I see practically nothing at all of them. Stewart goes every day to the Palais de Chaillot where speeches go on as continuous as Tibetan prayer wheels and with the same sort of hopes attached to them no doubt. He tries to keep the little Arab flock from following too many will o' the wisps (mostly Egyptian at this moment) – and comes back very exhausted. But my share is confined to an occasional lunch with Iraqi or Syrian, and the taking of a wife or two to a dress show. I go every morning and draw at Julian's, where my parents went fifty years ago. And I am getting great delight from it. I suppose it is like all creative art: what is in one pours itself out if one can only gain so much of the mechanic skill as not to be too much of an impediment to the soul inside. In two months before me I hope to be able to learn enough to bring you little sketches of Asia Minor next year that may give pleasure. I am not beginning any Turkish, as I can do that in Asolo in summer, but just concentrate on the drawing – and have not even been about Paris as we are desperately poor, having no French francs except quarter of Stewart's salary, which is all that our Government allows us.

Stewart sends love and I do, to both of you, and loving thanks again for the good days.

Your

FREYA

Paris

24 November 1951

Dearest Jock,

What do you think of 'The Arabian Tree' as a title for Volume III?[129] From Shakespeare's 'On the Sole Arabian Tree'. It would be very good as *sense*, if the sound is good too.

This hotel and all the surrounding streets have been looking like a Spanish melodrama with gendarmes in shiny black waterproof capes, and batons in their hands, and some with black steel helmets in groups of three dotted all about, ready – one felt sure – to break out in a chorus: not for us, or Princess Margaret, or even Mr. Eden in his suite at the top of this hotel – but for

[129] In the event, *The Coast of Incense*.

Dr. Adenauer.[130] The celebrities are all safely off now, except Princess Margaret, who is no doubt buying one last dress at Dior. We couldn't afford the ball: it was rather unenterprising as the sight must have been lovely. Perhaps if you had been here, with a few coupes beforehand, we might have gone. But we did see Mr. Eden: he asked us up for a drink yesterday morning before he left for Rome. He is such a pleasant man in himself, with an atmosphere of candour and warmth that must be useful to a Foreign Secretary. He wished pathetically that he could have three days for each problem clustering round. The Middle East is not the least tricky and one ought to deal with it not just here but simultaneously and coordinately from a lot of different and distant places. One should, long ago, have prepared a parrot cry to substitute that of 'Down with the British' – which has become like an advertisement, something that causes an automatic reflex which makes the sales go up but has nothing to do with reason. Mr. Eden said that they nearly lost the election because of the war-mongering scare, an appeal to mere emotion, rather surprisingly successful in a well-trained electorate, and I suggested that the down-with-Britain cry in the East is exactly the same sort of thing, and equally capable of being successful.

Dear Jock, one *can't* believe the UNO will do much better than poor old Geneva. I sat yesterday looking at all the faces going to and fro and not one that one would choose as the director of one's life. My studio is much happier – I get about ten to twelve hours a week, so I ought to be able to make a recognisable mark on a sketch book.

Love,

FREYA

LADY CHOLMONDELEY
Paris
26 November 1951

Dearest Sybil,

Two things have been spurring me to write, your dear letter, and a beautiful letter received from Queen Mary, all in her own hand, and with that wonderful stamp of definiteness and resolution about it, even about the handwriting, which is surely her own, and what one ought rightly to call 'royal'.

We are still here, and couldn't *afford* to live in a reasonable hotel, as this spacious room is paid for by H.M.G. and I am just allowed the spare bed as

---

[130] The West German Chancellor.

if I were one of Stewart's suitcases. We are too poor to dine in the hotel and go and look at the menus of bistros in the proper student way.

It seems to me that there is no hope for United Nations getting together for the purpose of airing their grievances: anyone in domestic life knows how that makes them grow. And all the churches of the world have known it: they get people together for praise or pleasure and the grievances are dealt with in quiet little corners, apart. But who would listen to anyone as sensible as you or me? The Middle East is a headache and we shall be *very* lucky if we weather it with any credit at all. I should have liked to see us out of Egypt five years ago: now it is difficult to do so, and no thanks if we do. The whole of Asia shutting again, gradually, like an oyster. I do hope Asia Minor will keep open – I am making beautiful plans for next autumn.

Love to you dear Sybil,

FREYA

BERNARD BERENSON

Paris

12 December 1951

Darling B.B.,

Thank you for your dear letter. The lace-like handwriting gives me such pleasure when I see an envelope in the post and open the news from Tatti: a little bit of it and you comes with it. I am so happy to think of you – so look forward to the spring and you and Nicky and the outline of the Settignano hill.

I am glad you liked the book. The letter form is difficult to weld into literature, but I saw no other way of producing that *double* voice of past and present of which our past is made: like music, some effects have to be got with the uniting of more than one note, and I felt I could get the effect by doing so. Anyway I am enjoying my holiday from writing and the Art goes on every morning for two or three hours. A certain semblance to the human form begins to appear: like learning the letters of the alphabet, one wonders if one will ever be able to use them to say anything. It is extraordinary how dead it all is till one does; but I suppose it is something to realise the deadness. I am delighted to be doing it, as it is giving me a great joy in *seeing*.

The Impressionist pictures from Germany are exquisite – and so are the early mss. in the English book exhibition. What loveliness, in those darkest centuries.

May all be happy for you and Nicky this Christmas.

Your loving

FREYA

18 December 1951
My darling Nigel and Marie,

I think of you so often here with Fadhil Jamali and Yusuf Ghailani and all wandering about, all the little echoes of Baghdad of which you are living with the voices. I would like to hear how it all is, a little gossip, and what you think of the general Mid-Eastern landscape, and how you like your life?

Stewart is here temporarily advising the British Delegation to UNO on Arab affairs, trying hard that is to stop the landslide in the direction of Egypt and Persia. Nationalism is like measles in a school: it is no good to try and check it, the best is for all to take the infection and get it quickly over. But if I were the god behind the British machine, I should leave Egypt and build the defence of the East through Turkey and Iraq, and leave the Canal well behind in the backwater. Can you see any reason against this stronger than the reasons for it? The military say it is too near Russia by air, but do they balance that disadvantage with the one of a hostile occupied country instead of an ally to have our base in? I don't believe for one moment that they do, but would love to hear what you have to say about it.

Dearest Nigel, I don't want ever any more to do Public Things. I want to make a Good End.

Love to you both,

FREYA

BERNARD BERENSON   Paris
15 January 1952
My darling B.B.,

A letter from you came weeks ago – in fact I found it here on our return from Christmas and New Year in England – and it was very dear and welcome, and sent me out at once to find Marie Bashkirtseff but she, alas, is *épinsée*. I must read her at I Tatti: we hope to be about early in March. We plan to go on to Ischia and could stop off on the way either up or down, but I long to see you as soon as possible.

The drawing goes on and gets a little better – but I hope to keep it severely in the 'documentary' state and not to let the agonies of art penetrate: as it is, it is a perfect escape from writing, an entry into a world of shapes that are not nagging with opinions, but just being, like the garden flowers. How lovely the line of the thigh to the knee, and the thinness of the upper arm, and the attachment of the neck. I am fascinated by the models too. The one we have now looks like one of those ladies of the Fontainebleau school, and is earning her day so as to spend the evenings learning 'magnetism for medical purposes'. Another was a lovely Dane, very like the Venus of Botticelli to look at and as young and innocent, stranded in Paris and anxious to become an air hostess; and in and out of these are tough little Parisiennes, most of them with something very engaging, though one can never get over the squalid contrast of their dingy clothes with the beautiful decency of the body that stands up out of them.

The Arabs are giving a lot of trouble, though I think much of it comes from our habit of trying to wave two flags at once – pure democracy and no one to interfere in the affairs of small nations; and then a fearful outcry when they do make their own decisions and we don't like them. It is a muddled world and very few with time to sit back and think even five years ahead.

Love to both of you, dearest B.B.,

FREYA

BERNARD BERENSON   Brussels
                                               6 February 1952
Darling B.B.,

The three months in Paris are over and I am on my way to London by Brussels where the Jellicoes, some old friends of the wartime in Egypt, are now stationed. Yesterday we went in the winter sun and looked over the field of Waterloo: it is still very haunted – the gentle slopes, so empty and easy for cavalry, and the little farms in their places, and the valley where Blücher came riding to meet Wellington in the afternoon, and, seeing the carnage, remarked, 'Quelle affaire!' One admires the soldier's *eye*, which, from that almost imperceptible fold in the surface of the ground, could realise it as the defence line of Brussels. A Belgian woman who dined here told me that her grandfather was taken by his father in a carriage to collect wounded on the field of Waterloo, and remembered a heap of tissue paper in one of the farms: he thought it snow, and was told it was the paper in which the cartridges were wrapped.

Paris has been full of many better things than the U.N. Assembly. *Britannicus* for instance at the Comédie – a moving experience, the 963rd representation of the play. What a tradition! Paris was divided over Jean Marais as Nero, but I think he must be rather like Nero inside and, being *his* part, did it well. And the decor was fine – with steps and an immense crimson curtain and a giant bronze crouching figure hiding its face. The other very moving evening was *The Consul* (after which I was unable to

259

sleep): the prima donna took her bows in tears. It was strangely poignant to hear the tradition of the Italian opera used for the saying of things that touch us so nearly. And then Chartres – what an audacity – daring to reach God face to face as it were. It was an icy day with snowdrifts in a grey sky, and those great wheel-buttresses naked against it.

I *must* stop but hope to see you soon. Tell Nicky please write and say if March, first week or last, would suit.

Love,

FREYA

LADY CHOLMONDELEY   I Tatti,
                                           Settignano
                                        15 March 1952

Dearest Sybil,

What a bad play and what a good party that was! It is good to say goodbye to England like that – an evening with one's true friends to remember, and all the agreeable things of life about it. I am so grateful to you, dear Sybil, for being around just then, when I was feeling almost as dead as the people in the play (but not quite).

I had five busy days in Asolo and came down, bursting into spring through the Apennine – all the blossom like little round bouquets among the olive trees.

B.B. is splendid, full of wit, like a straight little candle, very frail. He and Sydney are the two Miracles. He sends you many greetings.

I leave them on Monday and put in the fortnight before my house is free, walking round the Tuscan foothills from Montecatini, skirting Lucca, up by Massa and Carrara with the sea on one side and the marble hills on the other, to Lena Waterfield at Aulla. My legs may be a little weak at first, but I can take very easy days.

Dear love to you,

FREYA

BERNARD BERENSON   Near Lucca,
                                              Tuscany
                                        20 March 1952

Darling B.B.,

The first half of the walk was over at three this afternoon; I came down by the heads of valleys from S. Quirico to Bagni, by lonely little uninhabited paths under chestnut slopes. My legs ache, but the rest of me seems intact. I found however that I am too old to carry a knapsack, and young lads are found from village to village (also necessary in the higher places as there is no one about to ask the way). How lonely the Apennine is compared to Alps or Dolomites; but how *romantic*! The upper Val Pescia was full of clustered hilltop towns. They grow like the little clusters of violets, all from one root, gathered close together. They all still have bits of wall and an arched gate leading to the steep ribbed stone-flagged street and cobbled *piazza*.

The cold you predicted made me suffer, but a serious chill was averted by the *scaldini*[131] which they put in the beds. Such charming peasants I stayed with in S. Quirico: faces from the early pictures and the manners of kings and queens. We sat over their fire while the supper was cooking and I was glad to see this little bit of the life of these hills. When I climbed to the ridge this morning the whole top of Val Lima was spread out and snowy hills with heads in cloud.

Darling B.B., so much love to you and Nicky.

FREYA

JOHN GREY MURRAY   Monte Mattanna
                                        22 March 1952
Dearest Jock,

Isn't it extraordinary how the things one has thought about come along, years and years afterwards, but as if a gentle, unconscious pull were taking one towards them? When I was about fourteen, I used to look up at these fine marble mountains from Carrara and think how I should like to see them close by, and here I have come, walking two days from the Lucca valley, and am going to sleep here and walk a day or two along the ridges before dropping to Massa on the southern slope. I thought, as I put one slow step before the other up the worn stones of the mule-track, so smooth and round, what a pattern our footsteps would make: a sort of graph of our life, in and out, round and round, with a straight bit here and there, our own private drawing of our life, which everyone makes for himself. Perhaps the imaginary footsteps ought to count as well as the real ones?

I came yesterday by train and bus till the road stopped and then left my sack to be brought up by 'the mules' in the evening and walked for two hours beyond the reach of wheels, keeping along the edge of a valley filled with young chestnut growth where the Germans had cut the old trees of the gullies to get a clear view downward from this Gothic line. All is growing up again and the trees cover the round wounded trunks with new shoots and

---

[131] Small braziers.

look happy. What a difference when the wound is made from outside and *accepted*: a rush of life comes over it. It is the want of acceptance, the want of vitality, that makes all ill and dead. I comforted myself with this feeling about the chestnuts, because it has been such an effort to get going again in solitude, the aching legs and cold evenings, and energy necessary to pull oneself up by the roots and deal with new people every day; and now the rhythm is coming again, and the hills are not so steep and long, and a beautiful passivity comes with the body at peace in the sun or by somebody's fire. The life of the little places trickles in and one feels *convalescent*, a nice lizard-like feeling on any warm stone.[132] And the people are so nice in this remoteness as soon as one is away from mechanical things. The knapsack is left at a casual dark little shop and comes safely to the next village in the dusk, and my guide this morning is given 300 lire for his morning, a little boy who asked for 500 being sent about his business by my landlady. 'We have to keep the young ones down a bit,' she said to me with a flattening gesture of the soup ladle, 'or they take advantage of strangers and give the village a bad name.' We dined all together with the village schoolmistress and I slept in a bed warmed with the *scaldino*.

In the summer all these walks are in the shadow of chestnut trees, but perhaps it is lovelier now with the brown slopes and a clear view; the birds are all awake and lizards beginning, and you never saw such colonies of crocus, darker at the tips with clear eyes with dark lashes, smooth and silky, and lying in purple sheets and terraces here and there. Primroses, violets, anemones in the plain, and whole hillsides of green hellebore under the chestnut trees. As I came walking along, the wind blew the dead leaves in long processions like ghosts, with a dead brittle rustling. I felt I must be seeing just what Milton saw.

Arni

23 March 1952

This is such an exciting place, a circle all surrounded by peaks (1,500 metres) spattered with snow and streaks of marble. One comes up by a wild valley, the road keeping high and the hillsides now black and spongy brown and severe; and then through a tunnel of a mile or two, out into this amphitheatre where the village is scattered among trees and inhabited by marble miners. The hills are dotted with smooth marble squares like Assyrian rock-carvings before they were carved, and runways go down where the huge blocks are lowered on rollers. When I was a child at Massa, the place was full of people who had lost legs while placing the rollers – the hemp ropes

---

[132] The break with Stewart Perowne was being made.

would break. But now the ropes look like silver, all metal and strong, really steel. It is fascinating to be so out of the world, all very rough people, but now we are friendly over the stove and a widower has just told me he would like to marry a new wife, about sixty, but 'ancora fresca'.

The stove is a great democrat. One can't face the 'parlour' in the evenings and I sit in the kitchen and eat with the family and feel as if it were Arabia: the same ease and hospitality. Tomorrow I hope to go down over the wall of the ridge to Massa and on to Lena Waterfield's where there should be letters. I haven't had one since leaving London.

Aulla
25 March 1952

Arrived yesterday, such a day, and the only one without a view, alas. Just as we got to the place where all the western hills should open out, the mist came boiling up and has continued ever since. So it was just discipline, one foot before the other; one's thighs feel as if they would die going up, and one's knees feel as if they would break going down, and the thin places with nothing but steepness below give an air-raid sensation in the tummy. Why does one do it, at my age? But it is wonderful to have it done, and be safe down in the valley with the earth-surface solid and flat enough to feel safe. I luckily had a good young guide, for the path, such as it was – a little worm of worn stones scarce visible, had been sliced away for marble and there was a nasty smoothish slab. How surprised I was to find myself negotiating it, and so was the guide.

Massa was full of ghosts. I sat at the café where my father used to give us ices forty-five years ago, oh my! And there were all the little orange trees and the red palace with twenty windows with Roman Emperors above them taking all one side of the square, and the other two sides bombed. And I came here and carried my knapsack to the castle in the dusk and have been sleeping and writing all day.

Love,
FREYA

BERNARD BERENSON AND NICKY MARIANO Aulla
25 March 1952

Darling B.B. and Nicky,

I came down to Massa yesterday and up to the Castello with my knapsack in the dusk (the only bit of knapsack carrying as I find I am *past* being a snail), and you can't think what a wonderful place I ended up in: Arni, the centre of the marble mountains, two little villages sitting like mice in a

Stilton cheese, eating out the edges all around. The white triangles of broken marble pour in from every side and all around are the lovely peaks, the Altissimo and all the others, covered with snow. One reaches this place by a wild road cut in the mountain side in 1870 from Stazzema above Serravezza, and penetrating through a tunnel over a mile long: I walked down to Stazzema from Mattanna, and there took the bus, and it was the wildest mountain country you can imagine, ruinous and steep, and then the pastoral remoteness and the strange mining camp atmosphere in all that beauty, the mountain circle sheeted in snow. I came down over a pass – about 1,300 metres – to the Massa road at Forno, and thought I should never make it what with shoes too light and knees weak in the long descent: and today am relaxing with Lena and refusing to put my nose out even into the garden.

Thank you dear B.B. for your good words about the book. It comforts me for so much when you like it. I have been sad, thinking over things in solitude, but with no doubt that it is all right: but how hard, to pull out the eye that offends you: will one ever get over the pain of it?

Dear love and thanks to you both. How I hope Venice may draw you in the spring.

FREYA

STEWART PEROWNE Asolo
30 March 1952

My dear Stewart,

A letter of yours was here when I came yesterday and tells me what I am sure is true, that there is much in me to dislike. *Pazienza*! I don't mind being told now and if I had been told before, *lovingly*, I would have tried to alter; but I'm dashed if I see why I should be conjugal all alone (the very etymology makes it wrong). It all proves how right we are to be married no longer, and let us, for goodness sake, stop thinking of each other's faults and be good friends instead of bad spouses. I may say that I have only mentioned our separation as a mutual preference for friendship to matrimony, so that it carries no criticism either way.

Love,
FREYA

LADY ASTOR Asolo
5 April 1952

My dearest Nancy,

Your letter is very dear and I would love to talk to you, but I am not going to go back to matrimony with Stewart for a long time, if ever. He doesn't want *me*, he wants a home and a lot of odds and ends, and I would like to give him as much of that as I can, true friendship, a place to dump his things and come back to, a feeling of safety. But marriage is more than that. We must go back, and having made a false start, retrieve it by not undertaking more than we can. Friendship is as far as the thermometer will rise, and there it must rest for the present. And Stewart can come here and be most dearly welcome like any friend, but I think as things are, it would be a good idea to wait a bit.

I think of you in your loneliness so different from mine, for there something has gone that *existed* and that is very hard to bear.

Dear love,

FREYA

JOHN GREY MURRAY Asolo
15 April 1952

Dearest Jock,

This house is full with children in the garden, grownups painting, boys going up Grappa, and the spring has come and all the flowers rush out. One couldn't be mournful if one tried. Bill Astor is here for five days, and Patsy and Alan Lennox-Boyd for three, and I had a lunch for them. The children have had two egg-hunts with sack and potato races which the British all had the bad taste to win with uncivilised determination. The lilies promise well, and I have managed to go sketching twice and learnt 200 Turkish words.

I am wondering, if Stewart gets his Palestine job, as I do hope he will, whether I should urge him to come here on the way? I would like it to be a friendship. What do you think? He wrote that he was dining with you so you will have seen him.

A letter next time, dear Jock.

FREYA

SIR SYDNEY COCKERELL Asolo
24 April 1952

Dearest Sydney,

I have been very busy reading a fascinating book which had to be returned quickly to the library – J. L. Myres's *Who Were the Greeks?* Do you know it? It takes one into my favourite world, the early adventurous dawn of the

Levant with people in boats going from island to island and legends springing from all they do and say. One feels about it as about one's childhood: all we are is in it, but with a distant light upon it where anything may happen.

Most of my guests have left this morning. Wilfrid Blunt is coming to lunch and to stay tonight, and then I have an interval till four women arrive in May, three of them young girls who have never been to Italy before. I like to have lodgers. I now have my *beautiful* room upstairs and see no one till lunch time when I descend, and then it is pleasant to see people enjoying the garden and making this loveliness seem worthwhile.

Dearest Sydney, I begin to feel how really right this separation has been. One has so many cross-currents, there is no certainty while one is among them, and I am still sad about it all, and still hope that something may happen to change Stewart's feeling for what is worth having in the world. But while things are as they are, I am wonderfully relieved to be free again and feel like a cornfield just reviving and getting more or less upright after hail.

Are you able to go out now? I hope so and that there are warm afternoons to walk in the Gardens.

Dear love to you,

FREYA

LADY KEELING[133]   Asolo
27 April 1952

My dearest Martha,

How glad I am for you – to find what satisfies and gives you peace, that is the most precious thing that can happen to anyone. I remember once, when we were discussing what one would ask for if *one wish* could be granted, that I came to the conclusions that the thing to ask for would be the feeling of the grace of God around one – and that I suppose is what you have found. I think I have it, in a strange solitary way, because it has come to me not by a church but in lonely places: but what does it matter *how* it comes, if it is there? I am so glad dear Martha. I am alone again, but only for ten more days and then have a houseful of young girls, which I look forward to. Meanwhile I am busy, learning Turkish, just enough to get me about Anatolia in the autumn; and doing bad little drawings when I can. The garden is beautiful: and it doesn't rain every day, but more than it should.

[133] Wife of Sir Edward Keeling, a Conservative Member of Parliament.

Something has happened to the North Italian climate – or perhaps it is just April.

Love to you both,

FREYA

CHARLES RANKIN
Asolo

7 May 1952

Dearest Charles,

Asolo is heavenly now. Tulips over, roses beginning. Everyone getting very old, but gay – Malipiero and Cavalieri houses so full of animal smells that one almost faints going in. La Mura giving trouble as usual with Brian Howard[134] as a tenant, drunk or worse, and turned out of Harry's Bar[135] for jabbing at his boy-friend with a fork. Luckily I have avoided meeting him, but he has at last put the lid on the Lawrences as tenants and the Rucellai are looking for someone 'respectable' who will take it on a long yearly lease: they want to give only the front and will do it up for them. *Do* find me a pleasant neighbour!

Let me have a nice gossipy letter with news of yourself, Lulie and other friends. I wish it were to say you are coming in June. I shall be here till July 10th. Then Dolomites, Zante, Athens, Anatolia...the whole world.

Love,

FREYA

SIR SYDNEY COCKERELL
Asolo

7 May 1952

Dearest Sydney,

What a lovely letter you wrote me, but I don't like to think of the flowering gardens without you to enjoy them. You and they will always be linked together in my mind. I still hope that, as the year goes on, you may collect the strength to go, perhaps in a chair? The spring in England doesn't *begin* till May, and even here it had been raining and cold with sudden fierce little bursts of warmth that make everything droop.

I am busy with my Turkish and have got four hundred words, but not yet very good at putting them together.

I have my own name again (*Mrs.*, however) and feel more and more relieved. There was a terrible sense of insecurity, which after all is the exact

[134] An unprolific writer, but enough of a star at Eton and Oxford in the 1920s to make his failure a matter of interest.
[135] In Venice.

opposite of what marriage should give. And we write now and then and I hope may turn it all into a friendship. I suppose people are divided into those who can do with a compromise and those who can't, and I am one of the latter. At least I can compromise in the sense of accepting and giving less, but not of pretending. It makes life quite bitter to me.

Dear, darling, Sydney, bless you for all your affection, very precious to me.

Your

FREYA

JOHN GREY MURRAY   Asolo
                                                                14 May 1952
Dearest Jock,

The three débutantes are charming and cheering us all up a lot and look very nice among the roses. I am very happy with them, and hope that they are, though I have scoured the landscape and not a man of suitable age is to be found in it, so they have to do the best they can with Culture and Art.

I have had to refuse the lecture invitation to my secret relief. I feel that if I had been in England you might have bullied me to go! It would be nice to think of a life completely free from public speaking. Anyway, no one can be expected to combine it with Turkish verbs. *I* think that it is they that have affected my inside and made me ill. No one can imagine the amount of unnecessary verbal subtleties a primitive language is capable of producing.

Do you know Brian Howard? A huge posse of carabiniers from Castelfranco came to see me and asked what I felt about him. I answered with rare discretion and said I didn't know him and had taken a lot of trouble not to. But it would be nice to have someone next door who is not either drunk or wanted by the police, and if you hear of anyone who would be a pleasant neighbour, do send him along.

Did Stewart tell you the story of the woman in New Zealand whose son was killed in Greece? She dreamed the place so clearly that she was able to draw it and the officer in Greece who was looking for our soldiers' graves recognised Mount Olympus and found the grave. Those Ancient Gods!

I have a most exciting letter about Anatolian castles from a Mr. Thomson in Jedda who has been there and visited about twenty and says there must be as many more but that one has 'to hack away the brushwood for one's horse if one leaves the path', a thing I was never good at!

Dear Jock, what a scrawl, a little news, but much love,

FREYA

Asolo
21 May 1952

Darling Sydney,

I wish you could see my garden now. I believe it would make you forget Kew. All the roses are out, and it is like an avenue of uniforms all different and all splendid. I am slowly getting them better and better and putting the colours together, to make a pattern, and it is a constant pleasure. One has to spend at least a spring and a summer, and then a long autumn, to see how the garden lives through the year and plan it and beds accordingly.

This morning my three girls left for four days in Rome. I miss them; they are charming, easy, and cheerful, like spring in the house. I hope to be able to take them to the Dolomites for a day's drive. How nice it would be to have just a *little* more money! But how lucky I am to have enough to manage here, even though difficult now and then, and to squeeze in a journey to Turkey.

Love, dear Sydney,

FREYA

BRIAN HOWARD

Asolo
28 May 1952

Dear Mr. Howard,

I am sorry you had to write me that letter for it must have been very distressful for you, and I should be sorry, too, not to answer to thank you for the nice things you say and to explain to you how much I, too, regret that we have not been able to make a happy acquaintance. There is nothing personal in it I do want to say. I don't think it is safe for one human being to judge the actions of another, and especially in this case when I don't know them. It would be quite an absurd impoverishment not to know people merely because they do things one doesn't happen to like oneself. But, as you have been living in this little town and are thinking of writing about it, you may see how it is, a rather touching small knot of civilisation, carried down through all its troubles, yet more or less intact, for about two thousand years. I suppose the people who have guided it have never been much better or worse than our notables today, self-seeking, jealous, sometimes venal, yet with a little collection of things they cling to as having a sort of sanctity beyond their personal values. And these sanctities, now threatened not with new ideas but with an absence of ideas, they are trying to preserve as best they can. I suppose big cities have these knots of ideas by which they live, but they are too complex for me to see. But I have never been in a *small* place anywhere that did not live with some such core of discipline, very various in form, at its centre. It seems to me that if one wants to know a place, it is this core of (shall I say?) holiness that one must come to understand?

Now I don't really know how it has come about, but you seem to have offended against it here. And you can see in what a difficulty it places me. If it were anywhere else, where I have no ties, it could be disregarded. But here there have been three generations of British people who have gradually succeeded in abolishing the prejudice of nationalism so that, quite apart from politics and purely on their personal values, the English are looked upon as decent people with the local pattern of decency. Tourists who come and go can do what they like without affecting this position, but I have been made a part of the little town. I have been asked by practically every Italian here whether I know you. All my life I have watched things like drunkenness being fought against, preached against, and finally (if I think of the difference forty years ago) more or less suppressed. You may say it is a silly thing to think of as important, but it is one of *their* standards. If they see that I think nothing of it, the whole British position here is let down, and the people here who are keeping up their gallant little fight for their own decencies are weakened. Now what am I to do? I would like to see you. Would you come in, as you suggest, for ten minutes and see my garden when I get back from Venice early next month, and then perhaps your mother would come by herself to tea one day? And I hope we may meet more easily somewhere where I have no responsibilities.

Yours regretfully,
FREYA STARK

STEWART PEROWNE Asolo
29 May 1952

Dearest Stewart,

The little fork and knife have come and they are little dears. I am *so* pleased with them. Thank you *ever* so much. I shall have my initials and the date engraved on the little shields and only hope no Turk will take a fancy to them.

Lucy[136] is here with a nice friend, very sensitive and quiet, who was to have been a singer but got TB and married a devoted husband instead. But the dream of her life is missed and she has a gentle sort of melancholy about

---

[136] sc. Moorehead.

her. I suppose one's dreams are the most important things one has? I think I should try very hard to give my children if I had any the right sort of dream to keep them happy.

Love, dear Stewart,

FREYA

Asolo

JOHN GREY MURRAY

10 June 1952

Dearest Jock,

I am longing to see the beautiful bindings.[137] Perhaps someone will be coming out to be loaded? Dear Jock, thank you so much for getting them done. I had been wishing for it for years. What a wonderful thing to have letters collected from two such people. Nothing can really prevent my being one of the most fortunate of creatures.

To my immense relief Stewart has a job, and one with refugees which will be good for him. So all is well, I hope.

This place is full of pansies and Lesbians, some are charming, but some Go Too Far. I wrote a letter of what Stewart calls Vicarage Stiffness to Brian Howard. It has had the surprising effect of making him want to meet me more than before, so he came yesterday and rather pointedly drank no vermouth and is behaving like a Plymouth Brother. All the same, it would be nice to have a few normal people about.

I must send this. With love always,

FREYA

Asolo

JOHN GREY MURRAY

16 June 1952

Dearest Jock,

I have just had the Caccias here.[138] What a nice couple, and how refreshingly normal. They rejected Culture and sat in the garden, and have asked me to Vienna next spring. It was pleasant to be talking about world affairs again; suddenly made me realise how easy and comfortable it is to slide into one's backwater and stay there. I was asked to Arthur Jeffries's party for the artists of the 'Biennale', so back we drove to Venice and out again till 2 a.m. I really only wanted the pleasure of wearing my Paris dress for the first time. I think one party every two months is rather a pleasant average.

---

[137] F.S. had had bound her letters from Lord Wavell and W. P. Ker.
[138] Sir Harold (later Lord) Caccia was their Ambassador in Vienna.

The heat has come and we live under beautiful green striped awnings. How nice it is to be really hot.

Love,

FREYA

Asolo

8 July 1952

Dearest Jock,

I don't know what has come over Asolo: it has suddenly gone all 'Positano'. Archie Colquhoun went over to them the evening before yesterday, sat at the café till 1.30 a.m. and then couldn't turn the key in our door so went to sleep across the way. As I am lending him my flat to finish his book, I had to take a rather firm line and put it to him that acquaintance was one thing and intimacy another and he can't go making close Capulet ties from a Montagu house. He seemed quite hurt at the thought that no Italian would believe he slept out merely because he couldn't manage a quite normal Italian key (or ring the bell). On top of all this, an unknown Irish reader writes ten pages to tell me his life, how he is irresistibly drawn to little boys, and what is he to do about it. What have I done to be entangled in this desert of thorns?

Lots of love,

FREYA

SIR SYDNEY COCKERELL Albergo Solda

(by the Ortler)

15 July 1952

Dearest Sydney,

This is a high wonderful end of a valley with a glacier huddled over the edge of it and peaks of Ortler, Zebru, and others, all over 10,000 or thereabout, standing in a semicircle. I have been here three days and now Jim and Pamela Rose have joined me. He was literary editor of the *Observer* and is now doing an international journalist job in Zurich. They are a charming couple, gay and quick and kind, and it feels like a holiday of the old sort to be here, all glad to talk and with nothing but the choosing and planning of walks on our mind. It is a pleasant hotel, long and huge like a ship and not too grand. People come because they enjoy the mountains. It felt very high (1,900 metres) at first, but today we walked up another 1,000 to a hut on the edge of the glacier, and began to feel at home again in that thin air. What a terrifying sight a steep glacier is, with wedges of green livid ice, and tumbled falls onto the boulder-strewn ice below, and huge ledges where the torrent rolls out of green ice caves. There is a perfect description of our view in Tennyson's 'Come down, O maid, from younder mountain height'.

High up there the flowers are so bright, a whole slope of forget-me-nots growing among stones, and little troops of campanulas, dark blue or light like the Boat Race, and all the little cushiony plants of the rocks in blossom.

I wish I could think of you walking in Kew, dear Sydney. Perhaps you, too, have been having a wave of summer and have felt strong enough to venture out?

I go back to Asolo in ten days, to pack, to see B.B. in Vallombrosa, and to leave for Zante, and will write to tell you what I find there.

Dear love to you, dearest Sydney,

FREYA

JOHN GREY MURRAY   Grand Hotel, Solda
                                                18 July 1952

Dearest Jock,

Jim and Pamela Rose have left today after five perfect days – always out with two paper bags full of lunch in the knapsack and no rain ever until we were safely home. We ended up on a grand scale, five hours' solid walk up and up with only half an hour for food on the way. From that exalted place (Ryer hut), which looked just like those improbable Dürer backgrounds perched on rock, we saw what looked like the whole of Switzerland, spiky to a degree. One wide flat valley with lakes went north (towards the Arlberg), and all the rest was hills and hills and hills, some with snow and icefalls in their arms, some like saws with teeth against the sky, Bernina in the West, and Ortler just behind us, a three hours' snow-walk to the summit. I went up like a snail, but fancy getting up at all in one's sixtieth year: it seemed miraculous to capture the sights of one's youth. We waited on the sunset, and slept in the hut, and saw at 4 a.m. a tiny sickle moon holding the old circular ball in its curve and wandering about the hilltops with a star here and there – and got up and saw that miraculous moment when the top clouds grow suddenly lucent and the sky behind the cold night snow grows like violets and roses, and the highest peak – Ortler in this instance – shines out like a banner. There is no sight more *triumphant* I believe: like a sudden chord in Bach, like some victory of Michael and all the angels. Then the sunlight crept down, fold after fold of lower hills received it; the clouds rose

273

steaming and hid the highest peaks; and we drank hot tea and came trotting down in two and a quarter hours, just half the time of the ascent.

This is a delightful hotel, and 6,000 feet up already. It was like long-lost holidays in my youth, with not a care in the world. The cares are there now, but I forgot 'em.

Do you know that the doctor here takes his little boy of 4½ walking up to all the huts and glaciers? It is high time my godsons were brought to the Alps.

Dear love dear Jock,

FREYA

SIR SYDNEY COCKERELL   Rifugio G. Casati,
                                                     above Solda
                                                   20 July 1952

Darling Sydney,

I am writing to you from high in the mountains, a hut 10,400 feet up, with a rounded glacier covered with furrowed snow sweeping down from it towards all sorts of peaks and pinnacles, blackish and streaked.

They had an international ski-race this morning on the northern slope of what we are standing on, and it was a charming walk up between the high mountain walls, with a long zigzag of people on the steep path, young and old, children, skiers, soldiers, young couples in peasant dress holding hands, like some Greek festival in a remote shrine, or like life itself, climbing and climbing, through all its varieties of ages. The skiing was terrific, a smooth snake of flattened snow curving down at a terrific angle, with glacier cracks on either side, and little flags at the bends, with Alpine soldiers posted beside them. Some slight young girls came whizzing down. It looks super-human, and must be very dangerous. I had a guide and we plodded slowly up halfway beside the course and then left it to cross the pass at the head of the glacier, tied on a rope and thinking how strange to be digging my boots into ice steps after so many years. Alas, I used to be complimented on the climb, now it is like Dr. Johnson's dog on its hind legs, they are surprised at my doing it at all. Italian women don't climb at sixty, and one gets up into a very young world here, of people practising summer skiing on the glacier all rather strained and burnt and worn and not, it seems to me, as carelessly and civilisedly happy as we used to be. The point is that we used to talk of everything in this world and the next, and these only talk of skiing.

Very dear love to you, dearest Sydney,

FREYA

274

Solda
                                                                    21 July 1952

My dearest Charles,

Your letter came just as I was starting for the mountains and that has delayed my telling you how glad I was to hear. Of course you are right: the moment when one has doubts there is really no doubt left, although all the sorrow and effort of the decision remain to unwind themselves slowly. And some day it will all fit in and show itself in the pattern of your life, and make it richer – but oh my! what a *strain* it all is. I still feel sad and lost – and yet I know it was necessary: but it does *cost* so – an expense of spirit.

I have been walking all over the hills. My last this morning from a snowy peak and all the Alpine chain spread out around it. Such a delight when we left the glacier, crawling down like a reptile full of cracked chasms and wickedness – to step onto earth and mountain flowers and smell the scent of things that grow and die and don't just last or wear away. But all the same, my dear Charles, I am very lonely and do feel I need someone to look after. Life will provide it, but there is a horrid chasm to cross and I think of you crossing it too.

I had three days in Venice with the Navy and was invited to lunch with the Mountbattens in the *Surprise* – and heard all about his triumphant visit to Tito. What a strange person he is – I feel I have no key; and she with those *haunted* eyes. It was a wonderful setting, with the Doge's Palace in the background.

This is only to send love and friendship dear Charles – and to tell you to *trust life*.

                                                                    Love,
                                                                    FREYA

Zante
                                                                    9 August 1952

Darling B.B.,

What an enchanted island this is: I have never seen such sunsets except in Aden. All its lines are so beautiful, gentle, horizontal and breaking into waves as if the sea had grown solid and bore trees.

I came by two little trains along the edge of Peloponnesus and got into a caique by a jetty at Killeni with the Crusader castle of Toron on the ridge above. I wonder if it is very different, except that the caique had a motor, and the Americans are trying to grow rice in the lowlands of Messene.

This is one of the old Zante houses, with dilapidated remains of grandeur

– ballroom and columns white and gold, and florid Empire gilt furniture of the islands – and the sea winds and suns eating into all the walls, and bleaching the streets and porticoes: it is the Greek-Roman world, a little melancholy and dwindling, without that hard brilliance of the Aegean which triumphs over Life and Time.

Darling B.B., how happy I was to see you those two days. I will write again and think of you always. Love to you both,

FREYA

STEWART PEROWNE   Zante
14 August 1952

Dearest Stewart,

This island is strangely familiar: as I go about, I feel myself inside a Lear picture that has come to life! – the long, tilted but *almost* horizontal lines; the olives so pruned and old that they look more like the ideas of man than nature; the pointed black spires of cypress in small clumps also arranged for the artist; the dusty bad roads and lonely cottages with plaster crumbling and an animal or two in the foreground: and even the atmosphere, the gentleness of the colour, the white or red soil, all seem more like painting and less accidental than nature. We went yesterday right across the central plain to the western hills, by charming villages on the first rise surrounded by fruit trees and climbing to pines – by a lake now dried off, but which Herodotus mentions as producing pitch, and then up into the regular Mediterranean limestone, with small silky pines and all the scented shrubs and stony fields built up in the saddles of valleys – beyond a village with a good seventeenth-century church to a lighthouse. The cliffs break away sheer, and there is a Homeric look about it all, the pathway of the sun dazzling below on the sea. The guardian of the light had been put in his job by Dino's father, and we called on him and his family – all beautiful with that smiling Greek mouth which *must* have been what those archaic statues try to represent. They had had the Italians and then the Germans: and when the armistice of September 3rd was made, the former were gathered like sheep and shot by the latter, hundreds at a time. But before that they carried off all the village food, the animals, even the fish that the fishermen caught. The people talk of it dispassionately, as one might of an earthquake – but in their bare little house it is touching to see the prints of their king and queen, and Dino's father as minister, and the word 'no' ('OXI') which Metaxas said to the Italians, framed in a garland of fruit and flowers: and another little saying beside it, that 'Greece cannot die'. We came back in twilight –

276

the sea very quiet and pale, and the olives a sleepy grey, on whitish ground or pale stubble, such *classic* landscape, so austere and kind.

You must let me know if you want books sent and what sort? I am reading Jane Austen (it was about ten years since last time) and it is as fresh and exciting as always. Emma is a bit of a prig but Mr. Knightley is her best hero, and what a picture of the village! I am trying to think what gives this permanent freshness, and I believe that it is because with all her insuperable keenness she is not merely observant, she is interested in the meaning of the things she notes. I think that is the difference between her and the modern novelists who put the observations down without drawing final conclusions. Jane, you feel, thought the conclusion the most important part and that gets the whole picture into place and when the quiet little climax comes, Mr. Knightley's few words, Mr. Darcy's second proposal, there is a tremendous *meaning* packed into that simplicity. And she is always right; never deceived by sentiment, but never undervaluing the reality behind it: her world is still the real world and always will be, and so brought down to essentials that, in spite of the different setting, one need never make allowances (as with Brontës or Eliot) for differences of place or time. The people are just what they would be now if they lived now, because she is interested in the essential substance of them and her values are as permanent as those of Shakespeare or Homer. And what terseness: Mrs. Norris, the vicar's widow, and the new vicar who 'were seldom good friends: their acquaintance had begun in dilapidations and their habits were totally dissimilar'. There it is: with nothing to be added. It is such refreshment that I wonder if you would not like to have it as an Escape. Shall I write Bumpus[139] to send you a collected works for intervals of refugees?

Much love,

FREYA

SIR SYDNEY COCKERELL   Zante

19 August 1952

Dearest Sydney,

How beautiful these islands are, unlike both Italy and Greece, but made by both, and with an English-Napoleonic touch, too, solid mahogany furniture, and Zante noblemen painted by bad English painters of that time. There are beautiful houses, seventeenth- and eighteenth-century, with decorated façades now showing signs of wear (and some of the best destroyed by bombing). But the general feeling is of a small Italian town with a long

[139] London bookshop.

277

street of whitewashed porticoes; but not vivacious like Italy – there is such a feeling of decline that I would dislike it for living, and would certainly keep away from the town – and in the country, incredibly lovely, with olives, cypress, and pine, a long wilderness of vines, not tied up and regulated but growing in natural bushes. The tiny stoneless currant grapes are now drying on squares of hard earth outside the country houses and the owner sleeps above them in a hut lifted on poles, with a gun. Then they are shovelled into heaps and brought to be loaded on caiques, and that and the oil are the chief income on Zante.

I climbed up the highest hill of the island, not very high, having driven to where the road ends in a quarry and then followed a path up to the monastery near the top. It was still dark with a bright old sickle moon, and I watched the faint band growing in the east towards the dawn; and, just as the daylight began, came on a young herdsman washing his head at a little fountain, much surprised to see me, who led me beyond the monastery to the little rocky pinnacle where the path ends. He didn't think I could get up, but I did and found some goats there, and sat and watched the pink light creep into the sky and all the island appear, dove-coloured beneath it, and the sun like a torch with a long stab of orange light across the water, rising behind the mountains of Peloponnesus. What a beautiful world! I looked in to the monastery below, very poor and half tumbled, but with a beautiful icon of gilt silver on a silver pedestal, and then stopped on the way down to draw it while the herdsman watched me and took me by the arm in far too affectionate a way when I was starting on my way again. Pleased as I was to be thought so young, I said 'οχι' in a firm way and went on till we came to the fountain, and the herdsman gave me water from it in an old tin, and presently vanished into his island wilderness of rosemary, thyme, and thorny bushes. And what could have been more like Theocritus than all that? Though it also shows how useful it is to learn the word for 'no' at an early stage of a language.

Bless you, dearest Sydney,

FREYA

JOHN GREY MURRAY   Athens
                                                  1 September 1952
Dearest Jock,

I was in Delphi yesterday and thought of you and Himyar.[140] How lovely it was. Parnassus in the afternoon, dressed in veils and veils, and radiant

[140] Jock Murray had been there with F.S. in 1938. Himyar was a pet lizard F.S. had kept at the time.

through them, so that it seemed like sky solidified. And Helicon with, quite clearly marked along its higher levels, the valley of the Muses, a deep cleft. Delphi itself with its eagles, brooding over the floods of olive trees below, with the great hollow valley very still and the high lands opposite a tawny red, like ancient pottery with uneven glaze, the colour left by the gathered harvests. We deviated on our way home and went down to the sea at Anta-kira, which I had visited twelve years ago. It was as beautiful as ever in its still bay at the foot of an open valley of olives and corn. But one no longer rides along the edge of the water by a narrow track, stopping to drink ouzo under a sycamore; a new road runs higher up the hill to carry bauxite from a mine, and it is cutting into the old citadel itself on its headland.

We came back through Distomo whose ruined houses are mostly rebuilt, and its little square is called the Heroes' Square. The Germans gathered the men there and shot them, but a good many must have got away hiding in the hills, for there were *crowds* sitting at their cafés on the Sunday afternoon, and many of them middle-aged.

Did I tell you I had been looking at the Agora, shown by Professor Homer Thomson who is digging it out? And there is the portico (or at least a few stones where it *was*) where Socrates used to sit and talk, and, most strangely *actual* to look at, the potsherds on which the names of Themistocles, or Aristides, or Pericles were written for ostracism.

I hope to find letters in Smyrna. My tummy is absurdly delicate, but I hope to last out with yogurt and care.

Love,
FREYA

Index

284